THE POWER
OF
POSITIVE TEACHING

THE POWER
OF
POSITIVE TEACHING

Floyd G. McCormick, Jr.
Professor Emeritus
Department Head Emeritus
The University of Arizona
Tucson

KRIEGER PUBLISHING COMPANY
MALABAR, FLORIDA

Original Edition 1994

Printed and Published by
KRIEGER PUBLISHING COMPANY
KRIEGER DRIVE
MALABAR, FLORIDA 32950

FROM A DECLARATION OF PRINCIPLES JOINTLY ADOPTED BY A COMMITTEE OF THE AMERICAN BAR ASSOCIATION AND A COMMITTEE OF PUBLISHERS:

This publication is designed to provide accurate and authoritative information in regard to the subject matter covered. It is sold with the understanding that the publisher is not engaged in rendering legal, accounting, or other professional service. If legal advice or other expert assistance is required, the services of a competent professional person should be sought.

Library of Congress Cataloging-In-Publication Data

McCormick, Floyd G., 1927–
    The power of positive teaching / Floyd G. McCormick. — Original ed.
        p.   cm.
    Includes bibliographical references and index.
    ISBN 0-89464-831-4 (alk. paper)
    1. Teaching. 2. Learning, Psychology of. I. Title.
LB1025.3.M346   1994
371.1'02—dc20   92-42276
                                                              CIP

10 9 8 7 6 5 4

To the two women in my life—
my mother, Gladys,
and my wife, Connie.
Without these two wonderful individuals,
this effort would not have been possible.

CONTENTS

PREFACE

"Positive Teaching" as utilized in this book connotes the understanding, use, and application of those pedagogical competencies (knowledges, skills, attitudes) which promote permanent learning on the part of students. Positive teaching will

- motivate students to learn more and to better learn
- promote the development of positive self-concepts on the part of the student, and
- result in the type of behavior modification which is beneficial to students and satisfying to teachers.

The Power of Positive Teaching consists of four sections, while the Introduction describes my perception of the educational process.

Section I examines "A Philosophy for Positive Teaching" and consists of four chapters. Chapter 1 describes the characteristics of an effective teacher, while Chapter 2 identifies the ingredients of effective teaching. Chapters 3 and 4 deal with the establishment and management of a positive educational environment.

"A Psychology for Positive Learning" is provided in Section II.

Section III presents "A Delivery System for Positive Teaching." In this section, emphasis is placed upon planning, delivering, evaluating, and applying learning for a positive educational experience.

In Section IV the various components of a positive delivery system are discussed. This section consists of eleven chapters. Each chapter details one specific aspect involved in delivering a positive educational experience. Topics range from analyzing subject matter to concluding a lesson.

This book is designed to assist many different individuals who are involved in the teaching-learning process. The rationale, teaching practices, and techniques presented should help experienced teachers to further hone their teaching skills; it should serve as a valuable reference to prepare prospective teachers; and it should provide a major source of information for those people who enter the teaching profession with little or no preparation in the field of pedagogy but who possess vast experience in business and industry. In the final analysis, the concepts of teaching and learning covered in this book are applicable to any individual who desires to change the behavior of another individual or individuals in a positive manner.

Finally, this book was written so that students may experience the substance and rigor of a real education. It is hoped that people who read and study the pedagogy presented will be more dedicated and committed to the enterprise of teaching. If this were to happen, the dignity of teaching would be augmented. It is my firm belief that effective (positive) teaching is the first step toward educational reform.

ACKNOWLEDGMENTS

The author wishes to recognize those individuals who provided valuable input into this book: To Glen M. Miller for offering suggestions on specific chapters and to David E. Cox for providing the initial manuscripts for Chapters 16, 17, and 19. Special recognition is due to Clinton O. Jacobs and Angela L. McCormick Owen who meticulously edited the entire content of this book.

In addition, special recognition is given to those teachers who have practiced the pedagogy described in this book. Through their actions and efforts, they have helped to provide integrity and validity for the content of *The Power of Positive Teaching*.

INTRODUCTION

It is pertinent to define, at the very onset, the concept of the education process which will serve as the foundation upon which to build and discuss the sections and accompanying chapters contained in this book. It is essential that the *purpose of education*, in general terms, be described as I perceive it, as well as my interpretation of *teaching* and *learning*, since each will impact upon the philosophy of teaching and the psychology of learning presented herein.

The term "educational process" connotes different meanings to different people. In order to establish a common frame of reference in this book, this process is discussed as it relates to the following dimensions:

• The Purpose of Education
• Teaching and Learning
• The Teaching-Learning Process

What is education? What is it attempting to accomplish? Education, whether formal or nonformal, is a process. It is a deliberate act since it is planned to achieve specific objectives preconceived as desirable for others to achieve. Education, simply defined, is the *process of changing the behavior of people*. This process involves both decision making and the acceptance of the possible consequences of those decisions. As a result, both rewards and penalties are to be realized. The final outcome is based upon the type of decisions made and the actions taken.

A teacher is a "change agent"! To change the learner's behavior in a positive manner, the teacher must understand both the learner and the ways in which a person learns. Teachers must know their students. In essence, to be an effective change agent, teachers need to possess an understanding of "A Psychology for Positive Learning" so that they can apply those principles and laws which affect learning. To become an effective and positive teacher, it is absolutely essential that the teacher understand what learnings are to be achieved as a result of the educational process. Moreover, a teacher must possess and apply "A Personal Philosophy for Positive Teaching." As John Dewey so succinctly stated, "Education is that reconstructing or reorganizing of experience which adds to the meaning of experience, and which increases ability to direct the course of subsequent experiences" [1]. As will be demonstrated throughout this book, the educational process can best be accomplished through student *involvement* and *experience*! Students must be involved and engaged in their *own* education.

Individuals are the sum total of their experiences! As such, no thought or action experienced by the individual is lost or forgotten. All thoughts and actions are retained in either the conscious or subconscious part of a person's mind. A thought or action can be recalled rather easily from the conscious mind. On the other hand, thoughts or actions stored in a person's subconscious are not consciously available. For most effective recall, student involvement in an educational experience is essential. Thus, active participation on the part of the student in concert with relevant and positive educational experiences for the student is stressed throughout this book.

THE PURPOSE OF EDUCATION

In 1917, a National Commission on Education identified seven cardinal aims of education which are still sound today. This Commission believed an education should address and provide for the following. It should

1. Teach good health

2. Teach command of fundamental processes

3. Teach worthy use of leisure time

4. Teach vocation and career preparation

5. Stress citizenship

6. Contribute to worthy home membership

7. Develop ethical character

All of these aims are important today and should be provided in a well rounded education.

In addition, over time the purpose of education has evolved into the following broad aims:

1. To develop competencies within the learner which will assist that individual to solve problems encountered in life;

2. To bring about desirable changes in the learner through the development of effective (positive and useful) abilities, attitudes, understandings, appreciations, ideas, and habits.

Specifically, the main objective of general education is to develop a broadly educated person with additional competencies in a subject matter field. More specifically, the student should develop the ability to

1. Communicate ideas clearly and effectively

2. Develop and use a personal philosophy of living

3. Understand and apply democratic concepts to problems and situations

4. Think effectively in terms of local, state, national, and international issues

5. Participate effectively in civic affairs

6. Appreciate the cultural and aesthetic aspects of society

7. Appreciate and use the scientific approach in dealing with problem situations

8. Work effectively with people

In the final analysis, educational pursuits should be directed toward the development of an individual's ability to (1) function as a purposeful and useful citizen in a democratic society; (2) identify and solve problems encountered in life; and (3) cope with and appreciate the "reality of living."

To this end, the *central purpose* of education should be to develop within an individual

- Rational reasoning ability
- Ability to think
- Ability to solve problems

Numerous philosophical approaches may be utilized to accomplish the central purpose of education. It is beyond the context and scope of this book to discuss in detail these approaches. However, it is important for teachers to understand that several approaches may be utilized to achieve the aims and purpose of education. Whichever educational approach is used, it involves the "deliberate process" of changing the behavior of people. And to be positive learning for students, the process is designed to provide participation through

- Action
- Involvement
- Experience

TEACHING AND LEARNING

The educational process, as presented here, involves the learning process, the teaching process, and the teaching-learning process. The learning process describes how students learn, while the teaching process explains how teachers can create and promote an environment conducive to positive learning. Both the learning and the teaching process imply and require action. The teaching-learning process brings both processes together in a descriptive way.

People are in charge of their own lives, actions, and learnings. They must be aware of what they say and do for they are the ones ultimately responsible for the consequences of their own actions. This statement carries with it several implications pertaining to the interaction process referred to as the "Teaching and Learning" process.

The Learning Process

Teaching and learning are deliberate acts. A simple definition of learning is *a positive change in the behavior of an individual.* Learning is an active process; it is not passive. Moreover, learning is a lifelong process! Behavior connotes the manner in which an organism reacts or responds to stimuli. If a student's learning results in a change in behavior, then a positive change in behavior should result in the improved performance of that student.

Behavior can be expressed as either innate behavior (inherited) or learned behavior (acquired) or a combination of innate and learned behavior. Innate behavior is unlearned behavior [2]. Teachers should be aware of the importance of innate behavior in the growth and development of the individual. However, they should concentrate their efforts upon changing and modifying, in a positive way, those learned (acquired) behaviors which can be observed and measured.

Likewise, behavior can be covert and overt. Actual feelings, thoughts, fears, etc., of an individual cannot be observed. However, they exist. They are covert. Observable behaviors, such as actually doing or performing or acting are referred to as overt behaviors. They can be seen and, in most cases, measured. Learning can result in changes in both covert and overt behavior, and teachers should concentrate their efforts upon modifying, in a positive way, each of these behaviors.

Without a change in human behavior, learning has not occurred. Learning is a process. Learning connotes a change in performance. The degree of learning or behavior modification, and the degree to which learning is positive or negative, depends, to a great extent, upon the stimuli utilized to affect the desired change. In the learning process, the stimuli become the "sum total" of the teaching-learning environment. If the learning environment is conceived and maintained in a positive manner, the behavior modification of students will more likely develop in a positive vein. It must be remembered that change in behavior results in new learnings. Thus, behavior modification and learning are assumed to be synonymous.

An Educational Competency

Based upon the definition of learning presented here, learning results in behavior modification or change. Carsie Hammonds states that this change can be a "doing" behavior, or a "knowing" behavior, or a "feeling" behavior [3]. Educators have long classified learning into three domains of learning—the cognitive domain, the psychomotor domain and the affective domain. The "knowing," "doing," and "feeling" behavior changes expressed by Hammonds in concert with the three acceptable domains of learning provide a means to identify the types of learning essential to formulate a definition of an educational competency. This comparison is illustrated as follows:

Learning Behavior	Learning Domain	Learning Type
Knowing	Cognitive	Knowledges
Doing	Psychomotor	Skills
Feeling	Affective	Attitudes
		Appreciations
		Values

To help conceptualize these comparisons, the following "ASK" construct is provided:

The "ASK" Construct

Using the above construct, a working definition of an "educational competency" can be developed to encompass all aspects of learning. An educational competency connotes "a knowledge, a skill, or an attitude, value, etc., or a combination of the three." Since one of the aims of education is "to develop competencies," it is obvious all three types of behavior changes must be incorporated into a well rounded, quality educational program. In essence, students must possess the ability to know and understand (cognitive domain); the ability to do and perform (psychomotor domain); and the ability to appreciate or to possess positive attitudes or to value something (affective domain).

Individual Differences

In order for the learning process to be truly positive, it is essential that the teacher recognize individual differences among students. There is no such organism as an "average" student. No two people learn at the same rate. Teachers must modify their lessons to accommodate these learning differences. It must also be pointed out that each student has a predominate and preferred learning style. Effective teachers try to provide a variety of instructional strategies to meet each student's learning style needs.

Students' experiences and backgrounds are different. Teachers must be cognizant of cultural differences existing among students in their classes. It is important that teachers recognize and understand those cultural characteristics and/or features which are unique in their students. Teachers must plan, deliver, and, if necessary, adjust their educational experiences to avoid inhibiting the learning of those students who may not be familiar with certain conditions and concepts in the teacher's culture. Teachers who recognize these differences and plan their teaching accordingly will help students to better realize positive and maximum learning within their capabilities.

It is important that teachers determine the degree of difference existing between individual students and between groups or classes of students. These differences can be determined through (1) class discussions; (2) oral questions; (3) student records; (4) private conferences; (5) visits to students' homes; and (6) assessment of learning styles, to cite a few. Nothing is so unequal as the equal treatment of unequals; some teachers plan and teach classes in such a manner that all students in the class are considered to be equally intelligent, equally motivated, and equally prepared to learn new and different competencies. In a positive learning experience, individual differences must be considered.

The Teaching Process

Simply stated, teaching can be defined as a *directing of the learning process so the behavior modifications occurring in students are directed toward positive results and are of a permanent nature.* Teaching, like learning, can be negative, neutral, or positive. Positive teaching results in more and better learning. Teaching is a process just as is learning. It is a deliberate or preconceived act consisting of specific behaviors performed by the teacher. The teacher becomes the facilitator of the "change" process. Both learning and teaching imply and require action. However, learning and teaching are not separate acts. They occur in concert with each other. This is referred to as the teaching-learning process. As will be pointed out later, teachers are not only facilitators of the learning process, but are motivators and witnesses to the values in life which they consider are important to instill in students.

Positive teaching is a twofold proposition. In the process, teachers gain understanding as they plan and deliver a deliberate educational experience for students. It has been said that to teach is to learn a second time. Likewise, the student learns by acquiring new knowledge or skills or by establishing new attitudes, values, and goals. Both the teacher and the student gain as a result of positive teaching.

The effective teacher teaches something new at every class session. The student learns new knowledges, skills, attitudes, and values, etc., as a result of the interaction between the two.

THE TEACHING-LEARNING PROCESS

Since learning is a process and teaching is also a process, the combination of teaching and learning is likewise a process—a deliberate act. The teaching-learning process is nothing more than *a series of actions and interactions between the teacher and the learner* designed to change the behavior of people. It, like both teaching and learning, implies and requires action.

Based upon Figure I.1, the greater the interaction between the teacher and the learner, the greater the relative degree of change expected in the behavior of the student, assuming the interaction is positive and directed toward the achievement of educational objectives.

The Teaching-Learning Process Is An Active Process

"People learn by their own learning" [4]. Learning is an active process! It is not reactive! Individuals learn only through their own efforts! No one else can learn for another person. Learning cannot be given away! Nor can it be bought! Only the opportunity to learn can be pur-

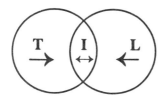

T = Teacher
L = Learner
I = Interaction
    (Learning)

Figure I.1   The Teaching-Learning Process

chased. Students learn through activity. And students do not learn as a result of what a teacher does—they learn as a result of what the teacher gets them to do! The best education is achieved. Certainly, most students "learn by doing."

In essence, the student who expects to learn by simply sitting back and listening is likely to be disappointed and, in all probability, will be bored because there is little or no "action" involved. On the other hand, the teacher who relies solely upon the "I'll lecture; you listen!" type of teaching *is not* likely to see much permanent learning take place. The lecture is a good way to present information; however, it is a poor way to teach students. Lecturing promotes memorization, not thinking, on the part of the student.

Since the teaching-learning process is an active process, the action must focus primarily on the student, not the teacher. The instruction must be "student centered," not "teacher centered" or "subject matter centered." The effective teacher thus plans a series and a variety of positive, participatory activities and experiences for students. Activities which promote "action" in a learning environment include the following.

- Observing
- Listening
- Thinking
- Remembering
- Imagining
- Writing
- Answering

- Questioning
- Feeling
- Touching
- Moving
- Agreeing
- Disagreeing
- Discussing

Those activities and experiences listed above promote the use of more than one sense and, at the same time, cause students to become involved. In essence, the more that students participate, the more they become involved. The more they become involved in the educational experience, the more they will use their six senses and, thus, the more likely it will be that residual learning will occur.

Change In Behavior Occurs In The Teaching-Learning Process

Since learning results in a change in behavior, students have not learned if they behave just as they did before the learning experience occurred. As pointed out earlier, however, these changes in behavior can be either positive or negative. Moreover, behavior changes do not truly become an integral part of an individual until those changes have been reinforced through use. Students must be involved in the process of learning. The importance of action and involvement of students in their own learning cannot be overemphasized as it relates to the power of positive teaching.

No discussion of the teaching-learning process would be complete without reference to the concepts, principles, and laws affecting how people learn. In Chapter 5, a concept of the teaching-learning process which incorporates these concepts, principles, and laws is presented in greater detail.

Throughout this book, reference is made to these "concepts," "principles," and "laws" affecting teaching and learning. These are defined as follows:

- A *concept* is an idea or notion conceived in the mind of one person which can be communicated either orally or visually to another person,
- A *principle* is a fundamental truth which is applicable to many different situations, and
- A *law* is an absolute truth which has withstood the test of time.

The psychological significance of each of the above as it impacts upon the teaching-learning process is illustrated in Figure I.2.

Students must be taught to think; therefore, teaching students those concepts, principles, and laws essential for them to develop the ability to reason logically and to make sound decisions is stressed throughout this book.

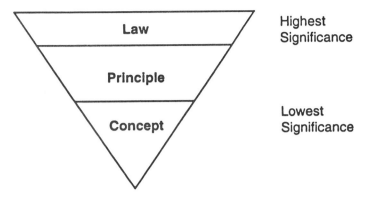

Figure I.2 Hierarchy of Concept, Principle, and Law as Each Affects Teaching and Learning

SUMMARY

This Introduction has presented my perception of the purpose of education, broadly defined. Likewise, the definition of learning, teaching, and the teaching-learning process has been presented in order to provide a foundation for the further discussion of *The Power of Positive Teaching*.

Education should provide experiences so students can develop to their maximum potential. Since teachers change the lives of their students forever, it is imperative that the educational process create a sense of excitement about learning and involve students actively in a mixture of intense hard work and enjoyment. Quality education must stress the development of reasoning, thinking, and decision making abilities on the part of students.

ENDNOTES

1. Dewey, John. *Democracy and Education*. The Macmillan Company, 1916, p. 76.
2. Hammonds, Carsie. *Teaching Agriculture*. McGraw-Hill, 1950, p. 1.
3. Hammonds, op. cit., p. 12.
4. Hammonds, Carsie and Lamar, Carl F. *Teaching Vocations*. Interstate Printers, 1968, p. 5.

SECTION I

A PHILOSOPHY FOR POSITIVE TEACHING

As a reader who has opened and begun reading the first section of a book entitled *The Power of Positive Teaching*, you have already identified yourself as an individual who is concerned about the effectiveness of teaching and learning in our schools today.

If you are a parent or an observer in the school system of your community or nation, this book is for you; it is important that you recognize good schools and good teaching and it is important that you recognize when real learning is taking place.

If you are an administrator in our nation's schools, this book is for you; it is important that you support positive teaching and positive learning in your program.

If you are a teacher in those schools, this book is, indeed, for you, because while every concerned teacher aspires to be a better teacher, most wish to be the best teacher they can possibly be. If you are a teacher, this book can help you to attain that goal. And, for several reasons, this book is written especially for you.

First, on a very personal level for you as a teacher, being a "good teacher" and attaining success with your students and in your classroom are essential to your emotional survival. Feelings of failure and chaos caused by consistently frustrating experiences with students can destroy the self-concept and self-confidence of any teacher; living with these feelings can create real personal stress. On the other hand, instructors who feel successful in their classrooms gain a sense of control over their lives and develop a sense of security and confidence. This book can help you to gain even more of that sense of control, security, and confidence.

In addition, effective teachers who provide their students with valuable tools, opportunities, and experiences as they prepare those students for the future earn for themselves both extrinsic and intrinsic rewards. Extrinsic reward for you as a teacher comes when your peers recognize you for doing a quality job of preparing students; extrinsic reward is earned when clear-thinking students, parents, and the community appreciate you for doing an important job well. This book can help you to earn even more the respect and appreciation of others who care about quality in our schools.

And, finally, for many, many teachers, feelings of real success come best with the intrinsic reward that develops from doing an important job . . . and from knowing that it has been done well, from giving of themselves to better another or to strengthen our society. This book can help you to attain that most meaningful of rewards.

If good teaching is both an art and a science, a significant part of superior instruction can be broken down into observable parts and arranged into steps which can be followed, one after the other. Read carefully the sections of this text step by step, analyzing your existing teaching style and modifying it when appropriate to create YOUR own personal Power of Positive Teaching.

This text will help you to develop the characteristics of an effective teacher. It will help you to determine your philosophy for positive teaching and the psychology for positive learning, finally guiding you as you create an orderly system for effectively delivering positive learning to your students.

To begin, you must have a personal philosophy, and, to be effective, that philosophy must be a philosophy for positive teaching.

Philosophy, as used in this book, connotes "the beliefs, values, perceptions, concepts, and attitudes held by an individual." Thus, a philosophy of teaching reflects how a teacher views, values, perceives, and/or understands students as that teacher directs learning experiences which promote positive changes in student behavior.

The first section of this text addresses the topic of a philosophy for positive teaching and the following topics are dealt with in the four chapters of Section I.

- Describing the Characteristics of an Effective Teacher
- Identifying the Ingredients of Effective Teaching
- Establishing a Positive Learning Environment
- Managing a Positive Educational Environment

Some might argue that establishing and managing a positive learning/educational environment should be included under the later section on "Psychology For Positive Learning." This may be so; however, these two topics have been placed under Section I dealing with "A Philosophy For Positive Teaching," since it will be the beliefs and values and attitudes held by the teacher which, in the final analysis, will most influence how well positive learning environments are established and maintained.

The terms "student" and "learner" are used synonymously in this publication. Some would argue that every person is a "learner" while some would believe everyone is a "student." To dispel any misinterpretation, in this text the terms student and learner are used interchangeably to mean the same.

Likewise, the terms "student" and "learner" are used to describe any person of any age who is involved in the educational process. The pedagogical concepts, practices, and techniques presented in this book are applicable for planning and delivering educational experiences for students at any educational level. Regardless of the educational level, the teacher will need only to modify the degree and intensity of specific concepts, practices, and techniques used depending upon the maturation of the students being taught.

The terms "effective teaching" and "positive teaching" are used to describe the phenomenon of facilitating the learning process to achieve the desired outcome.

As discussed in the preface, *positive teaching* connotes the understanding of, the use of, and the application of those pedagogical competencies which promote more and better learning on the part of the student. Positive teaching will (1) motivate students; (2) promote the development of positive self-concepts on the part of the student, and (3) result in behavior changes which are beneficial to students and satisfying to the teacher.

CHAPTER 1

Describing the Characteristics of an Effective Teacher

What is one of the greatest things that can be said about a person? Ranking high on the list would be that this person is a good teacher! It is the responsibility of every person to teach others in some way, and it is the priviledge of many to teach as professionals. So what is meant by the term "a good teacher?" How would one describe a good teacher? What are the characteristics of a good teacher? Why is it important that an effective teacher be discussed in the first place?

Pedagogy is the art and science of teaching. It is an art because of the methods used by a teacher to plan and deliver a lesson. Effective teachers involve and utilize the "interactive" process. On the other hand, it is a science due to the fact that research proven principles and laws of learning are applied in the teaching-learning process.

Effective teaching is a learned trait that can be perfected and improved with practice and experience. Teaching can be enhanced by the application of learning principles. It has been said of teachers, "We all know how to teach better than we do!" Very few teachers teach as well as they know how to teach.

CHARACTERISTICS OF AN EFFECTIVE TEACHER

There are numerous opinions on what constitutes a good teacher. Are there certain attributes which tend to separate the "good" from the "not so good" teacher? It is important that those characteristics of a good teacher be discussed at the onset, since it is known that one of the most important factors in determining the success of any educational program is the *quality of the teaching*, which is a direct reflection upon the quality of the teacher. If the teaching is effective, desired behavioral changes will be developed in the students. The student who has learned will think, feel, and act differently. Most people have an idea of who they consider to have been one of their "good" teachers. What did these teachers possess which makes them remembered? Could answers to the following questions help identify the characteristics of a "good" teacher?

Feeling

- How did this teacher treat his or her students?
- Did the teacher show empathy and/or sympathy towards the students?
- What feelings did this teacher demonstrate towards students?
- Did this teacher believe in the "worth" of the individual student?

Class Control

- Who was in command of the learning environment—the teacher or the students?
- Who was the master of the teaching-learning process?
- Was instruction handled in a businesslike manner?
- Did the teacher command or demand respect of the students?
- Did the instruction have purpose and direction?
- Did the students know when they had mastered the subject matter being taught?
- What characteristics did this person possess regarding classroom management and student behavior?
- Were student and class expectations communicated to the students by the teacher?

Attitude

- What type of attitude did this teacher possess?
- What type of attitude did this teacher attempt to instill in students?

- Did this teacher look upon teaching as a chore?
- Did this teacher enjoy teaching?
- Was this teacher well prepared for teaching?
- How often did this teacher complain about the "long hours" and the "low pay"?
- Did this teacher smile and use humor in class?
- Was this teacher an "upbeat" or a "downbeat" type of person?
- How would you describe this teacher's attitude toward teaching?

Subject Matter

- Did this teacher enjoy learning about the "unknown"?
- Did this teacher create a desire on the part of students to learn?
- Was this teacher excited about new things or about gaining new experiences?
- How would you rate this teacher regarding knowledge of the subject matter taught?

Value and Relevance of Learning

- Was the time spent with this teacher boring or exciting?
- Was the content taught useful?
- Did this teacher help students to establish goals and then teach to assist students to achieve these goals?
- Were the students' needs satisfied?
- Did this teacher explain the value and usefulness of the subject matter being learned?
- Did the instruction have value to help students solve problems or to cope with life's challenges?
- Did this teacher make learning meaningful and useful?
- How would you classify the time spent with this teacher—useful or useless?

From the above sets of questions, it is apparent that effective teachers possess certain attributes which distinguish them from "other" teachers. How important is it for a teacher to demonstrate positive feelings toward students or to be in control of the learning environment in a *positive* and yet enjoyable manner? Certainly the attitude toward self and toward teaching is critical for effective teaching to result. Teachers cannot teach something they do not know or understand. Likewise, what is taught should satisfy student needs, be enjoyable, have value, and be useful. If these assumptions are correct, then it is possible to describe the major attributes of an effective teacher.

MAJOR ATTRIBUTES OF AN EFFECTIVE TEACHER

Most successful individuals, regardless of the endeavor, possess essential abilities such as the ability to communicate ideas on an eye-to-eye basis with others; the ability to reason; the ability to organize; and the ability to have a positive attitude about new ideas. In addition to the above abilities, effective teachers possess certain attributes which distinguish them from other teachers.

1. Effective teachers have strong, positive feelings for students and are not afraid to demonstrate these feelings; they show the students that they "love" them in a platonic manner. These teachers like students. They respect students. These teachers create an atmosphere of caring about students.

2. Effective teachers are effective disciplinarians without being overly authoritative. They are "master of their classrooms" but do not turn students off. They stress a disciplined learning environment mixed with compassion and provide "no nonsense" educational opportunities leavened with kindness.

3. Effective teachers possess a positive attitude toward teaching and let the students know that the instructors enjoy what they are doing. These teachers are enthusiastic about teaching and enthusiastic about their students and themselves. These teachers establish high expectations combined with much helpfulness. They are teachers both in and out of the classroom. They radiate a "winning" attitude. They not only possess a positive attitude toward teaching, but toward students and themselves, as well. These teachers attempt to instill this same positive attitude in their students by serving as a role model.

4. Effective teachers are enthusiastic. They show excitement about what they teach. They are excited about their students. These teachers know that their enthusiasm is related to students' achievement. Enthusiasm is the most important ingredient of effective and positive teaching. The enthusiastic teacher conveys a great sense of commitment, excitement, and involvement with the subject matter content. Animation on the part of this teacher is expressed by nonverbal communication and gestures. Lessons are imaginative, stimulating, and students respond in a positive manner and appear to enjoy the educational activity.

5. Effective teachers know the subject matter being taught. These teachers encourage students to become scholars.

6. Effective teachers make learning relevant. Their teaching is meaningful and useful. They teach to satisfy students' needs. These teachers stress application of what has been taught to assist students in learning to think, reason, and make decisions.

7. Effective teachers are attentive listeners. The ability of the teacher to listen to students is a golden quality.

Effective teachers are positive people who believe in the worth and dignity of the student; these teachers are excited about what they do and they know how to manipulate students so the learners will produce or perform at their maximum level of ability.

OTHER IMPORTANT ATTRIBUTES

Other important attributes associated with an effective teacher are "caught and not taught" as a result of experience and education. Some of the more salient are listed below.

Initiative

Effective teachers work at the job of teaching. They initiate new teaching practices and procedures in their teaching. They are hard, but smart, workers. They are considered to be innovators by their peers.

Resourcefulness

Effective teachers are always looking for new ideas, teaching materials, and techniques to incorporate into their teaching. They are creative and can envision how a particular situation or problem can be utilized to make their teaching more relevant and useful.

Maturity

The abilities to make rational decisions and to use "common sense" are important attributes of effective teachers. They know when to react and when not to react.

Humility

The ability to be humble, yet to be confident in one's capabilities, is a valuable attribute for effective teachers to possess. They know the feelings of their students and realize when a student must be treated with humility.

Self-esteem and inner pride

Positive self-concepts are essential for any individual to live the happy life. Effective teachers possess self-esteem and are confident in their abilities. They know, without being told by someone else, when they have done a good job. They believe in themselves.

Feeling for Others

The demonstration of empathy is of paramount importance for the effective teacher. Since all people have feelings, it is essential that a teacher know how students feel and then practice the art of showing feelings for them. An effective teacher is "someone who cares!"

Ability to Set the PACE

Most of the attributes cited above as being essential for an effective teacher to possess and utilize also hold true for any purposeful, successful, and happy individual. These attributes are not unique to teachers. They are advocated in this chapter, however, because teachers need to exhibit these characteristics if they are going to be able to instill these and other values in their students. Students tend to emulate those traits (both positive and negative) demonstrated or practiced by their teachers. Therefore, it is imperative that teachers possess and then reflect in their own teachings those attributes important for students to mimic and utilize.

In essence, those attributes, values, and attitudes possessed by a particular teacher not only direct that teacher's thoughts and actions, but, more importantly, provide the basis for that teacher's approach to teaching. For the most effective teaching to occur, it is obvious that the power of positive teaching should be the model. Positive Attitudes Change Everything. Teachers must *Set the PACE!* A teacher must serve as a positive role model for students.

BEHAVIORAL CHARACTERISTICS OF EFFECTIVE TEACHERS

Students should receive a positive and quality education. Effective teaching can result only when the teacher plans for teaching and then uses these plans and appropriate techniques to teach students.

Those teachers who understand and practice the power of positive teaching demonstrate these behavioral characteristics. They

1. are willing to change their ideas, dress, and behavior when appropriate

2. are able to see the other person's point of view and are open-minded

3. complain only when there is a real grievance

4. enjoy working with people and are cooperative

5. have faith in the worth of the individual and faith in the value of teaching as a help to developing individuals

6. are honest about situations and do not make excuses

7. use tact when criticizing others

8. maintain good eye contact when talking with other people, knowing that the eyes are one of their most effective teaching tools

9. respect opinions and ideas of other individuals, yet make it clear that they are also allowed to have opinions

10. have a wide variety of interests and the ability to utilize their interests to excite and motivate students

11. smile easily and have a good sense of humor

12. accept responsibility

13. understand people and their development

14. exhibit desirable moral character

15. have the ability to communicate effectively

16. exhibit good citizenship in the school and community

17. have the ability to evaluate objectively

18. are sincere, dedicated, and committed

19. exhibit the ability to establish and maintain standards

20. set a positive example for students

Do effective teachers like to be liked? Sure, but only if it does not distract from or hinder their positive classroom management and positive student control. Too much familiarity breeds deceit. Effective teachers demonstrate these ways to make people like them in a positive manner. They

1. become genuinely interested in other people

2. remember that a person's name is to him or her the sweetest and most important sound in the English language

3. become good listeners, encouraging others to talk about themselves

4. talk in terms of the other person's interests

5. make the other person feel important and do it sincerely

Being able to identify the characteristics of an effective teacher is one thing; being able to put these characteristics into practice is quite another. Learning *why* to teach students and learning *how* to teach students should provide a basis for developing those characteristics desired in an effective teacher. It is essential for teachers, both current and future practitioners, to understand and exhibit those characteristics which constitute good teaching. In the final analysis, the effective teacher is a *human engineer!*

SUMMARY

This chapter has identified those attributes and characteristics of an effective teacher (both tangible and intangible) which are essential if positive teaching is to occur. However, those characteristics described for the effective teacher would also apply to any professional who "works with people." In the final analysis, those intangible traits identified in this chapter are probably more important than the tangible ones when it comes to planning and delivering a positive educational experience. Since the intangible traits are difficult to teach, it is imperative they be identified so that teachers can exert time and effort to perfect these attributes in order to be successful as facilitators of a positive teaching-learning process.

Effective teachers exhibit passion for teaching and compassion for those they teach. There is no secret to being an effective teacher. However, those teachers who can be classified as *effective* have the desire and motivation to teach; they learn and perfect teaching behaviors which are effective; they are dedicated and committed to teaching; and they possess talent, natural ability, and drive. Effective teachers

- believe in themselves; they are proud to teach
- hold good self concepts
- have positive attitudes about themselves, their students, and the teaching profession
- know that it is up to them to succeed
- give of themselves to their students
- develop and improve teaching techniques
- listen attentively to their students

CHAPTER 2

Identifying the Ingredients of Effective Teaching

Based upon the qualifications of an effective teacher, it is rather easy to synthesize a list of basic ingredients of effective teaching. It is important to identify and discuss these basic ingredients of effective teaching since they provide the foundation for the eventual utilization of approved teaching practices and techniques.

BASIC INGREDIENTS

Effective teaching requires the use of all of the following.

- *A pre-plan or guide to direct the learning*
  Teaching without a delivery (lesson) plan is like telling time with a clock without hands.
- *Well defined educational objectives*
  Students have the right to know what is expected of them. A more positive learning environment is created when educational objectives are defined early in the lesson.
- *Instruction based upon the student's needs*
  Positive teaching is promoted when teachers teach to satisfy students' needs.
- *Strong lesson introductions which build a case for learning*
  Effective teachers make a concerted effort to get students to "buy

into" the lesson. These teachers are excited about what they teach and they know that there is a direct relationship between their enthusiasm and student achievement. Teachers stress their enthusiasm and the utility and value of the lesson being taught during the introduction.

- *Active involvement of students*
  An education is achieved by participation and active involvement; it is not received. Student-centered instruction promotes positive learning. The more senses used, the more and better the learning.
- *Oral questions*
  The use of effective thought provoking oral questions is one of the easiest and most effective teaching tools available to teachers.
- *Problem solving teaching*
  Students should gain experience in using the decision making process. They need practice in the application of this process. Problem solving teaching provides positive learning activities associated with lifelong learning.
- *Instructional realia*
  As the old adage states, "One picture is worth a thousand words!" Realia, any resource materials that relate instruction to real life, tend to stimulate student interest and promote more active involvement in the lesson.
- *Appropriate reference materials*
  Students need to learn how to glean information and knowledge from reference materials. One of the great outcomes of positive teaching is to teach students how to study, how to take notes, and how to evaluate reference materials.
- *Supervised study*
  Since students learn from their own actions, it is essential they be provided the opportunity to study under the guidance of the teacher. They need to learn how to "discover the unknown." They must learn how to learn.
- *Complete conclusion for each lesson*
  If one or two key points or concepts are taught to students each class period, a great deal will be achieved during a school year. It is important for the teacher to summarize and conclude each day's lesson by highlighting the key points learned.
- *Application of concepts and principles taught*
  No learning technique is as effective as real experience. Nothing

"fixes" learning like the actual application of newly acquired competencies to real life situations.

- *Appropriate classroom management and student control*
The teacher designs and utilizes an environment conducive to positive learning. Students appreciate knowing what is expected from them regarding mannerisms and conduct.

USING THE BASIC INGREDIENTS OF EFFECTIVE TEACHING

Since effective teachers use these thirteen ingredients of effective teaching, it is essential that each be discussed in sufficient detail so teachers understand *why* they contribute to positive teaching and *how* they can be utilized to promote effective learning. Once the "why" and the "how" are established for each basic ingredient, it is possible to synthesize a list of approved teaching practices and techniques which can be used by the teacher to promote positive teaching and effective learning. In the final analysis, effective teachers would utilize these ingredients in their day-in, day-out teaching.

The constant use of these basic ingredients of effective teaching will promote the most effective and longest lasting behavioral modification of students by changing the way they think, act, and feel. In addition, their use will make teachers more effective in promoting the development of positive attitudes, understandings, values, and appreciations within their students. Basic ingredients of effective teaching promote the power of positive teaching and at the same time assist students to observe a systematic approach to solving problems. Thus, the delivery system utilized in the day-in, day-out teaching of the instructor will make a significant contribution to students' grasp of how the problem solving process is applied.

SUMMARY

Just as there are certain characteristics which an effective teacher possesses, there are basic elements which, if properly utilized, will contribute to more effective and positive teaching. Effective teachers know what these ingredients are and possess the ability to put them into practice in the learning environment.

Each of the basic ingredients identified in this chapter is discussed in greater detail in a later chapter of this book. Section IV is devoted to a detailed discussion of these critical elements of effective teaching.

CHAPTER 3

Establishing a Positive Learning Environment

Positive teaching should promote positive learning. Positive learning should result in desirable changes in student behavior which should produce improved performance. This concept is illustrated as follows:

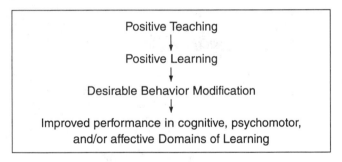

Positive Teaching
↓
Positive Learning
↓
Desirable Behavior Modification
↓
Improved performance in cognitive, psychomotor, and/or affective Domains of Learning

LEARNING ENVIRONMENT

Biologically, an environment refers to the surroundings in which an organism lives and relates to other organisms. Thus, a "learning environment" connotes the *sum total* of all physical, cultural, social, and emotional factors influencing or surrounding an individual placed in a learning situation. Learning environments are not necessarily confined to classrooms but can be found in school laboratories, in the field (field trips), in the community (businesses, etc.) and in any location wherever there is interaction between a teacher and a learner.

Why is it important to build a positive learning environment for students? What should teachers do to establish an environment conducive to positive and effective learning?

POSITIVE CRITICISM

Very few individuals like to be criticized, particularly in front of their peers or in public. Criticism connotes improper behavior or performance. However, people probably learn as much from negative experiences as they do from positive ones. Criticism offered in a constructive manner is a very effective teaching tool. The proper use of criticism becomes a very challenging responsibility for a teacher. In essence, positive learning can occur through a teacher's skillful use of positive criticism.

However, most people do not like to be told what to do or how to act by someone else. When this happens, it tends to impinge upon one's own ego. There is probably nothing more damaging than deflating an individual's ego. There is a direct correlation between one's ego and one's self-esteem.

Deflating Egos

The following examples will help illustrate how loss of self-esteem can or could happen. Most people have experienced similar situations.

Example 1.   How do teenagers react when they are told by their parents to be home by 10:00 p.m. when other youngsters are allowed to stay out until 1:00 a.m.? Do they feel that their parents do not trust them?

Example 2.   How do employees respond when they are told by the "boss" that they are doing a poor job? What tends to happen to their future performance when no positive reinforcement is provided?

Example 3.   How do students perform on a paper and pencil test when the teacher tells them, "There is no need for you to take the test because you cannot pass it anyway"?

Example 4.　How does a class react when it is told continuously, "You are the dumbest group of students I've ever had"?

These examples illustrate not only how a student's ego and self-esteem can be "deflated," but also how to provide a negative learning environment for students. Under no circumstances, however, should students be led to believe that they possess abilities or capabilities which they do not have, nor should they be told they are "better" than they actually are. Students need to be informed of their capabilities and of the results of their performance as accurately and correctly as possible, but in a positive manner. Emotional tension on the part of the student should be kept to a minimum. Emotional tension decreases efficiency in learning.

Natural Hostility

Because it relates to building a positive learning environment, it must be pointed out that there is a "natural hostility" which exists between a teacher and the students. This same kind of hostility exists between parents and their children, between employers and their employees, and between any two organisms when one tends to threaten the independence of thought, action, or behavior of the other organism, or when one organism gives an indication to inflict evil, injury, or damage to another. People are organisms; therefore, people possess these natural hostilities.

Whenever an individual's ego is threatened by being told or made to do something that the individual does not want to do, whether it be by parents, teachers, police, or the "boss," this hostility may surface. Most people control this hostility because they have learned that harm or damage will result if they resist doing what they are told to do. For example, when a teacher makes a homework assignment, students' natural resistance is aroused since they do not want to take the necessary time to complete the assignment—doing the work will take away valuable time which could be used to do those things they want to do after school.

Unstable or immature students may revolt by either complaining loudly or by failing to complete the homework. On the other hand, mature, sincere, and committed students think through the consequences—if they do not do the work, they fail the assignment, if they do the work, they succeed. Although they may not want to do the assignment or they may not be too happy about the assignment, they do it anyway. They have learned to cope with the system, to work within it, and not to fight it!

POSITIVE LEARNING ENVIRONMENT

Why is it important to build a positive learning environment? The answer is obvious! *A positive learning environment will promote positive student achievement,* lessening the hostility natural between learner and teacher. What should teachers do to maintain an environment conducive to positive and effective learning?

In the final analysis, it is the goal of education to affect student achievement in such a manner that desirable educational objectives will be achieved. To maximize student performance, attention must be paid to creating a positive learning environment. Knight suggests that there are at least two major psychological notions which provide the foundation for building and maintaining positive learning environments [1].

Pygmalion Effect: The Self-fulfilling Prophecy

The Pygmalion Effect can be simply stated: "people tend to live up to what other people expect of them!" How people perceive others influences how they treat these people, how they talk to them, and how they feel about them. The same thing holds true for teachers. If teachers perceive their students as individuals with worth, these teachers will strive to assist their students to develop and perform to their capabilities. On the other hand, if teachers perceive their students as losers and failures in a classroom setting, the students will, in reality, be losers and failures. How a teacher perceives students is extremely important since this perception will influence the kind of learning environment that teacher creates for the students. Students' performance and achievement are influenced significantly by the perceptions their teachers hold of them. Teachers with high expectations promote maximum student achievement, while those with low expectations promote minimum student achievement.

Positive teaching utilizes those positive actions, oral expressions, and activities which radiate positive perceptions for both the students and the teacher.

Self-Image/Self-Esteem Concepts

Closely related to the Pygmalion Effect are the "self-esteem" and "self-image" concepts. The self-image/self-esteem concepts state that how people perceive themselves and how they feel about themselves influence their behavior as well as their achievement.

As Knight points out, "How students perceive themselves (self-image) and feel about themselves (self-esteem) will influence their behavior as well as their achievement" [2]. If students perceive themselves as productive, they will tend to be productive. If they feel they are worthwhile and valuable, their actions will reflect this positive feeling. On the other hand, if students perceive themselves to be "worthless" or "stupid," they will react accordingly; their behavior and attitude will reflect their self-image and their self-esteem. Self-image and self-esteem held by students, according to Knight, are probably the strongest indicators of their academic success, more than any other variable impacting how much and how well students learn.

Of additional consequence, the self-image and the self-esteem held by a student may influence how a teacher feels about the student. Conversely, how teachers feel about themselves and how teachers feel about students may become a vicious cycle: the teacher who has poor self-image and poor self-esteem may reflect that to students; students may be influenced by this and may fail to treat the teacher with respect; the teacher may resent the student behavior at the same time that this behavior reinforces the teacher's original poor self-concept. However, this cycle can be either positive or negative. Positive teaching promotes positive "self-image" and "self-esteem" on the part of both the students and the teacher.

HUMAN RELATIONS STRATEGIES

While dealing with the Pygmalion and the self-image/self-esteem concepts, human relations strategies can be utilized by the teacher to establish and maintain a positive learning environment [3]. Those teachers who establish positive learning environments do the following; they

1. *Make Students Feel They are Worthwhile and Valuable*
   - Everyone is "worth" something. Every person has something to contribute. Everyone has the right to feel important because everyone is important.
   - Positive teaching makes students feel worthwhile by the way they are treated within the learning environment. Students are treated as human beings; they are listened to; they are given responsibilities; they are praised for doing a good job; and students are told they are worthwhile and valuable.

2. *Make Students Feel Welcome in the Learning Environment*
   - Teachers make students feel that they are held in high regard and are welcome in the class. Likewise, students know and feel that teachers want them in their classes. Students feel respected.
   - Teachers employing a positive learning climate greet their students pleasantly as they enter the classroom.
   - When using oral questions, students are allowed ample time to think about the answer to the questions. If students cannot answer the question, they are given clues or the question is restated, redirected to another student, or the teacher answers the question. Thus, a pleasant, not threatening, atmosphere is maintained in the classroom.
   - The manner in which the teachers convey empathy for the students, how students are evaluated, and how they are talked to all contribute to making students feel welcome to the class.

3. *Deal With Needed Behavioral Changes in Students from a Positive Point*
   - It is man's tendency to condemn and not offer praise. This tends to be human nature. Criticism is negatively correlated to learning. On the other hand, positive reinforcement and appropriate praise promotes learning.
   - Positive teaching requires continuous use of positive reinforcement. Effective teachers look for "what is good," not "what is bad" in students as they create a positive learning climate.
   - Teachers who look for and use positive approaches in the teaching-learning process promote positive learning environments. Positive teaching requires that ample time and effort be spent on reinforc-

ing and praising positive behaviors of the student. In essence, "Accentuate the positive and eliminate the negative," as the saying goes.

4. *Make Use of Appropriate Nonverbal Clues*
   - As noted in this text, people learn more and better with their eyes than with any of their other senses.
   - Teachers who smile, nod their heads when a student answers a question, give a wink, or give students a pat on the back are creating a positive atmosphere.
   - The teacher's neat, clean, attractive classroom, the teacher's pleasant voice, the use of hand gestures and the teacher's choice of dress all provide nonverbal clues about how teachers feel about their students, their profession, their school, and themselves.

5. *Know Students, Their Interests and Needs and Home Situations*
   - Showing students that the teacher is sincerely interested in them goes a long way to promote a positive climate for learning. Caring enough to learn all the teacher can about his or her students illustrates to students that the "teacher really cares about me!" Thus, the students will be more likely to care about the teacher. Mutual liking, mutual respect, and mutual understanding between the teacher and the student create positive educational outcomes. This mutual relationship will promote effective teaching and learning. "If I care, you care!" When teachers know students well, students come to realize that their teacher is someone who cares about them!
   - Knowledge about students will be extremely valuable when it comes to dealing with such concerns as unacceptable or inappropriate student behavior.
   - Although extra effort is required to gain personal knowledge of each student and his or her parents through home visits, the value far exceeds the cost in time and effort.
   - The personal interest of the teacher is a positive indication to the student and the parents of the value the teacher places upon the student. The only thing that can possibly result is a positive learning environment.

6. *Learn to Empathize*
   - Empathy connotes the ability to understand the feelings of another person. Effective teachers practice the three F's—Fair, Firm, and Friendly.

- Of all the attributes that a teacher possesses, the one that students will tolerate the least is "unfairness." Thus, "fairness," where the teacher treats all students the same, is the key to educational success. And the only way a teacher can be fair is to be able to *empathize*!
- In order to empathize, teachers must get to know their students. They need to learn why students act the way they do based upon such things as the family and home situation, etc.
- If students behave in a particular way, the teacher needs to learn the causes—what conditions caused the students to act the way they did! For example, a student is constantly late for class. Instead of treating the symptom (tardiness), the teacher should ascertain the cause—it might not be the fault of the student.

7. *Establish Acceptable Standards of Behavior and Workmanship for Productive Performance*
   - "Man is fickle; Man needs direction." People learn more and better when they know what is expected of them. Students like and need some degree of structure or discipline to guide their learning.
   - Students learn more and better and behave more positively when boundaries (not rigid rules) are clearly established.
   - Positive teaching requires that guidelines are established that clarify "what is expected!"
   - Letting students "do their own thing" will not result in learning of any particular value. For permanent learning to occur, adequate time on task must be afforded students.
   - Those teachers who provide clear and concise directions, teach to a student's needs, utilize assertive discipline, stress educational objectives, and evaluate in the light of those educational objectives are establishing conditions which result in successful and positive learning for students.

8. *Make Instruction Student Centered*
   - Since learning is an active process, students learn best when educational activities are focused upon the students. Students learn by their own activity.
   - Teachers must teach students; they must not just teach subject matter.
   - Instruction which is designed to assist students to achieve their needs and which provides utility will more likely be accepted by the student. Students needs must be satisfied.

9. *Know the Difference Between Discipline and Punishment*
   - Discipline is a learned behavior; thus, discipline should be considered as a "teaching tool." It should be positively oriented.
   - Discipline should not be punishment!
   - Effective teachers deal with the causes of "inappropriate" student behavior in lieu of addressing the symptoms. They avoid the establishment of rigid rules and stress agreed upon guidelines of student behavior and classroom management.
   - If unwanted student behavior does develop, teachers act to resolve the problem on a one-on-one basis; they avoid peer influence and public confrontations. Effective teachers recognize the power of peer pressure as it relates to student-teacher relations.
   - Those teachers who de-escalate or defuse the situation; who eliminate the demonstration of any emotion in a given situation; who know when there is a discipline problem and not just normal or anticipated student behavior; who know when the discipline situation is over and then "forgive and forget"; who know when a student is misbehaving because the student is "starved for affection"; and who have the ability to solve the problem before it occurs (prevention vs. cure) are utilizing discipline as an effective teaching tool.

10. *Exhibit an Enthusiastic Teaching Style*
    - Teacher enthusiasm is one of the most effective techniques to promote student achievement. Enthusiasm begets enthusiasm. Enthusiasm "rubs off" on others.
    - Teaching enthusiasm can be reinforced by the teacher knowing the subject matter; by being well prepared and well planned; by asking questions; by being committed to teaching; by demonstrating organized and businesslike mannerisms; by "loving" students; and by enjoying teaching and the teaching profession.
    - Being proud to be a teacher and being prepared to teach students from both subject matter and pedagogical points of view will help create a positive teaching experience.

MAINTAINING PROPER PSYCHOLOGICAL DISTANCE

More effective and positive learning will usually occur when students fully understand what is expected of them. Teachers' behaviors and actions influence, to a great extent, how students perceive what they are to do or how they are to behave. One serious concern confronting some teachers is just how close a personal or social relationship should be established and maintained between teachers and their students. It is a fact that a favorable learning environment is enhanced by friendly, warm, and caring teachers. The problem becomes one of recognizing how this friendliness, warmth, and empathy should be conveyed to students.

Maintenance of the proper psychological distance between teachers and their students is a critical consideration for the educator, one which can cause tremendous student behavior repercussions for teachers who do not establish and maintain that proper distance. The relative degree of psychological distance varies with the type of learning environment or the kind of teacher-student interaction at hand. Effective teachers have learned when to narrow and when to broaden and widen this distance. They know that they can narrow the psychological distance when advising students on a one-on-one basis or when offering individual counsel. On the other hand, they realize that a wider distance must be maintained during periods of formal instruction or when correcting undesirable student behavior.

Effective teachers recognize that too much familiarity with students tends to promote disrespect; thus, they are constantly adjusting the psychological distance in the learning environment or interaction process. This is an acquired skill which can be perfected through actual teaching experience. In the final analysis, the maintenance of the proper psychological distance promotes a more favorable learning experience for students because it better communicates to them when and how to react and respond to various teacher behaviors. Likewise, it projects to students the type and kind of respect and relationship expected at any given time.

TECHNIQUES FOR ESTABLISHING
A POSITIVE LEARNING ENVIRONMENT

Establishment of a positive learning environment is a deliberate happening. It requires time, effort, talent, and "common sense." It involves providing the type of atmosphere in which both the teacher and the students can interact to their fullest. It means setting high standards of performance and expectations for students and then helping them achieve these educational goals. It means using common sense and human kindness as teachers interact with students.

Teachers who continuously use positive recognition of students' achievements promote a positive learning environment. Recognition of another's strengths is one of the primary motivational factors available to teachers. It is also one of the basic developmental needs of people. Effective teachers praise students for performing as expected.

It is easier to assess behavioral changes associated with the cognitive (knowledge) and the psychomotor (skill) domains of learning than those in the more intangible affective domain. It is expected that a teacher will administer examinations, assign homework papers and problems, and observe safe and proper completion of manipulated skills, practices, and operations. However, it is much more difficult for teachers to assess objectively those behavior modifications associated with the affective domain. Any good teacher knows that students' attitudes, students' values, students' maturity, students' initiative, students' resourcefulness, students' self-concepts, etc., are important attributes which learners must develop in positive ways. These *intangible* behaviors are probably more important than those in the cognitive or psychomotor domain. In the final analysis, it is the students' intangible attributes, especially ATTITUDE, which most influence student achievement and performance. Certainly, it is the "intangibles" which affect the type of learning environment established.

What can teachers do to establish and maintain effective student-teacher relations essential to promote the positive development of both tangible and intangible attributes of students? Cited below are some useful techniques.

1. *Use and give out "Happy Grams"*
   • Let students know the teacher is pleased with their performance; let their parents and other teachers also know of their achievement.

CONGRATULATIONS

YOUR POSITIVE
ATTITUDE —— BEHAVIOR —— PERSONALITY
EARNS YOU THIS

H A P P Y G R A M

---

2. *Use "Student of the Month" recognition*
   - Give these students a certificate which specifies the fact they were selected "Student of the Month for _____."
   - Place student's name in a place of recognition in the classroom such as on a bulletin board or a chalkboard.

3. *Send Letters to Parents*
   - Send letters to parents complimenting their student for exemplary behavior, attitude, personality, and performance.
   - Send a copy to building principal or supervisor.

4. *Use "Questions for (name)"*
   - Instead of writing "Questions for Study" on chalkboard, write "Questions for Student's Name."

5. *Use Telephone*
   - Call home to inform parents "how great" their children are.
   - Also call students with positive messages.

6. *Use In-School Announcements*
   - Put student names on morning announcements recognizing them for their achievements.

7. *Utilize Committees*
   - Whatever the task to be accomplished, form a committee and name a chair. Praise the "chair" for the accomplishment of a job well done.

8. *Recognize Students*
   - At the beginning of class, take a moment to recognize students who are doing a good job in anything!

9. *Use Extra Work*
   - Use "crew" structure for outside work. Use this as an opportunity to praise those who excel as "boss"—this is a chance to reward those "other" skills and attitudes students possess.

10. *Shake Hands*
    - Shake students' hands occasionally.

11. *Let Students Know*
    - Let students know that they are the best and that the teacher appreciates them.

12. *Use Verbal Expressions*
    • Never forget to say: "You're a good person"; "Thanks for the good work"; "I'm proud of you"; "You're all right." Remember, proud people produce!

SUMMARY

The affective domain must be developed positively before the teacher can make any contributions to the students' cognitive or psychomotor domain. Otherwise, students are learning in spite of the teaching, not because of the teacher.

Remember, before a mother or father can teach his or her child to walk, talk, ride a bike, etc., there must be love, trust, and respect on the part of the child for the parents. These same conditions must be present for positive learning to result in the classroom.

Students need to experience some type of success in order to build self-confidence and self-esteem. Effective teachers help their students develop confidence in themselves by employing those human relations strategies discussed in this chapter. In essence, high standards and high expectations on the part of both the students and the teacher result in quality education of a positive nature.

ENDNOTES

1. Knight, James. "Strategies for Improving Instruction." *NACTA Journal*, Vol. 32, 1988, pp. 13–15.
2. Knight, op. cit.
3. Adapted from material by James Knight in *The Visitor*, 71, 3, University of Minnesota, Summer 1984.

CHAPTER 4

Managing a Positive Educational Environment

As previously pointed out, a teacher is the *facilitator* of the learning process. As the facilitator, the teacher is not only a teacher, but an advisor, a counselor, a supervisor, a manager, and an evaluator among other things. It is the teacher's responsibility and obligation to *manage* the educational setting, whether it be in the classroom, in the laboratory, in the field, or in the community, providing an educational atmosphere conducive to effective learning.

Managing a positive classroom does not just happen; it requires an understanding of how and why students behave the way they do. It also requires ample planning and supervision. Effective teachers create their own learning environment. Moreover, when the teacher manages an educational setting in an orderly, businesslike manner, this should not impose threat, harm, or punishment to students. It should provide the kind of environment where students can learn in an enjoyable and relaxed atmosphere. Nevertheless, a certain degree of discipline is essential and required for a teacher to manage a positive classroom situation.

DISCIPLINE AS A TEACHING TOOL

Discipline is not punishment when it comes to positive teaching. The notion that discipline is the same as punishment must be dispelled at all costs.

Discipline is derived from the word "disciple." A disciple connotes an individual who, through self control and orderly behavior, learns, accepts, and disseminates the doctrines of another. Thus, discipline, in the teaching-learning process, must be looked upon as a teaching tool to assist teachers in bringing about desirable changes in students, especially those changes pertaining to the affective domain of learning.

Discipline is a management tool as well as a teaching tool. Discipline, at its best, assists individuals in establishing desirable habits of life. Discipline, effectively administered by a teacher, provides for the management of a positive "classroom." Since students learn mainly by their own activity, this same phenomenon holds true for the use of discipline as a management/teaching tool: for learning to be most effective, students must also be involved in the management of their learning environment. Thus, discipline, at the optimum, is carried out by the students under the guidance of the teacher. Effective teachers see that when it comes to discipline, the so-called "monkey" is placed upon the shoulders of the students, not upon their own shoulders. Good discipline begets good student morale. Self-discipline develops self-control which develops positive values, appreciation, etc. Students must accept responsibility for their own behavior.

DISCIPLINE AND CONTROL OF THE CLASS

Someone is always "in control of the class!" That someone must be the teacher, not the students. The ability to maintain effective discipline has long been considered one of the leading measures of *teaching competency*. Parents and school administrators evaluate teachers' success upon their skill in establishing and maintaining positive student behavior and student morale. Likewise, from the teacher's point of view, good classroom discipline has strong implications for the

- students' learning
- teacher's job satisfaction
- teacher's mental attitude
- teacher's teaching effectiveness
- teacher's ability to maintain a teaching job

Too, most students appreciate and profit from mature, intelligent teacher leadership in the maintenance of classroom conditions which prevent a needless waste of time and confusion in their work. On the other hand, effective teaching requires much effort and energy, even when student behaviors are under complete control.

DISCIPLINE AND CORRECTING THE BEHAVIOR PROBLEM

Positive teaching stresses the need for and value of praising and recognizing students for satisfactory achievement and performance with their education. The point has been made that teachers should tell students that they appreciate them, love them, and want to help them reach their greatest potential. At some time, some students will occasionally misbehave and this undesirable behavior must be corrected. However, in this process, teachers must stress that they *dislike the behavior of the student at that point in time, not the student personally*! This is a very key point in managing a positive classroom. Remember that a natural hostility does exist at all times between the teacher and the student, and the teacher must continually work to defuse that hostility.

Another key point for teachers to learn is to ascertain when there is a behavior problem and when the activity is a natural student behavior. The lack of the ability to make this distinction has probably caused more new and inexperienced teachers to fail than any other one thing. The ability to make this distinction is a learned behavior; it is one of the "arts" of teaching. Teachers, over time, learn to contemplate "behavior problems" of students the same way medical doctors attempt to prevent the spread of an infectious disease. They learn to identify the cause before the behavior becomes a problem. They learn to prevent the problem by minimizing or eliminating the causes.

DISCIPLINE IS AN INDIVIDUAL PROPOSITION

Now on to the crux of the matter of managing a positive educational environment by controlling student behavior. How can and should this task be accomplished? There is no one best way; every teacher will handle each situation differently. Student control and management is an individual proposition. Teachers must develop their own techniques which will work best for them. However if one believes that an individual's behavior addresses that person's needs and that valuable learning experiences for students can result when they are actively involved in managing their own behavior, there is one management approach which supports these two beliefs.

ASSERTIVE DISCIPLINE

The concept of assertive discipline promotes a "take charge" approach by the teacher in which students assume the major responsibility for their own behavior [1].

Three major components are inherent in the *Assertive Discipline* approach. These components will be referred to as "action steps" which teachers must take in order to employ the assertive discipline concept.

ACTION STEP 1: Establishing and Teaching
Expectations (Standards of Performance)

- Teachers must think through and then decide what they expect regarding student performance and what they will or will not tolerate relative to student behavior. Teachers have needs and wants, the same as students. These should be communicated to students in a specific manner; there is no room for vagueness in this regard.
- Teachers teach students exactly what they want and expect from the students. The teacher must be specific, not vague!
- Teachers establish standards of performance based upon their expectations for students. It should be remembered that it is easier to "ease up" than to "get tough" later. The teacher must set the stage at the beginning of each new class. The need to begin the first few classes in a school year in a firm, yet fair and friendly, manner cannot be over-emphasized.
- In establishing standards of performance, the teacher must be thorough and cover all aspects as completely as possible. If new and/or

different situations arise, the teacher must establish new standards and then take class time to teach these new standards of performance to students.

- Every attempt should be undertaken by the teacher to seek agreement from students that the standards of performance are acceptable and workable since they will benefit the students in the final analysis. The teacher must explain *why* the standards of performance were established. If the students "buy in" to the standards, the student-teacher relationship regarding the management of a positive educational environment will be more effective, more beneficial, and less threatening for both the teacher and the students.
- The teacher must thoroughly explain the consequences (the penalty resulting) if the standards of performance are not met.

ACTION STEP 2: Providing Positive Recognition

- When students perform or do what is expected of them, the teacher provides *positive enforcement* for proper behavior and performance.
- The teacher praises the students during class when they have earned praise.
- The teacher always gives the students a "plus," the extra compliment, when they deserve it.
- The teacher brags upon students when they do as expected.
- The teacher provides awards and incentives in recognition of exemplary behavior.
- The teacher sends notes to parents, principals, etc., praising student behavior and performance, and the teacher visits the students' homes to review student behavior with parents and/or guardians. The teacher also utilizes those techniques presented in Chapter 3.

ACTION STEP 3: Enforcing Consequences

If students do not perform (from a behavior standpoint) or do not do what the teacher wants or expects (within limits), they suffer the consequences. (NOTE: This has implications for establishing parameters regarding student behavior early by the teacher.)

- The teacher must "stand firm." The teacher cannot deviate from the *standards* established and verbally communicated to the students in Action Step 1.
- The teacher must take action, if necessary, when undesirable behavior or unsatisfactory performance occurs. However, the teacher must be sure to stress that the action taken is because of student's behavior or performance, not because of the student per se.

Assertive Discipline is not the only method to monitor and control student behavior, but it does provide a system whereby students become responsible for their own behavior. Moreover, it is a positive approach for managing a positive educational environment.

PROMOTING POSITIVE STUDENT BEHAVIOR

In essence, a student's behavior, at any given point in time, addresses his or her needs. The effective teacher manipulates student behavior in such a way that positive and productive behavior results in the type of performance that satisfies students' needs. Positive behavior can satisfy students' needs just as effectively as can undesirable student behavior. In the final analysis, more effective learning will result from learning environments conducted by teachers who stress positive student behavior and who manage positive learning experiences for their students.

However, it must be remembered that, even under the best of conditions, student behavior must be monitored continuously by the teacher in order to detect "symptoms" which might erupt into undesirable and distracting situations affecting the learning environment. Student behavior can be controlled or manipulated in a positive manner. For both students' and teachers' success and happiness and for teachers' job satisfaction, positive student behavior must be maintained to enhance maximum student learning and to maintain teachers' sanity.

Effective teachers apply the principle of learning that students learn more and better when a favorable climate of success is maintained. Maintaining positive student control and classroom management help promote the favorable results of this principle. Remember, there is a natural hostility between the students and the teacher. The key is to maintain it with minimum stress!

TECHNIQUES FOR
MANAGING STUDENT BEHAVIOR

No set of rules for managing student behavior can be followed in all cases. Each student is a different individual and each must be dealt with individually. However, there are numerous techniques a teacher can utilize to promote and maintain desirable student behavior.

The effective teacher should utilize the following techniques.

1. Before teaching begins thoroughly think through what will be the teacher's expectations for students.

2. Consult experienced teachers to determine appropriate standards of performance to stress.

3. Take action immediately when symptoms of potential problems are observed.

4. Never back away from established standards of performance.

5. Avoid one-on-one confrontations with students in class or in public.

6. Work with disruptive students on an individual basis and in private.

7. Never argue in class with a student.

8. Contemplate potential behavior problems of students before they happen or occur. Be observant!

9. Never "lose one's temper" in front of a class.

10. Never show anger in front of students.

11. Never become tested by the students in a classroom situation.

12. Learn when class interruptions are normal student behavior and when they are "problems."

13. Always speak in a normal tone of voice when correcting student disturbance.

14. Speak more quietly as a student talks more loudly.

15. Keep students actively involved in their learning.

16. Start teaching *only* with the undivided attention of all students.

17. Handle routine details such as roll taking quickly.

18. Never be led astray from the lesson by the students.

19. Stop teaching when an undesirable behavior evolves in the class and correct the situation immediately.

20. Always be aware of what is occurring in the classroom.

21. Avoid responding to behaviors and comments of disruptive students.

22. Avoid calling on or involving those students creating management (behavior) problems until these students begin behaving as expected.

23. Usually do not involve a student again during the class period once the student has been reprimanded for undesirable behavior.

24. Establish procedures regarding when students are allowed to answer questions or respond in class.

25. Do not call on disruptive students unless these students are sincerely interested in the lesson.

26. Become forceful, if necessary.

27. Be prepared to handle disruptive students.

28. After a class interruption, do not move forward with the lesson until the attention of *all* students is directed on the teacher and the lesson.

29. Be in command of the educational environment at all times.

30. Handle student behavior problems; a teacher should not expect someone else to do it. However, there are situations where the school administrator must be involved.

31. Visit the homes of disruptive students if the situation cannot be corrected at school.

32. Involve the school administrator only as a last resort.

33. Never ignore the problem; it will not go away!

34. Avoid too much familiarity with students.

35. Realize that disorder is more easily prevented than remedied.

36. Have classwork well planned in advance.

37. Provide adequate physical facilities.

38. Avoid making rules.

39. Cultivate desirable traits such as unaltered firmness, genuine sympathy, unwavering consistency, and human kindness.

40. Avoid negative traits, such as
    - low, weak voice
    - objectionable mannerisms
    - unbusinesslike attitude
    - bluffing
    - false dignity
    - partiality
    - use of sarcasm
    - holding grudges
    - emotional instability
    - dishonesty

41. Know that all behavior activities, both desirable and undesirable, are a part of the environment of students and that they have an influence upon student growth and development.

42. Know that no two students are alike; therefore, punishment will not follow a set of rules.

43. Never appear to students to show partiality.

44. Treat all students as if they were honest and truthful. If they prove otherwise, never tell other people about the happening.

45. Be firm—"no" should mean no.

46. Give a clear assignment and enough work to keep students busy and learning.

47. Set a positive example in speech, dress, health, and manners.

48. Assign responsibility to students who seem to create problems.

49. Study each individual—assess each student's home conditions, motives, and interests; such facts may often reveal what the teacher needs to know to help the student.

SUMMARY

Used in a positive environment, discipline is an effective teaching tool. In essence, teachers' discipline is essentially self-discipline. Teachers who are hopeful yet fearful, ambitious yet humble, idealistic yet practical, with everything to give and with everything to lose, will find their success in proportion to their ability to know themselves and to use that knowledge in personal and professional growth.

Effective teachers have the ability to manage a positive educational environment by controlling (manipulating) student behavior. They manage in a businesslike yet friendly manner. They avoid placing undue pressure upon students for they realize that pressure causes tension. Tension in an educational environment minimizes the quality of learning. Also, they realize the power of peer pressure from both a positive and negative point of view.

ENDNOTE

1. Canter, Lee and Canter, Marlene. *Assertive Discipline.* Canter and Associates, Inc., Santa Monica, California, 1992.

SECTION II

A PSYCHOLOGY
FOR POSITIVE LEARNING

What one believes influences what one perceives and vice versa! Since perceptions are, in reality, truths to the perceiver, it is important that a discussion on "Psychology for Positive Learning" be presented before examining how to best deliver positive educational experiences for students.

As utilized in this book, a discussion on the psychology for positive learning centers upon how people learn with reference to the application of principles and laws of learning and teaching.

This section addresses the following major aspects, each of which impacts upon how students learn best:

- Motivation
- Principles of Learning
- Psychological Laws Affecting Learning and Teaching
- A Model of the Teaching-Learning Process

The above sequence of topics will provide a logical discussion of how people learn by first examining student motivation and the principles and laws affecting teaching and learning, culminating in a description of the teaching-learning process.

CHAPTER 5

Examining a Psychology for Learning

How do people learn? What influences how people involve themselves in the teaching-learning process? There are time proven principles and laws of psychology which will, if utilized in a positive way, influence *how much* and *how well* people learn. For a principle to be a "true" principle, it must be applicable to many situations. A principle, as used in this book, connotes a "fundamental truth which is applicable to many situations." Principles differ from laws since a law is "an absolute truth which has withstood the test of time."

Since the art and science of teaching is a "learned" or an acquired ability, it can be perfected and improved through (a) actual experience in teaching, and (b) the application of psychological principles and laws of learning which affect how people learn more and better. Learning principles, either individually or in concert with each other, when applied in a positive learning environment tend to "turn students on!" The prerequisite to good teaching is an enthusiastic teacher who can interest students in the subject matter being presented! Before learning can occur, however, students must want to learn. They must be motivated to learn! Students only learn through their own efforts. Teachers cannot learn for their students—they can only provide the opportunity for students to learn! What makes students want to interact and to learn?

MOTIVATION

Motivation is the most basic element of learning. This is a most provocative statement. Why can it be made? For one thing, without motivation in learning all else is of little or no importance. No one learns without feeling some urge to learn. The greater the urge, the more people will learn on their own. What is motivation? Motivation is that internal element that forces a person to move towards a goal. It is motivation that makes a student want to learn, want to know, want to understand, want to believe, want to act, want to gain a skill, or want to achieve an educational objective.

Can teachers motivate students? By applying some motivational techniques, the effective teacher can create in a student motivation designed to satisfy a personal need. What are some of these personal needs?

- *The need for security.*
  People need to feel free from harm and threats. They go to great lengths to avoid those things which impinge upon their security. When the natural impulses that people possess are addressed, people feel more secure.
- *The need for new experiences.*
  One only needs to reflect upon America's attempt to conquer outer space to appreciate the motivational force associated with experiencing new and different things.
- *The need for recognition.*
  The human being is a goal seeker! Most people strive to achieve so they can be recognized. The need for recognition is a powerful incentive for most people.
- *The need for self-esteem.*
  Self-concepts are important for all people. Attaining strong, positive self-image and self-esteem attributes will force people to achieve.
- *The need for conformity.*
  Most people need limits set regarding their behavior. People like to know "where they stand in the scheme of things."
- *The need to help others.*
  Helping people stimulates people to act and to react in a positive and constructive manner.

Since motivation is the one intangible which must be present to release the potential in each student, teachers must be able to activate within their students one or more of the factors that satisfy the above needs. However, realizing what tends to motivate students is one thing, but the ability to apply these factors in day-in, day-out teaching activities is what is really important. What are some examples of how these factors can be applied?

By relying upon some of the basic human needs, desires, and impulses the teacher can divert these into a motivational pattern. For example, curiosity is present in nearly every student as is a desire to participate in something new. The need for new experiences is an important factor affecting motivation. If the teacher captures and guides the basic needs, desires, and impulses of students and uses any and all of the pedagogical tools available, the student will usually be motivated. When teachers bring instruction to life by using teaching situations, realia, and real experiences, they are employing tactics to take advantage of those basic needs, desires, and impulses of the students. As a result, students "get turned on" to what is being taught—the power of positive teaching is being employed.

SOME PRINCIPLES OF LEARNING [1]

There are numerous theories on how students learn best. There are just as many interpretations of what constitutes the principles of learning. How principles are phrased is not as important as whether they are utilized properly in the teaching-learning process. Understanding the basic principles and psychological laws affecting learning will be of little consequence unless the teacher learns how to apply them as they influence ways in which students learn. Simply reading this book will not make an effective teacher; suggested techniques utilizing "psychological truths" of effective teaching and learning must be put into positive practice to be of value in bringing about behavior modification in students.

> PRINCIPLE 1: STUDENTS LEARN MORE AND BETTER WHEN THERE IS INTEREST

What is meant by interest? Lancelot describes interest as "the inner springs of thought and action" [2]. It is interest that stimulates and guides peoples' thinking. Interest begets motivation. Can teachers create interest on the part of students? The effective teacher can create interest by understanding and applying the following approaches which promote interest [3].

Interest Approach 1

Interest approaches which refer to the natural impulses, urges, and drives of human beings tend to stimulate student interest.

These impulses, urges, or drives include

- Love of nature
- Creativeness
- Gregariousness
- Activity
- Curiosity
- Desire for approval
- Altruism
- Self advancement
- Competition
- Ownership

Interest Approach 2

Interest approaches which affect us, others about us, or humanity at large tend to interest students.

Interest Approach 3

Interest approaches which build upon things which students are already interested in tend to create more interest.

Interest Approach 4

Interest approaches which build upon students' abilities or skills tend to increase interest.

Interest Approach 5

Interest approaches should begin with interesting ideas which, in turn, flow into important but uninteresting ideas whenever the two are clearly connected in thought.

Interest Approach 6

Interest approaches which require thinking are more interesting than those requiring memorization.

Interest Approach 7

Interest approaches can become contagious since one person can "take interest" from another person.

Interest Approach 8

Interest approaches should provide a sense of progress towards a goal since progress stimulates interest.

Interest Approach 9

Interest approaches should provide suspense.

Interest Approach 10

Interest approaches should build upon an idea which is already accepted by students so it becomes a new interest center for other ideas.

Interest Approach 11

Interest approaches should employ the novel and unexpected.

Interest Approach 12

Interest approaches should utilize humor since humor creates interest.

Interest as Power

These interest approaches can be applied by effective teachers to stimulate the thinking of their students which, in turn, will tend to excite students in the learning process. It is important to point out that once interest is stimulated, it is the teacher's responsibility to maintain students' interest by providing positive learning activities.

It should be remembered that interest in something (anything) is an indicator of growth and development of an individual. Teachers, however, do not teach simply to get interest, but if interest is *not* present, teaching will *not* be as effective.

In essence, interest becomes a source of power in motivating students to learn. When students are interested in a subject, they feel a part of it. Effective teachers lock their teaching to whatever students feel they are already a part of and build upon this point as they develop and deliver their lessons. This ability to find out what students already know, already feel, or already believe about the subject at hand becomes one of the greatest powers teachers have at their command. The importance of oral questioning techniques cannot be overemphasized as a teaching tool to ferret out how students feel about a particular thing or subject.

> **PRINCIPLE 2:   STUDENTS LEARN MORE AND BETTER WHEN NEEDS ARE BEING SATISFIED**

How do teachers create a feeling of need? For positive teaching to occur, students' needs must be satisfied. Unless teachers create a feeling for the need to learn, students will not perform to their maximum potential. It is imperative that teachers know the basic developmental needs of students and then take those actions necessary to assist students to satisfy these needs. This is where the "art" of teaching comes into play. A teacher's initiative, resourcefulness, and creative ability must be utilized to the fullest degree in order to adapt and to make application of the basic needs of students to the subject matter at hand. The effective teacher soon learns this competency. In essence, for positive teaching to result, the teacher must help students discover what their needs are so that students come to realize that the lesson will help them satisfy their needs.

What are the developmental needs of people? People need

- to belong
- to be a part of something worthwhile
- to receive recognition for accomplishments and achievements
- to select and train for an occupation
- to strive for goals which make sense and are within reach
- to accept and share responsibility
- to do those things which have real purpose and value

Teaching and learning activities which address one or more of these developmental needs of people will tend to (1) create interest, (2) motivate students to want to learn, and (3) make the learning of a more permanent and positive nature since it will be useful and relevant to the student's growth and development.

Figure 5.1 shows Maslow's hierarchy of human needs [4]. It will be noted that "basic" needs must be satisfied before "security" needs are met and so forth.

Effective teachers operate in the realm of "self-achievement needs" since they are creative and imaginative in planning and delivering relevant and meaningful instruction. Certainly these teachers are contributing to society and are helping students grow and develop.

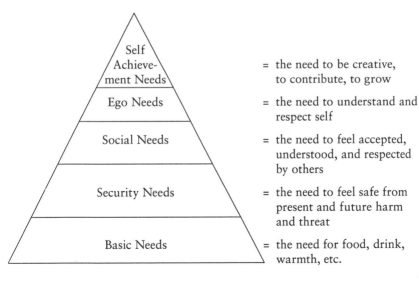

Figure 5.1   Maslow's Hierarchy of Human Needs

Are the needs of youth different from those of other people? Most people who involve themselves with teenagers can tell you what the needs of young people are and what motivates them to do the things they do. Students have many needs which influence their attitudes, drives, habits, and goals. Most students are concerned with

- making money
- securing a job
- doing something worthwhile
- satisfying personal developmental needs
- developing self confidence
- obtaining job satisfaction
- assuming responsibility
- developing self esteem
- seeking economic independence

Effective teachers realize the importance of identifying student needs, both individually and collectively as a class, so the teachers can plan and use those activities and experiences essential to assist students to meet their needs. Learning experiences which help students satisfy these basic needs will usually be readily acceptable. Students want to function in the "real" world. Positive teaching will afford students the opportunity to gain competencies essential to help them satisfy some or all of their basic needs.

In order to satisfy students' needs, teachers need to answer these questions as they plan an activity for instruction:

1. Is it useful to students?

2. Does it help accomplish goals and educational objectives?

3. What pedagogical tools are available to help satisfy student needs?

PRINCIPLE 3: STUDENTS LEARN MORE AND BETTER WHEN
             THINKING IS STIMULATED

Although thinking is more interesting than rote memorization, most people think only when they must or when they are required to. Teaching students how to think is one of the primary purposes of education. Positive teaching results in the ability of students to apply the decision-making process in such a manner that students learn how to think and not just learn how to memorize facts which they can recall if asked. Positive teaching places major emphasis upon the development of understanding rather than memorization. It is understanding in the form of knowledge which is the basic ingredient of thinking. As pointed out earlier, thinking is basically interesting.

Adults only need to reflect back upon their own learning experiences to recall which type of teaching resulted in the most effective educational experience. Those educational experiences which stressed *only* "facts and more facts" were not the most pleasant and satisfying, especially if the facts were not organized or connected to something relevant or significant. Very few facts, in and of themselves, help to satisfy students' needs, let alone assist students in learning how to think.

On the other hand, those educational experiences which involve a real life situation or a problem to solve were, in all probability, more interesting, more relevant, and better remembered.

The problem-solving approach to teaching promotes the development of thinking competence on the part of students. Of more consequence, this type of teaching will more likely help satisfy students' needs. Certainly, teaching for problem solving will provide a more sound psychological basis for developing those competencies essential for students to cope with life's problems and, at the same time, provide them with experiences in developing (1) rational reasoning abilities; (2) abilities to think; and (3) abilities to solve problems. Students do learn more and better when thinking is stimulated.

PRINCIPLE 4: STUDENTS LEARN MORE AND BETTER WHEN THEY PARTICIPATE ACTIVELY

As already noted, learning is an active process. Students learn by their own involvement in their education. The more activity, the greater chance learning will occur. For optimum learning to take place, students must participate in the "interaction process" with their teachers. Positive teaching results in the maximum amount of interaction between the teacher and the learner.

Effective teachers know that the interaction process must be focused primarily upon the students, not upon the teacher. Focusing attention on learning activities involving the student will promote "student-centered" teaching which will result in a more permanent change in students' behavior.

It must be remembered, however, that students do not learn by what the teacher does; students learn more effectively by what the teacher gets them to do! Students learn more and better by "learning to do by doing!" Positive teaching is directed at those educational activities focused upon the students which will yield the maximum amount of positive behavior modification in the students. If this behavior modification is directed toward the achievement of predetermined educational objectives which promote the maximum development of students and, at the same time, assist in satisfying students' needs in an interesting manner, positive teaching is occurring.

There is a tremendous difference between "telling students" and "teaching students." If telling were the same as teaching, we would all be so smart we couldn't stand it! Teaching is facilitating, directing, and guiding the learning process. Teaching is not learning! The student must learn; the teacher cannot learn for the student. Students learn through their own activity, not through the activity of the teacher. The teacher who believes that lecturing (telling) is the best approach to changing the behavior of students will short change the students in the final analysis. However, teachers who know that students learn more and better from their own activity, assuming the students are interested in the subject matter, will promote positive teaching which will be of a more permanent nature.

To further illustrate the importance and value of this principle of learning, reference is made to the Dale Cone of Educational Experiences as shown in Figure 5.2 [5]. This illustration shows the influence of various teaching activities upon learning effectiveness and abstractness.

Learning effectiveness, according to Dale, increases with an increase in activity and participation while abstractness of the learning process increases as the teaching tools employed become less activity oriented and more teacher centered.

PRINCIPLE 5:   STUDENTS LEARN MORE AND BETTER WHEN
TWO OR MORE SENSES ARE USED

People have five basic senses. These are seeing, hearing, smelling, tasting, and feeling. The principle "the more activity focused upon the learner, the more learning is likely to occur" has been discussed. Thus,

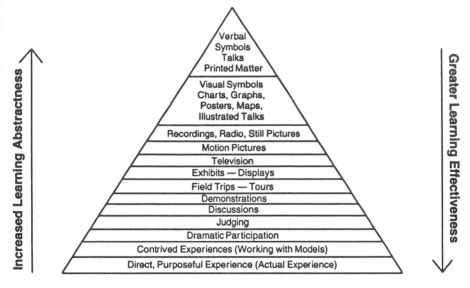

Figure 5.2 The Cone of Educational Experiences

the more senses that a student can utilize in the learning process, the more learning is likely to occur. Positive teaching employs those activities which will enable students to utilize as many of their basic senses as possible in the learning process.

Have students take notes; recite in class; view images projected by an overhead projector; view slides, filmstrips, or motion pictures; read reference materials or textbooks; smell new odors; touch real objects or taste new foods. These are all ways to involve students' senses in the learning process.

To illustrate the importance of the basic senses and how they impact upon permanent and positive learning, reflect upon the following two points which should involve experiences most people have had.

First, recall your first date with a member of the opposite sex.

Next, recall the first time you solved an algebraic equation.

Which one did you recall the quickest and the easiest? Why were you able to recall this experience more vividly than the other? Were smelling, feeling, seeing, hearing, and possibly tasting more involved in the experience recalled most readily?

Research points out that the ability of learners to retain information studied increased with greater participation and involvement associated with the use of more senses [6].

Percent Retained by Student	Activity Involved
10%	of what they READ
20%	of what they HEAR
30%	of what they SEE
50%	of what they SEE and HEAR
70%	of what they SAY as they TALK
90%	of what they SAY as they DO a thing

Thus, it is evident that the ability of students to retain information increases with greater participation and involvement associated with the use of more of their senses. Students do learn more and better when they use two or more senses in their learnings.

The importance of this principle of learning is further illustrated as follows.

TELL ME; I FORGET.
SHOW ME; I REMEMBER.
INVOLVE ME; I UNDERSTAND.

PRINCIPLE 6: STUDENTS LEARN MORE AND BETTER WHEN A POSITIVE CLIMATE OF SUCCESS IS MAINTAINED

One of the important characteristics of an effective teacher is that the teacher possess strong positive feelings for students and not be afraid (or ashamed) to demonstrate these feelings towards students. Positive teaching also radiates empathy and sympathy for students. Just as do teachers, students have feelings which must be reckoned with as teachers design teaching strategies to affect positive changes in students' knowledges, skills, and values and attitudes. Demonstrating empathy for students, being sensitive to others' feelings, is one of the first prerequisites of positive teaching. If a teacher does not possess a sense of caring for and about students, all else will be of little or no avail. The "love" a teacher shows for students is critical since (1) not only is a human a goal seeker, and (2) a human is an "ego-seeking" individual, as well.

The effective teacher maintains a positive climate of success for students' growth and development by being well prepared for teaching; by sharing the educational intent (objectives) with the students; by having a stimulating introduction; by basing instruction upon students' needs; by providing active involvement for students' participation; by asking questions; by using problem solving methods of teaching; by utilizing instructional realia; by using appropriate authoritative references; by effectively concluding the lesson; and by stressing application of subject matter taught. Also, the effective teacher maintains a neat, clean, attractive classroom setting with up-to-date bulletin boards, current displays, and proper heating, cooling, and ventilation. The learning environment is conducted in a positive and pleasant manner employing a businesslike approach.

In maintaining a climate of success, the teacher constantly praises the students' progress and achievements. Students are recognized for their intellectual accomplishments, as well as for the patterns of behavior they exhibit. Moreover, students sense a high degree of personal achievement since the effective teacher continuously reinforces what has been learned with what is currently being taught. The teacher stresses how the competencies (knowledges, skills, attitudes) being taught and learned can be used to cope with life's challenges and problems and, at the same time, to help satisfy students' needs. In essence, when the basic ingredients of effective teaching are used by a teacher, a favorable climate of success is maintained.

Summary

The above six principles will affect *how much* and *how well* students learn. They will provide a sound basis for effective learning and positive teaching. However, they will be only as effective as the emphasis placed upon each of them as they are applied and utilized in the teaching-learning process.

SOME BASIC PSYCHOLOGICAL LAWS AFFECTING LEARNING AND TEACHING

In addition to the six principles of learning cited, several basic psychological laws control, influence, and affect students in the learning process and make learning experiences more effective, more lasting, more enjoyable, and more positive for students. The major psychological laws of learning discussed are the *law of effect*, the *law of association*, the *law of primacy*, the *law of exercise*, the *law of disuse*, and the *law of intensity*. In addition, several other psychological laws of learning should be mentioned.

The Law of Effect: *People tend to accept and repeat those experiences which are pleasant and satisfying and to avoid those which are annoying or unpleasant*

Positive experiences are more pleasant and satisfying than are negative experiences. This is not to say that all negative experiences are bad! People learn, in all likelihood, as much from negative experiences as they do from positive experiences; but these negative experiences are not likely to be pleasant or satisfying experiences and they will cause the learner to avoid rather than repeat them in the future. This law could also be called "the law of satisfyingness."

An educator who emulates the characteristics of the effective teacher and who employs the ingredients of effective teaching is making application of the law of effect. Reading from an authoritative textbook followed by a class discussion of the key concepts or points contained in the reading will tend to promote pleasant and satisfying experiences for students. Contrast this situation with one where the teacher makes a reading assignment in a book and immediately follows the required reading with a written quiz. In essence, the effective teacher employs those positive experiences and activities to involve students which yield more pleasant and satisfying learning experiences for students. Positive experiences are those which satisfy the needs of students and which demonstrate the value, relevance, and utility of the lesson being studied.

The Law of Association: *Experiences which occur together tend to reoccur together*

Again, experiences can be both positive or negative. Examples of positive experiences occurring together might include anticipated test questions evolving from lesson objectives; class notes consistent to questions asked on a test; positive reinforcement of students' behavior with businesslike manner and effective work habits; teaching to educational objectives which help satisfy students' needs; an introduction which explains why the lesson is being taught; the habit of bringing a pencil so class notes can be taken; and orderly conduct associated with achievement of educational objectives, to cite a few. It is important that one activity or method used in the teaching-learning process *not* negate the positive aspects of another activity or method: for example, a teacher's failure to share unit objectives with students might cause those students to prepare for the wrong focus on the unit evaluation.

The Law of Primacy: *First impressions are the most lasting*

As Will Rogers said, "You only get one chance to make a good first impression." This principle has many implications for the effective teacher who wants to provide positive teaching. Being well prepared for teaching, completing daily classroom announcements in an orderly fashion, providing a stimulating introduction which stresses *what* is to be accomplished and *why* it is important for the students to learn are some examples of how the law of primacy can impact positive teaching. Also, a teacher's dress, speech, and stage appearance (mannerisms) provide additional examples of how this psychological law can impact teaching and learning.

The Law of Exercise: *The more often an act is repeated, the more quickly a habit is established*

This law could be referred to as the "law of practice" or the "law of repetition." Repetition is a vital teaching tool. A person only needs to recall the number of falls from a bicycle in mastering the skill of riding a bike to appreciate the importance of the law of exercise in the teaching-learning process. This law is utilized continuously as the effective teacher reviews the previous day's lesson; concludes the lesson by calling for key concepts or key points covered in the lesson; reviews for quizzes and examinations; discusses the assigned reading; assigns homework; requires term papers or reports; requires students to have pencil and paper before class starts.

Some educators refer to this law as the "law of repetition" since a learning activity experienced (repeated) many times tends to be remembered longer and recalled more quickly and easily. The law of exercise is of additional importance when teaching students how to perform psychomotor skills and when teaching the use of *safe* operation of tools and equipment.

Behavioral changes do not truly become a part of a person until "they are reinforced through use" and this further exemplifies the importance of this law in providing positive teaching.

The Law of Disuse: *A skill not practiced or a knowledge not used will be largely lost or forgotten*

Unless the change of behavior "sought and taught" is constantly reinforced by use or application, in most instances it will become non-observable or non-measurable. This law has tremendous implication for the value and use of repetition in the teaching-learning process. If the knowledge or skill or attitude is being or has been taught *only* for the sake of teaching, then there is no need to be concerned about the utility of the law of disuse. However, if what is or has been taught students is of value and relevance, if it is useful, then it must be repeated until it becomes a habit which can be utilized or recalled at a moment's notice. Positive teaching stresses those changes in behavior which are of value, utility, and relevance to the students to help them develop the ability to reason, think, and solve problems. If something is taught students just to be teaching, the results will be much less effective. One of the major problems facing public education today is the fact that students see or realize little or no utility in what they are being exposed to and taught in most classes. Positive teaching must be directed toward satisfying students' needs. It is the teacher's responsibility to assist students in realizing what their needs are and then teaching to satisfy these needs.

There is a great difference between "teaching students" and "entertaining students." However, positive teaching can also be entertaining. Creating a pleasant and satisfying learning environment by an enthusiastic teacher who really wants to assist students as they strive for "the better life" can be enjoyable for both the students and the teacher.

The Law of Intensity: *A vivid, dramatic, or exciting learning experience is more likely to be remembered than a routine or boring experience*

As discussed earlier, enthusiasm is one of the characteristics of an effective teacher. Also, the fact that interest is contagious since it can be taken from another person further illustrates the power of the law of intensity on the educational process. Man is a "curious animal." Curiousity is one of the natural human impulses affecting the ways in which a person acts and thinks. Too, people tend to like and enjoy excitement. What happens when people hear a fire siren? Usually they interrupt what they are doing and look to see if they can locate the fire! Positive teaching employs interest approaches which create and sustain a state of suspense. Student interest and curiousity are stimulated by vivid, dramatic, or exciting activities and experiences.

The Law of Readiness: *Learning will not readily occur unless the person is ready or willing or able to learn*

The teacher can prepare and deliver a lesson, but the student will not change behavior (learn) unless that student wants to. This law could also be referred to as the "law of timing." It implies that the teacher should "strike when the iron is hot" or that the teacher should be alert to and ready to respond to the students' willingness to learn.

The Law of Reward: *Rewards in general tend to maintain and strenghten any connection which leads to them*

Reinforcing positive learning with rewards and praise will result in more positive learning.

The Law of Motivation: *Without drives, an organism does not behave and hence does not learn*

Refer to the discussion on "Motivation" presented at the beginning of this chapter for more detail.

The Law of Appreciation: *Previous learning always sets the stage for subsequent learning*

Effective teachers tie today's lesson to yesterday's lesson.

The Law of Transfer: *A person learns through transfer to the extent that the abilities aquired in one situation help in another*

Transfer of learning is an important component of the educational process.

The Law of Recency: *The more recent an experience, the more readily it can be recalled*

Summary

As with the principles of learning, the value and usefulness of the psychological laws of learning discussed herein will be realized only if they are applied in practice. Understanding them is one thing; applying them in the teaching-learning process is quite another. If a teacher masters the ability to apply one or more of these psychological laws of learning in day-in, day-out teaching, more effective learning and positive teaching will result. The use of these laws will add magic to teaching!

SOCIETY AND EDUCATION

It has been said that public education is the largest enterprise in this country. Certainly the concept of a "free education for every citizen" is a tremendous economic undertaking. Since education is a reflection upon society and, conversely, society is a direct reflection upon the educational system in operation, it seems appropriate at this juncture to point out briefly the implications of the educational process that aims for the betterment of society. The concept of the impact of education upon society and society upon education is presented below.

Education  Society

To this end, the teacher should

1. Make the educational investment in time and money count

2. Help those who have handicaps

3. Try to draw out the full capacities of every student

4. Teach people to do better those desirable things they are going to do anyway

5. Make what is taught useful and teach it so that it will be usable

Effective teachers should both understand and utilize sociological factors impacting teaching and learning as they plan and deliver instruction and, also, they should assess the impact they are causing as they strive to develop a better citizen for a democratic society. Education should contribute to the economic growth and development of the individual student in particular and to society in general. Too, education should be "cost effective." Professional educators should create "wealth" in the form of changed behavior in the students they teach commensurate to at least the cost of operating the educational process they are associated with.

A CONCEPT OF THE
TEACHING-LEARNING PROCESS

Since teaching is the "Mother of All Professions," it is now appropriate to synthesize the concept of the teaching-learning process.

Those principles and psychological laws affecting learning and teaching which a teacher really believes to be effective will determine the method and teaching techniques employed by that teacher. Methods and teaching techniques connote those teaching tools and practices utilized by the teacher to facilitate learning. If a teacher believes that students learn more and better by using two or more senses, that teacher will be likely to incorporate several varied instructional realia, such as various forms of audiovisual aids, into the teaching procedures that will be utilized. Likewise, if a teacher believes in the value of the "law of exercise," that teacher will likely make provisions for "actual practices in class" or make homework assignments to utilize this psychological law to promote effective teaching and learning.

Influence Of Psychological Principles And Laws

Naturally, the methods and techniques utilized by a teacher will determine, to a great extent, the effectiveness of the teaching. If those methods and techniques are selected and utilized which yield the most pleasant and productive learning, the teaching should be interesting, develop thinking and understanding, meet the needs of students, promote active participation, recognize individual differences, and promote the values of society, to name a few educational results. It seems justifiable to repeat that the teacher is not only the facilitator of the learning process, but the motivator toward and a witness to the values in life which that teacher considers important.

The relative effect that principles and psychological laws of learning can have upon the teaching-learning process is illustrated in Figure 5.3.

As illustrated in Figure 5.3, it is the application of psychological principles and laws of learning which influence the teaching methods employed and the teaching-learning techniques utilized. The methods and techniques employed by the teacher will impact upon the quality and effectiveness of the teaching.

Influence Upon An Individual's Teaching Philosophy

The beliefs, concepts, and attitudes held by an individual influence how that individual thinks. This philosophy also provides a basis for selecting the best teaching approach to direct the learning process. If a teacher believes that students learn more and better by creating and maintaining a positive climate of success, this belief will become part of the teaching philosophy of that teacher. In the final analysis, it is the teacher's beliefs about the characteristics of effective teachers and of the

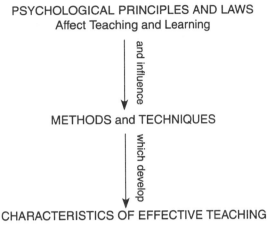

PSYCHOLOGICAL PRINCIPLES AND LAWS
Affect Teaching and Learning

and influence

METHODS and TECHNIQUES

which develop

CHARACTERISTICS OF EFFECTIVE TEACHING

Effective teaching
1. Is interesting
2. Develops thinking and understanding
3. Serves a useful purpose based upon need
4. Makes use of available resources
5. Promotes wide participation
6. Recognizes individual differences
7. Evaluates fairly
8. Promotes the values of society

and results in

MORE AND BETTER LEARNING

Figure 5.3   Influence of Psychological Principles and Laws on Effective Teaching

ingredients of effective teaching which influence and "set" or establish that individual's teaching philosophy.

Of more consequence, a teacher's philosophy will influence the desired outcomes expected of the teaching; these become the individual teacher's objectives in teaching. Assuming that the teacher has a positive philosophy with positive educational objectives, the end results should be more

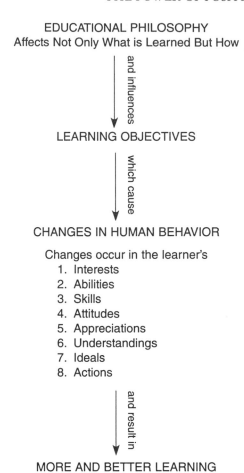

Figure 5.4   Influence of Philosophy on Objectives and Eventual Behavior Modification

and better learning in the form of behavioral changes relative to students' interests, abilities, skills, attitudes, appreciations, understandings, and ideals.

Figure 5.4 demonstrates the ways a teacher's philosophy influences teaching objectives, which in turn affect the behavioral modification of students.

Relationship Between Principles and Laws of Learning and Teaching Philosophy

In the final analysis, the degree of "sincere positiveness" projected by the teacher will influence the degree of positiveness reflected in the changes in human behavior. For example, teachers who possess and demonstrate a positive attitude will tend to instill this same positive attitude in their students. Likewise, a teacher who stresses neat and accurate work habits will likely instill these same habits in the students. The example set by the teacher has awesome influence upon students. Positive teaching requires a teacher who "sets a positive example."

As illustrated in Figure 5.3, those psychological principles and laws of learning influence the type of teaching methods employed which, in turn, impact the quality of teaching. This is the *first* relationship in the teaching-learning process.

On the other hand, the influence of a teacher's philosophy upon the preconceived educational objectives that particular teacher will advocate and utilize is illustrated in Figure 5.4. This is referred to as the *second* relationship in the teaching-learning process. In addition, the effect of a teacher's desired outcome of teaching is reflected in the quality of learning which results in observable and measurable changes in student behavior.

Both relationships are of major importance since each influences the end result of teaching. The teaching-learning process has been described as a series of actions and interactions occurring between the teacher and the learner. The type, quantity, intensity, and quality of these actions and interactions are the direct influence of, and have as their original foundation, the teacher's psychology of learning and philosophy of teaching.

Teaching and learning are complex processes because so many relationships come into play at the same time. On one hand

Relationship #1

- Principles and Laws of Learning that the teacher applies
    Influence the
- Type of Selected and Utilized Methods and Teaching Tools
    Which Affects the
- Characteristics of Teaching

while on the other hand:

Relationship #2

- The Teacher's Philosophy
     Influences
- The Objectives of Teaching that the teacher advocates
     Which Affect
- The Quality of Learning

Teaching is directing the learning process. Figure 5.5 shows a construct illustrating how the above two relationships are "tied together" in the teaching-learning process. This concept points out the need for the teacher to understand and apply the psychological principles and laws of teaching and learning and also to develop and nurture the type of teaching philosophy which will result in more and better learning on the part of students.

Referring to Figure 5.5, it is obvious that teaching and learning processes are deliberate acts which require the teacher to employ numerous psychological principles and laws of teaching and learning. Likewise, the teacher's philosophy on education is of major importance.

SUMMARY

This chapter has examined a psychology for learning. It has addressed the importance of motivation as a basic element of learning. Numerous principles and psychological laws of learning and teaching were discussed in order to provide the foundation essential to establish a useful concept of how they can be applied to the teaching-learning process. Several examples and techniques were presented to illustrate how the various principles and laws could be incorporated into a teacher's methodology.

An understanding of and the application of those psychological principles and laws affecting learning and teaching will result in more and better learning for students.

ENDNOTES

1. Adapted from class notes taken in Dr. Ralph E. Bender's Methods of Teaching class at The Ohio State University.

TEACHING IS DIRECTING THE LEARNING PROCESS

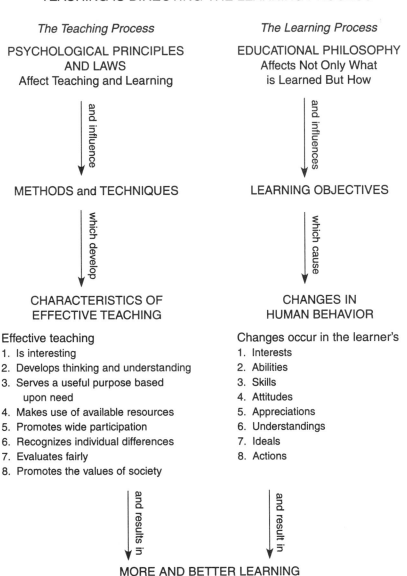

The Teaching Process	*The Learning Process*
PSYCHOLOGICAL PRINCIPLES AND LAWS Affect Teaching and Learning	EDUCATIONAL PHILOSOPHY Affects Not Only What is Learned But How

and influence ↓   and influences ↓

METHODS and TECHNIQUES   LEARNING OBJECTIVES

which develop ↓   which cause ↓

CHARACTERISTICS OF EFFECTIVE TEACHING   CHANGES IN HUMAN BEHAVIOR

Effective teaching
1. Is interesting
2. Develops thinking and understanding
3. Serves a useful purpose based upon need
4. Makes use of available resources
5. Promotes wide participation
6. Recognizes individual differences
7. Evaluates fairly
8. Promotes the values of society

Changes occur in the learner's
1. Interests
2. Abilities
3. Skills
4. Attitudes
5. Appreciations
6. Understandings
7. Ideals
8. Actions

and results in ↓   and result in ↓

MORE AND BETTER LEARNING

Figure 5.5 Construct Illustrating the Parallel Teaching-Learning Process

2. Lancelot, W. H. *Permanent Learning*. John Wiley and Sons, Inc., 1944, p. 31.
3. Lancelot, op. cit.
4. Maslow, A. H. *Maturation and Personality*. Harper and Row, New York, 1954. Copyright © 1970 by A. H. Maslow. Reprinted by permission of HarperCollins Publishers.
5. "Cone of Experiences" from AUDIOVISUAL METHODS IN TEACHING, Third Edition by Edgar Dale, copyright © 1969 by The Dryden Press, reproduced by permission of the publisher.
6. Minnesota Mining and Manufacturing Company.

SECTION III

A DELIVERY SYSTEM
FOR POSITIVE TEACHING

It has been implied throughout the preceding chapters of this book that the application of educational theory in the form of principles and laws affecting how people learn will assist the teacher to realize the desired outcomes of teaching and learning. Granted, an individual teacher must possess a thorough understanding of the "why and how" people learn and also be knowledgeable of the characteristics and ingredients of effective teachers and teaching. But, in the final analysis, the real and time proven tasks of the teacher are *to use* those knowledges, skills, and attitudes affecting the teaching-learning process day-in and day-out if positive changes in human behavior are to result.

For the desired outcome to be realized, the teacher must design a delivery system. The most effective teachers are those who develop teaching strategies in writing and then use them. Positive learning is the direct result of positive planning and execution of those plans by the teacher.

A *Delivery System* as used in this book connotes a strategy for

- planning,
- delivering,
- evaluating,
    and
- applying

a positive educational experience for students.

Section III examines, in some detail, how teachers can facilitate positive teaching and learning. The following aspects are presented:

- Planning a Positive Educational Experience
- Delivering a Positive Educational Experience
- Evaluating Learning to Assure a Positive Educational Experience
- Applying Learning to Assure a Positive Educational Experience

The various components presented in this section provide a systematic approach for any teacher to follow regardless of the educational level of the students being taught.

CHAPTER 6

Planning a Positive Educational Experience

Planning an educational delivery system implies developing teaching plans. These plans are developed to teach students large, broad blocks of subject matter, such as algebra or chemistry, commonly referred to as courses or areas of instruction. Areas of instruction are further broken down into units of instruction, referred to as teaching units. Teaching units consist of written plans for teaching students a specific block of subject matter such as "solving algebraic problems" or "utilizing the periodic table." Teaching units contain a series of individual teaching plans. A teaching plan as used in this book is defined as an organized, written plan for teaching one aspect of a subject matter unit for one or two class periods. A teaching plan is developed to achieve certain specific educational objectives.

In order to provide a positive educational experience for students, it is imperative that teachers be prepared for teaching. The quality of teaching will be a direct result of the quality of planning for delivering an interesting and exciting learning experience. Effective teachers always enter the learning environment with a well thought out written teaching plan. In the final analysis, a teaching plan is a plan for learning.

TYPES OF TEACHING PLANS

Which type of teaching plan is the best? There is no one best type of teaching plan. It is important for the teacher to use a variety of plans since the continuous use of any one type of plan will tend to create a stereotyped delivery. Positive teaching requires the use of a variety of approaches and teaching plans. Whatever plan is developed, it should contribute to the development of students' reasoning, thinking, and problem-solving abilities.

FACTORS INFLUENCING TYPE OF PLAN

The type of plan finally selected for delivering the desired educational experience will depend upon several factors. Some of the more important are listed below.

- *Time Available for Instruction*
  The length of time (minutes) for each class period will dictate, to a large extent, the amount of subject matter which can be covered. It will also influence the number of participating activities that students can be involved in within the actual time available for instruction.
- *Situations or Conditions under which Instruction Will Occur*
  The reason(s) why the lesson is being taught, the degree of interest which can be generated for the subject being taught, the adequacy of the student reference materials, the utility and value inherent in the lesson for the students, and the location where instruction will occur are some of the situations which will influence the type of teaching plan developed.
- *Educational Objectives to be Achieved*
  The desired educational objectives sought will influence the type of lesson plan selected. A different type plan will be required if students are to learn to perform a skill than if the objectives of the lesson are designed for students to achieve knowledge or arrive at a decision.
- *Application Sought*
  Application of subject matter taught requires time. If students are expected to make application of the subject matter taught at a school

laboratory in contrast to their home or somewhere in the community, this will affect the type of teaching plan selected. Also, the level of application will dictate the type of lesson plan to select.

- *Students' Abilities*
  A teacher would not expect students to make complex decisions without first acquiring the necessary background information. Different type plans would be required for each level of learning.
- *Students' Levels of Experience*
  Students' experience in learning can impact upon the type of plan developed. In many instances, students must acquire background information before they can perform a skill or make realistic decisions.

The type of teaching plan finally selected for use in a given educational situation should contribute to the kind of change in human behavior desired. In essence, a teaching plan is developed so a "lesson" can be taught.

Several types of teaching plans are at the command of teachers. Since all learnings can be grouped into the three broad categories—the cognitive, psychomotor, and affective domains of learning—and since the primary purpose of education is to develop competencies within an individual which will assist that individual to solve problems encountered in life, the type of teaching plan developed should contribute to the maximum development of those knowledges, skills, or attitudes (values, appreciations, etc.) sought. The relationship between the domains of learning, desired competency development sought, and the type of teaching plans to use is illustrated below:

Domain of Learning	Desired Competency Development	Type of Teaching Plan to Use
• Cognitive	• Knowledges	• Informational
• Psychomotor	• Skills	• Operational
• Affective	• Attitudes, Appreciations, Values	• Managerial

The remainder of this chapter will be devoted to a detailed discussion of the three basic types of teaching plans:

- Informational
- Operational
- Managerial

EDUCATIONAL FUNCTION
OF EACH TYPE OF PLAN

Most formal teaching plans will fall into one of the above types. Needless to say, there are numerous variations to each of these plans. All of these plans have advantages in appropriate situations. Teachers should not become stereotyped to the point they utilize only one type of teaching plan and fail to use the others. "Variety is the spice of life!" Of more consequence, teachers need to consider the *applicability* and *adaptiveness* of the specific plan for the subject matter they are teaching.

Each type of teaching plan has specific educational functions. These are shown as follows:

TYPE OF TEACHING PLAN	EDUCATIONAL FUNCTIONS IN TEACHING AND LEARNING
Informational	1. To acquire information. 2. To analyze functioning facts. 3. To use facts (understandings) to do a job or perform an operation.
Operational	1. To do a task or job correctly. 2. To perform a skill or operation (practice) satisfactorily.
Managerial	1. To arrive at an intelligent decision. 2. To develop thinking and decision making ability.

TEACHING PROCEDURES

The following outline illustrates the uniqueness of the teaching procedures for each type of teaching plan.

TYPE OF TEACHING PLAN

TEACHING PROCEDURE	INFORMATIONAL	OPERATIONAL	MANAGERIAL
Step I	Introduction and Motivation	Introduction and Motivation	Introduction and Motivation Statement of the Problem
Step II	Development of key questions for study and discussion	Demonstration by Teacher (Instructor does and tells)	Identification of the factors to be considered and the kinds of information needed to arrive at the decision
Step III	Supervised Study	Supervised Practice	Supervised and outside study
Step IV	Discussion of Questions	Application	Discussion to establish basic facts and evaluate factors.
Step V	Application and follow-up	Evaluation	Make a decision
Step VI	Evaluation		Application and Evaluation

COMPONENT PARTS OF A TEACHING PLAN

Although the educational functions and teaching procedures differ somewhat for each type of teaching plan, the component parts of each are basically the same. These parts are as follows.

- Identification
- Situation
- Objective
- Introduction

- Procedure
- Realia
- Concepts Reinforced

To utilize the type of delivery system or plan to provide the most positive teaching and learning experiences, it is essential for the teacher to include each of the above component parts. The educational function of each of the component parts of the three basic teaching plans are as follows:

COMPONENT PART OF PLAN	EDUCATIONAL FUNCTION OF EACH COMPONENT PART
I IDENTIFICATION	• To provide an organized system for identifying, classifying, and/or codifying teaching plans in a course of study or subject matter area. • To identify those competencies to be taught as a result of the educational experience (lesson).

> • Included in the IDENTIFICATION portion of the teaching plan should be:
>
> AREA: Broad area of subject matter, e.g. Chemistry
>
> UNIT: Specific concentration of subject matter, e.g. Gases
>
> LESSON: Specific topic, e.g. Physical Properties of Gases
>
> COMPETENCIES TO BE TAUGHT: Describes specifically what students are to be able to do or demonstrate or perform at the conclusion of the lesson.

II SITUATION	• To state or identify the conditions under which instruction will take place. • To explain *why, where, when,* and *how* the lesson will be taught.

- In preparing the SITUATION for the plan, the following points should be stressed.
1. List the important "teaching situations"*; this step is useful to explain why the lesson is to be taught.
2. Identify pertinent local situations which have a bearing upon the value and usefulness of the lesson.
3. List important points which relate to community and student needs

* "Teaching Situation" refers to an experience, a case study, a case situation, an example, an incident (real or fictitious), a problem which focuses on/illustrates/demonstrates the topic of the lesson.

- Clarifying the SITUATION portion of the teaching plan helps the teacher make instruction more relevant and more specific to students' needs. Communication of this information to students makes it easier for students to grasp why the lesson is important and why it is being taught.

III OBJECTIVES (Educational)

- To identify the terminal behavior desired (change in behavior) in the students as a result of instruction.

- A complete OBJECTIVE should also state the *conditions* under which the terminal behavior is expected to occur and the *criterion* by which the terminal behavior is to be evaluated.

IV INTRODUCTION

- To identify specific procedures, and/or interest approaches used to stimulate or arouse interest so students become motivated to participate in the educational activity or lesson.

V PROCEDURES

- To cite those teaching methods* to be used to achieve the educational function of the plan.
- To identify the desired subject matter content (including educational objectives) to be taught.

		* Teaching methods imply those activities, techniques, and procedures teachers use to facilitate learning.
VI	REALIA	• To list all resource materials including real materials, real situations, audiovisual aids, resource people, direct experiences, and activities used by teachers to relate instruction to real life situations and to reinforce the basic principles and laws of learning.
VII	CONCEPTS REINFORCED	• To list those science and math concepts which are included in the lesson and which are stressed and/or reinforced as a result of the lesson being taught. • If applicable, to cite those communication (reading and writing) concepts which are included, stressed, and/or reinforced in the lesson.

> • It is the aim of education to develop the "whole person." Every teacher should contribute to and reinforce each and every discipline which impacts upon the growth and development of the student.

> • Every student needs to be able to read, write, compute, and perform as a useful and purposeful individual. To achieve this, all teachers must recognize the need to identify those science and math and communication concepts that their instruction reinforces.

> • Teachers have the obligation and responsibility to inform their students of those complementary concepts being taught, stressed, and/or reinforced in their lesson.

As one studies the educational function of each component part of the teaching plan, it can be seen that each plan, assuming all seven component parts are utilized, will contain (1) specific procedures (teaching methods) to be followed to complete a total lesson and thus accomplish the educational objective(s) of the plan, and (2) the desired subject matter content to be taught in a lesson. In essence, each plan becomes a teacher's teaching tool to specify both *procedure* and *content* associated with the desired educational experience sought.

The quality of planning is extremely important. A well organized, thought-out teaching plan will help students think through *why* they should learn, *what* they should learn, and, also, *how* they can use and apply what was learned to solve problems encountered in life. Adequate planning will also increase the confidence and effectiveness of the teacher.

INFORMATIONAL TYPE OF TEACHING PLAN

Many educational problems and teaching situations arise where the important learning value lies in the acquisition of specific, up-to-date facts, knowledge, and information essential to achieve the educational objectives and, at the same time, satisfy the needs of the students. These problems and situations require "functioning" information. It is assumed that if students are to carry out a specific task, skill, or operation, they should be able to do it or at least understand how it can be done if they possess the necessary information. Oftentimes, such teaching also requires some manipulative skills and perhaps some decisions need to be reached, but the primary emphasis of informational teaching plans is placed upon the acquisition of knowledge through the media of information, facts, etc.

The important teacher preparation for informational teaching plans is a complete lesson outline which includes a thorough analysis of the information (subject matter content) necessary to achieve the stated educational objectives.

A sample format to be used in developing informational teaching plans is shown in Figure 6.1.

OPERATIONAL TYPE OF TEACHING PLAN

There are many important educational practices and activities where the learning value for the students is essentially manipulative or motor skill development. Whenever this ability and "know how" is necessary in order for the students to be able to do or perform the practice and/or

UNIT: _____

LESSON: (Number and Title) _____

COMPETENCY(IES) TO BE TAUGHT: _____

SITUATIONS TO BE DEALT WITH:
   List the important ones.

LESSON OBJECTIVES:
   1. What the students should know as a result of instruction.
   2. What the students should be able to do.

INTRODUCTION: "Building a Case for Learning"
   1. Clearly explain objectives.
   2. Bring out why lesson is important through questioning.
   3. Stress immediate or future application.
   4. Identify student and community situations.
   5. Use realia.

PROCEDURE:
   1. *Questions for Study and Discussion:*
      a. Through discussion, with the assistance of students develop a list of study questions.
      b. By suggestive questioning, list additional questions which need to be answered if objectives are to be achieved.
      c. List study questions on board and have students copy these in their student notebooks.

   2. *Supervised Study:*
      a. Distribute reference books/materials/resources.
      b. Provide time for students to find solutions and/or answers to the study questions identified above.

   3. *Discussions:*
      a. Through students participation, discuss their findings relative to key questions.
      b. When correct solution or answers have been agreed upon, list on chalkboard or overhead.

    c. Provide time for students to write correct answers in their notebook or worksheet.

4. *Conclusion:*
    a. Review lesson based upon objectives.
    b. Summarize the key points of the lesson.
    c. Involve students in developing a concensus statement which concludes the lesson.
    d. Write the concensus conclusion on the board/overhead and have students write it in their notes.

5. *Application and Follow up:*
    a. Make specific homework assignment(s).
    b. Identify specific activities students are to complete which will reinforce (apply) information learned.

6. *Evaluation:*
    a. Include key information on unit examinations and/or daily quizzes.
    b. Periodically, review and grade notebooks for completeness, neatness, and organization.
    c. Observe students' performance.

REALIA:

List specific references to textbook, bulletins, software programs, visual aids, and other instructional materials to be utilized.

SCIENCE / MATH CONCEPTS REINFORCED:

List specific concepts contained in the lesson.

Figure 6.1   Sample Format for an Informational Teaching Plan

skill according to standard specifications, these lessons should be taught from the *operational* point of view. The students should learn to do these jobs or tasks efficiently, and the teacher's objectives for students for this type of teaching plan are (1) to develop the ability to do the task or job correctly, and (2) to develop the ability to perform a skill or practice satisfactorily.

Developing questions for study, making reading assignments, using class discussions or recitations based upon assigned study *are costly* and *time consuming* in this type of teaching plan. Furthermore, lecturing on plans of this nature is even worse. "One learns to do by doing" in operational lessons. Too much time is wasted in teaching operational "jobs" by talking about them. Students should be shown how to do such skills and then provided *ample practice time* to learn how to do them. Operational teaching plans should be delivered by demonstration, not by talking about how to do the job or perform the skill.

If certain knowledge and/or information is required for the students to understand before a skill or practice can be developed, this information should be taught students first using an informational teaching plan. It is important that teachers determine what basic information and/or knowledge students must know before they can do a job correctly or perform a skill or practice satisfactorily. This information should be taught first and then the job, skill, or practice to be performed should be taught next. Teaching tends to become confusing when a teacher attempts to teach students in both the cognitive and psychomotor domains concurrently.

The most important teacher preparation for the operational teaching plan is to make a *complete step by step analysis* which outlines an up-to-date, economical, and efficient way for doing the job or performing the skill according to acceptable standards of performance. These are commonly referred to as "operation sheets." They should then be utilized by the teacher when conducting the demonstration. Refer to page 271 for a sample of an operation sheet.

In conducting demonstrations, the following three steps are suggested.

Step 1.   Teacher does and tells.
Step 2.   Teacher does and student tells,
                          OR
          Student does and teacher tells,
                          OR
          Student does and tells.

(NOTE: At the conclusion of Step 2, the teacher distributes the operation sheet to students for use in Step 3).

Step 3.   Students practice under supervision of the teacher. (NOTE: This is commonly referred to as "supervised practice.")

A suggested teaching plan format for developing operational teaching plans is shown in Figure 6.2.

MANAGERIAL TYPE OF TEACHING PLAN

Since the ultimate purpose of education should be to develop within an individual (1) rational reasoning ability, (2) thinking ability, and (3) the ability to solve problems, students need to learn how to do these things through actual participation and practice. Teachers who promote positive teaching utilize managerial teaching plans whenever possible. These plans not only expose students to the decision-making process, but also provide them with actual involvement in decision making which requires reasoning and thinking abilities.

Managerial lessons are taught to help students make intelligent decisions and to provide them with training in decision-making ability. By and large, managerial "jobs" are mental in nature. In all teaching situations where a clear-cut decision needs to be made, the lesson should be taught from the managerial point of view. Students learn to think efficiently by solving real "lifelike" and worthwhile problems—problems that students face and that affect them. Learners tend to better develop this decision-making ability by following a rational thinking procedure.

Students have many real lifelike and worthwhile problems and decisions confronting them. Due to the origin of these problems and the need to seek sound solutions, such problems are of vital interest to these students. Thus, teachers have a built-in mechanism for teaching students how to apply the decision making process. Those teachers who provide the most positive learning experiences for their students utilize managerial teaching plans since these plans are one of the most effective techniques for providing experience in thinking and also for helping students solve their important managerial problems.

Before presenting a sample teaching plan for managerial lessons, the steps involved in the decision making process should be understood. The steps are as follows.

UNIT: _____

LESSON: (Number and Title) _____

COMPETENCY(IES) TO BE TAUGHT: _____

SITUATIONS TO BE DEALT WITH:

    List the important ones.

LESSON OBJECTIVES:

    1. Development of skill to do a job or perform a task satisfactorily according
       to standard specifications.

INTRODUCTION:

    1. Why is the lesson to be taught?
    2. Bring out the importance of skill.
    3. Show examples of use of the skill.

PROCEDURE:

    1. *Demonstration by Teacher:*
       a. Teacher demonstrates how to perform skill as outlined on the operation sheet.
       b. Teacher explains clearly each step of operation and gives reason why.
       c. Student should demonstrate how to perform skill while explaining each step.

    2. *Supervised Practice:* (Laboratory or Field)
       a. Students practice skill under supervision of teacher.
       b. Teacher assists students.

    3. *Conclusion:*
       a. Review lesson based upon objectives.
       b. Summarize the steps involved and review safety when appropriate.
       c. Involve students in developing a concensus statement which concludes the les-
          son and identifies ways to use the skill.
       d. When appropriate, write the conclusion on the board/overhead.

    4. *Application:*
       a. As students complete skill practice, assign a production job or exercise to be
          completed according to specifications.
       b. Provide additional assistance as needed.

    5. *Evaluation:*
       a. Include psychomotor development activities on unit examinations.
       b. Score the quality of work of the job or exercise performed by student according
          to specifications.

REALIA:

    List specific references, instructional materials, operation sheets, tools,
    and equipment to be used in teaching the lesson.

SCIENCES / MATH CONCEPTS REINFORCED:

    List specific concepts contained in the lesson.

Figure 6.2   Sample Format for an Operational Teaching Plan

Step 1. *Experience a provoking situation*: determine a need to resolve a difficulty.

Step 2. *Identify the problem*: state the decision which needs to be made.

Step 3. *Determine the factors*: isolate the factors which need to be considered before a decision can be made.

Step 4. *Arrive at the decision*: gather the necessary information; evaluate the factors; come to a conclusion.

Step 5. *Take action*: develop a plan and execute the plan.

Step 6. *Accept the results*: evaluate the decision in terms of benefits; assess the thinking process involved; reap the benefits or suffer the losses.

In the classroom, the decision-making process is usually carried to the fifth step. The decision is made when action is taken. Evaluating the results of the decision is done when the complete "project" is analyzed and comparisons are made to standards and/or predetermined goals.

In order for the students to be provided effective and positive experiences in decision making, they must individually engage in each of the steps. However, the activity is primarily mental. As with informational teaching plans, the important preparation for developing teaching plans of this nature is a *complete lesson outline* which includes a thorough analysis of the problem in question. This should include (1) the statement of the problem to be solved or the decision to be made, (2) a complete listing of all factors to be considered if the problem is to be solved, and (3) a complete analysis of the information pertaining to each factor to be evaluated. If teachers have a comprehensive analysis, it will be comparatively easy for them to develop on the chalkboard or overhead, with the aid of the students, the analysis of each managerial teaching plan discussed in class.

A suggested format to be used in preparing managerial teaching plans is shown in Figure 6.3.

DEVELOPING TEACHING PLANS

There are logical steps to be followed in the evolution of a worthwhile teaching plan. In developing a teaching plan, several "do's" and "don'ts" should be considered in systematic planning.

UNIT: _____

LESSON: (Number and Title) _____

COMPETENCY(IES) TO BE TAUGHT: _____

SITUATIONS TO BE DEALT WITH:
List the important ones.

LESSON OBJECTIVES:
1. To develop thinking ability.
2. To arrive at an intelligent solution to a problem.
3. To develop sound decision-making ability.

INTRODUCTION:
1. Build a case for the problem.
2. Set up a situation or simulated activity.

PROCEDURE:
1. *Identify problem to be solved/decision to be made:*
   a. Through student participation, formulate a group statement of the decision that needs to be made.
   b. Place problem statement on chalkboard or overhead projector.

2. *Determine the factors:*
   a. List all pertinent factors on chalkboard/overhead which need to be considered.
   b. Determine the information needed to evaluate the factors.
   c. Have students copy in their notebooks.

3. *Supervised study:*
   a. Students gather facts and information necessary to evaluate factors using all available resources.
   b. Students record data for later use.

4. *Discussion:*
   a. Identify and discuss the more important functioning facts.
   b. Through group participation, arrive at conclusion for each factor.
   c. Evaluate factors, solve problems, and arrive at a decision.

5. *Conclusion:*
   a. Review lesson based upon objectives.
   b. Summarize the factors which were identified and information which was gathered.
   c. Involve students in developing a concensus statement which concludes the lesson.
   d. Write the concensus conclusion on the board/overhead and have students write same in their notes.

6. *Application and testing:*
   a. Students develop plans for putting decision into operation.
   b. Students put plans into operation.
   c. Teacher observes students' performance as it relates to application of decisions arrived at in class.

REALIA:

List specific references, instructional materials, software programs, resources, and equipment to be used in teaching the lesson.

SCIENCE / MATH CONCEPTS REINFORCED:

List specific concepts contained in the lesson.

Figure 6.3   Sample Format for a Managerial Teaching Plan

The following suggestions for preparing a teaching plan should serve as a guide and are not offered with the idea of providing a rigid format or an inflexible teaching pattern that must be adhered to. The eventual teaching plan developed (including realistic teaching situations; observable and measurable educational objectives; interest approach(es); approved procedures; and visual aids and resource materials) will vary with the type of lesson (informational, operational, or managerial), the desired behavior modification sought, and the needs and interests of the students.

Points to Consider in Systematic Planning

1. A plan is based upon specific behavioral objectives which have been predetermined by the teacher.

2. A plan provides specific teaching methods and procedures for attaining the desired behavioral objectives.

3. The content of a plan should be carefully and thoroughly developed.

4. A plan is a definite and particular *way* for doing a definite and particular *thing*.

5. A plan is developed with regard to complete, up-to-date, and accurate knowledge; appropriate materials; and a summary of basic concepts to be taught.

6. A plan should deal with dynamic and not static teaching situations.

7. A plan should provide for flexibility to deal with unexpected developments and situations.

8. A plan should be well balanced with regard to the component parts of a teaching plan.

9. A plan should be made in writing so it may be examined critically for improvements and revisions.

10. The plan should not be changed except after the most careful reasoning.

11. A plan should be kept in operation until it is revoked or replaced with a better plan.

Things to Avoid in Planning

1. Avoid unnecessary planning. All situations do not require detailed plans. The experienced teacher can very often deal successfully with situations without detailed plans.

2. Do not use some other person's plans. A good plan for one situation may be a poor plan for another situation.

3. Avoid writing too complicated plans. It is a good practice not to work out a plan in such detail that it cannot be made flexible as new teaching situations develop.

4. Avoid hurried planning. Unless sufficient time is taken to work out the plan, it will probably be a poor plan.

5. No matter how good teachers think their plans are, they should not "fall in love" with their plans to the point that they cannot keep an open mind to modify or change the plan. Teachers should be prepared to meet the actual teaching situation as they find it and to take advantage of what others have done or can contribute to the effectiveness of the plan.

6. Avoid having no plan at all. There is always a very thorough plan behind any well organized effort. Opportunists and people who trust to luck are too numerous already and make very poor teachers.

SUGGESTIONS FOR PLANNING THE VARIOUS PARTS OF A TEACHING PLAN

I. *IDENTIFICATION*
   a. Identify the unit and lesson title as clearly and completely as possible in order to communicate the subject matter intent of the lesson.
   b. List the competencies to be taught in this lesson.

II. *SITUATION*
   a. List the important teaching situations which can be used to explain *why* the lesson is to be taught. A teaching situation is an experience, a case study, a case situation, an example, an

incident (real or fictional), or a problem which focuses upon or illustrates or demonstrates the educational intent of the lesson.

b. Identify pertinent local situations which have a bearing upon the value and usefulness of the lesson.

c. List important points which relate to community and student needs.

An example of a SITUATION for the plan "Identifying the Mouth Parts of an Insect" is shown below.

SITUATION

- This is the third lesson taught on insects.
- The class has been taught a lesson on the economic importance of insects and one on the major body parts of an insect.
- Both mounted and fresh insects will be used in insect identification.
- Students interest should be high.
- This lesson is important because students need to be able to determine whether insects are harmful or beneficial.
- The way an insects feeds will determine how to best control the insect.
- Students will be required to make an insect collection following a field trip.
- Instruction will occur in the biology laboratory for two class periods.

NOTE: Effective teachers never walk into a classroom *without* a teaching situation.

III. *OBJECTIVES FOR THE LESSON*
List those educational objectives which have been identified for the individual teaching plan.

An example of EDUCATIONAL OBJECTIVES for a teaching plan on "Identifying the Mouth Parts of an Insect" is shown below.

EDUCATIONAL OBJECTIVES
Students will be able

1. To describe three major types of mouth parts of insects based upon information presented in class.
2. To identify the types of mouth parts of ten different insects.

IV. *INTRODUCTION OF THE LESSON*
   a. Identify routine chores such as taking roll, making assignments, etc. which must be handled. NOTE: This information will be used when preparing the daily plan (see page 99).
   b. Review previous day's lesson. Relate to the conclusion of prior lesson (when applicable).
   c. Write IDENTIFICATION on teaching plan. Clearly identify the lesson or job. List area, unit, lesson number, and title.
   d. Identify reasons *why* lesson is important and place on SITUATION portion of the teaching plans.
   e. Cite the Interest Approach(s) to be used. Identify the teaching situation.
   f. Identify the desired outcome of the lesson. Place on OBJECTIVES portion of the teaching plan.
   g. Formulate list of questions to
      • find out what students already know about the lesson topic
      • establish why the lesson is important
      • develop interest or develop a provocative situation or identify a problem
      • analyze the teaching situation involved
      • get students to "buy into" the lesson
   h. Identify realia to be used in the lesson and place under the REALIA portion of the teaching plan.

   NOTE: The procedures and devices used for introducing the lesson should be varied frequently in order to create and maintain interest. Refer to Chapter 13, "Building a Case for Learning" for additional information.

V. *PROCEDURE (Body of the Lesson)*
   a. Develop questions for study and discussion. Identify key questions and/or problems for study and discussion which must be answered if the educational objectives are to be achieved. In the case of an operational plan, develop an "Operation Sheet" for presenting the demonstration.

Examples of Questions for Study and Discussion for a teaching plan on "Identifying the Mouth Parts of an Insect" are shown below.

QUESTIONS FOR STUDY AND DISCUSSION

1. What are the major types of mouth parts found in insects?
2. Name one insect with each type of mouth part.
3. List the various *parts* of the mouth part of an insect.
4. How can the major types of mouth parts be identified?

NOTE: The following factors should be considered in developing study questions for students:
   a. Answers should be available in the references listed for the lesson.
   b. Questions should deal with pertinent information in the lesson.
   c. Questions should be brief, concise, and written in simple terms.
   d. Information called for by the questions should aid in the attainment of the lesson objectives.

   b. Plan *analysis of answers to questions*. Develop a complete and thorough analysis of the information necessary to answer the key questions and/or solve problems.
      The Analysis (short answers to Questions for Study) is placed directly below the list of Questions for Study.

An ANALYSIS for the key questions contained in a teaching plan on "Identifying the Mouth Parts of an Insect" is shown on the next page.

ANALYSIS

1. Major types of mouth parts
   - Chewing
   - Piercing-sucking
   - Rasping-sucking
   - Sponging
   - Siphoning
   - Chewing-lapping
2. Insect with each type
   - Chewing: grasshopper
   - Piercing-sucking: mosquitos
   - Rasping-sucking: thrips
   - Sponging: housefly
   - Siphoning: butterflies
   - Chewing-lapping: honey bee
3. Parts of the Mouth Part:
   - Mandible ⎫
   - Clypeus ⎪   As each part is
   - Labrum ⎬   listed, show a
   - Labial Palpus ⎪   sample of each
   - Maxilla ⎭   using the over-
        head projector
4. Identification of Mouth Parts can be completed by
   - Use actual pictures to show samples of each mouth part, pointing out each part for each type. After all parts have been identified, distribute one sample of each type of mouth part to each student.

NOTE: The ANALYSIS is placed directly below the QUESTIONS FOR STUDY AND DISCUSSION.

c. Plan supervised study. Make the assignment; distribute reference books and materials; establish time schedule.
d. Provide for Discussion. Identify those procedures and materials to be utilized by the teacher to assist students to answer the questions and solve the problems for study. Make provisions for using real materials, charts, pictures, films, mimeographed materials, demonstrations, field trips, etc.
e. Develop a specific Conclusion. List those basic concepts which should evolve from the lesson. During the conclusion of the

lesson, the concepts should be identified and listed on the chalkboard or overhead.

An example of the CONCLUSION for a teaching plan on "Identifying the Mouth Parts of an Insect" is shown below.

CONCLUSION

1. Review key points discussed
   - Types of mouth parts
   - Insects with each type
   - Parts of the mouth part
   - Identification
2. Concepts to be taught
   - All insects have mouth parts.
   - Each insect has the same basic mouth parts; however, some parts have been modified to serve specific functions.
   - The major type of mouth part can be identified by observing real insects.

---

f. Determine application and follow up. List techniques which will be stressed and utilized to make actual application of concepts and subject matter taught in the lesson. Identify exercises where application can be made; stress practice.

An example of the application portion for a teaching plan on "Identifying the Mouth Parts of an Insect" is shown below.

APPLICATION:

1. Following a field trip, student will identify the mouth parts of the insects collected.
2. In a later lesson, students' knowledge of insect mouth parts will be used to determine the type of chemical control to administer.
3. Students will use information on mouth parts to assist them as they classify insects in their insect collection.

---

    g. Provide evaluation. Identify procedures to be used to assess student achievement of educational objectives: use of written or oral tests; approved practices being used by students, etc.

An example of the evaluation for a lesson on "Identifying the Mouth Parts of an Insect" is shown below.

EVALUATION

1. Administer a two question quiz on mouth parts of insects at the beginning of the next class period.
2. Include actual identification of at least five mouth parts on the unit examination.

VI. *REALIA*
    a. List all resource and reference materials which will be used by teacher and students in the lesson.
    b. Include all visual aids, mimeographed materials, etc., which will be needed.

VII. *CONCEPTS REINFORCED*
    a. List all science and math concepts which are included, stressed, and/or reinforced in the lesson.
    b. If applicable, include all communications concepts (reading and writing) included, stressed, and reinforced in the lesson.
    c. If applicable, cite all concepts included and reinforced in the lesson which promote thinking, reasoning, problem solving, and "working with people" abilities.

Two additional steps are required to develop a complete teaching plan. These are:

VIII. *TIME BUDGET*
    a. After the mechanics of the teaching plan have been developed, establish a time schedule for the different activities included in the plan.
    b. Indicate estimated time schedule on the left-hand column of the plan.

IX. *DAILY PLAN FOR TEACHING-LEARNING ACTIVITIES*
   a. The final step in planning will be to develop a daily plan. The daily plan should include the time schedule and a list of major student and teacher activities to be completed. A daily plan will be prepared for each class each day and destroyed at the end of the class. Prepare a new daily plan for the next day's presentation. A sample plan is found in Figure 6.4.
   b. A suggested format for planning for an informational lesson is found in Figure 6.5.

SUMMARY

Planning for instruction is one of the major and time consuming responsibilities of a teacher. Effective teachers select, develop, and utilize the type of teaching plan which will yield the maximum amount of learning. They realize that only through the development of teaching plans can they provide organization for meaningful learning. In this chapter, three basic types of teaching plans were discussed in detail. Each type is designed to address one of the domains of learning.

Numerous suggestions and procedures were presented to assist teachers develop the most effective type of teaching plan. To provide a positive educational experience for students, effective teachers use written teaching plans which have been thoroughly developed.

Budget time for study assignments, group and individual work assignments, main questions for class discussion, re-introduction, review points, supervised study, discussion periods, showing real material, charts, graphs, films, field trip plans, demonstrations, etc. (Show possible omissions or additions in parenthesis.)

TIME BUDGET   MAJOR STUDENT AND TEACHER ACTIVITIES

Figure 6.4   Sample Format for Preparing a Daily Plan for Teaching-Learning Activities

99

AREA:

UNIT:

LESSON:

COMPETENCY(IES) TO BE TAUGHT:

SITUATION:

LESSON OBJECTIVES:

INTRODUCTION:

QUESTIONS (OR PROBLEMS) FOR STUDY AND DISCUSSION:

Figure 6.5   Sample Format for Planning an Informational Lesson

SUPERVISED STUDY:

DISCUSSION:

SUMMARY AND CONCLUSIONS:

APPLICATION AND FOLLOW UP:

EVALUATION:

REALIA:

MATH/SCIENCE CONCEPTS REINFORCED:

Figure 6.5   Sample Format for Planning an Informational Lesson (*continued*)

CHAPTER 7

Delivering a Positive Educational Experience

Although adequate planning is a prerequisite to positive teaching, how the educational experience is delivered (taught) is just as important and as critical. In pedagogical terms, teaching methods, commonly referred to as "methods," connote those activities, procedures, and/or techniques that teachers use to teach. How well teachers select and use appropriate teaching methods will influence, to a large extent, the quality of the educational experience provided students.

THE O.P.E. CONCEPT

As explained earlier, a concept is an idea or notion conceived in the mind of one person which can be communicated either orally or visually to another person. When a concept is conveyed visually, it is usually done by the use of a "construct." As used herein, a construct is a visual drawing, a symbol, or a graphic illustration which conveys the concept in question.

Putting together a complete lesson should be the goal of every teacher. This goal should be sought and, it is hoped, achieved each time students and teachers interact. Teaching a complete lesson is the job of any teacher. Effective teachers put complete lessons together consistently!

A simple way to convey the idea of teaching a complete lesson can be illustrated by the O.P.E. concept. This concept expresses what is required to put a complete lesson together.

The O.P.E. concept conveys the idea that at least three events are required to deliver a complete and positive educational experience. *First*, every lesson has an "opening," a "procedure," and an "ending." *Second*, this concept stresses that "objectives," "a plan," and "evaluation" are vital parts of the teaching-learning process. *Third*, this concept stresses its continuous use. The O.P.E. concept is utilized for every educational experience that students are involved in. In essence, it advocates a cyclic effect which is repeated over and over each class period. Employing the O.P.E. concept allows for the review and expansion of subject matter content each time students and teachers interact.

This cyclic effect is illustrated below by four circles which represent four class periods. The circles overlap to reflect (1) the notion of review (repetition) of what was learned previously, and (2) the expansion into new subject matter content.

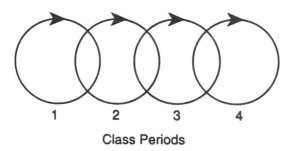

Class Periods

A general discussion of teaching methods will be presented in this chapter. However, the "Critical Incidents of Teaching" are presented in detail in Section IV of this book under the heading "Components of a Positive Delivery System." One component or critical incident of teaching is highlighted in each of the chapters in Section IV. These components are described in a manner designed to assist teachers as they put the O.P.E. concept into actual practice in any educational setting.

TEACHING AN INFORMATIONAL LESSON

The term "lesson," as used in this book, means the delivery of an educational experience. Many educators would refer to a lesson as instruction or a plan. A lesson is more than a lesson plan; it also involves teaching. A lesson is a plan for learning put into action.

Lessons which have exciting introductions (openings) based upon students' needs; are built around observable and measurable objectives; utilize appropriate procedures germane to the educational intent of the objectives to be achieved; are backed by well developed teaching plans and draw conclusions (endings) which make reference to the educational objectives identified in the introductions; and, finally, advocate student performance evaluated in the light of their achievement of the educational objectives will promote positive teaching and effective learning.

In Chapter 6, planning for teaching was discussed in some detail. Examples of teaching plans were provided to illustrate ways in which teachers could develop a plan for teaching each of the three domains of learning.

Assuming an adequate teaching plan for teaching students new information has been developed, how should this plan be used to teach a lesson? The "start of class" bell rings; it is time for class to begin! The following teaching procedures might be used to put together a complete lesson:

COMPONENT PART OF AN INFORMATIONAL LESSON	SUGGESTED TEACHING PROCEDURES
	1. Handle routine chores • Take roll • Make announcements • Collect assignments, etc.
INTRODUCTION	2. Review previous day's lesson. Ask student to cite concepts taught in last lesson.

3. Place Identification portion of lesson on chalkboard or overhead.

4. Discuss reasons *why* lesson is important by reviewing points contained in the Situation portion of the lesson.

5. Present the Interest Approach by citing teaching situation. This could be an individual student problem, a community situation or problem, a teacher's experience, or a current event which focuses upon the lesson topic. Refer to Interest Approaches in Chapter 5.

6. Explain desired outcome of lesson. Draw educational objectives from students. If appropriate, write objectives on chalkboard or overhead.

7. Ask leading questions to
   • find out what students already know about the lesson topic
   • establish why the lesson is important
   • develop interest or develop a provocative situation or identify a problem
   • analyze the teaching situation involved
   • get students to "buy into" the lesson

8. Show realia (real specimen, visual aids, etc.). Ask leading questions about realia shown to stimulate student interest and suggest need to study the lesson.

9. To complete the Introduction, the teacher should ask or refer to the Questions for Study; moving from leading questions to asking the key Questions for Study; especially those questions which must be answered if

the educational objectives are to be achieved.

NOTE: When asking or referring to Questions for Study, the teacher should *not* provide answers to study questions in the Introduction, nor should the teacher teach in the Introduction.

DEVELOPMENT OF KEY QUESTIONS FOR STUDY

10. As the teacher asks the Questions for Study, either the actual questions or key word(s) can be placed on the chalkboard or overhead. These words can be used by the teacher at the conclusion of the Introduction to phrase the actual Questions for Study.

11. At conclusion of the Introduction, write the Questions for Study on the chalkboard or overhead. If Identification or Objectives have not been placed on the chalkboard or overhead, the teacher should do so at this point.

    Many teachers desire to complete the entire Introduction before they write anything on the chalkboard. They believe that students become distracted in the Introduction when they stop to write.

12. Have students copy Identification, Objectives, and Questions for Study in their notes.

SUPERVISED STUDY

13. Distribute reference materials (textbooks, magazines, etc.) for students' use in seeking answers to Questions for Study.

14. Inform students how they are to record their answers.

15. During Supervised Study, the teacher moves around the classroom quietly to assist those students who need as-

sistance and also to monitor student progress in seeking answers to Study Questions.

Many teachers desire for students to answer questions on "scratch" paper during Supervised Study. They believe students might copy incorrect answers in their notes unless the correct answers are discussed first.

16. When most students have completed the Supervised Study portion of the lesson, the teacher begins the Discussion portion.

DISCUSSION

17. Through the use of oral questions, the teacher solicits the correct answer to each Question for Study.

Effective teachers make the Discussion a group process. When agreement has been reached regarding the correct answers, the teacher writes the answer on the chalkboard or overhead. By following this procedure, the teacher can be more confident that students are recording the correct answers in their notes.

CONCLUSION

18. When all Questions for Study have been answered, the teacher begins the Conclusion of the lesson by
   • either reviewing the key points covered, or having student cite these points
   • determining if the Educational Objectives were achieved

19. After key points of the lesson have been reviewed, the teacher, through oral questioning, involves students in developing a consensus statement which reflects the major concept(s) taught.

20. Once an agreement has been reached, the concepts taught are written on the chalkboard or overhead by the teacher and students write the same information in their notes.
21. If appropriate, the teacher conveys to students those complementary concepts reinforced in the lesson.

APPLICATION
22. If applicable, the teacher stresses Application of what was taught by
    • making specific homework assignment(s)
    • identifying specific activities or projects students are to complete

EVALUATION
23 The teacher communicates to students specifically how their performance will be assessed.
24. The teacher dismisses the class, as the end of class period bell rings.

A review of the twenty-four specific procedures presented above might seem burdensome. However, most of the methods shown become habit with the experienced teacher. The lesson has an "opening" and objectives, a "procedure" and a plan, and an "ending" and evaluation. The O.P.E. concept for a complete lesson will be achieved by following the procedures outlined.

It must be pointed out that the above sequence of teaching procedures is only one way to teach an informational lesson. Numerous variations can be utilized; however, the above example does cover the suggested teaching procedures as presented in Chapter 6.

APPROVED PRACTICES FOR TEACHING AN INFORMATIONAL LESSON

Several approved practices should be used in teaching a complete Informational lesson. Some of the more important are listed below.

1. The teacher should vary the Interest Approaches used in the Introduction.

2. The teacher should continue the Introduction until a majority of the students have "bought into the lesson." On the other hand, the Introduction should cease when students are motivated to receive learning.

3. The manner in which the teacher requires students to keep notes should be varied. Instead of always writing objectives and questions for study on the chalkboard, the teacher may hand out a piece of paper with these already printed on it with sufficient space for students to record answers and concluding statement.

4. By referring to or asking Questions for Study in the Introduction, the teacher provides a smooth transition between the Introduction and the Body of the Lesson.

5. The Introduction of the lesson should be used to motivate and stimulate interest. The teacher should *not* "teach" in the Introduction by answering Questions for Study; if the teacher does teach in the Introduction, students will not be provided the opportunity to become involved in answering questions or solving problems or learning how to do a job. Anyone who has taught knows it is easier to "do" for the students than it is to teach the students "how to do."

6. In the Introduction, when asking Questions for Study, if most students already know the answer to one of these questions, there is *no* need to have students find the answer to that question during Supervised Study. Therefore, that particular question should not be used in the lesson. Don't insult the intelligence of the students. A teaching plan must be flexible; teachers must adjust the plan to fit a particular situation.

7. On the other hand, leading questions which cannot be answered by the students should be included as Questions for Study, especially if the answer to the question is necessary to achieve the educational intent of the lesson.

8. Asking Questions for Study as one of the last parts of the Introduction accomplishes two things: (1) it helps tie the Introduction to the

Body of the Lesson, and (2) it provides the teacher with a quick assessment of whether students already know the answers to any of the Questions for Study.

9. If a teacher does not know why a lesson is being taught, how can that teacher expect students to buy into the lesson. An Introduction should point out at least three reasons *why* the lesson is being taught.

10. Printed materials in the form of books and bulletins are not the only means for students to seek answers to Questions for Study. For example, slides, movies, field trips, resource people, etc., could be used by the teacher to help students seek answers to questions or to solve problems.

     Effective teachers utilize a variety of realia during the Supervised Study portion of the lesson.

11. Not all information lessons lend themselves to immediate Application. However, there should be application made of subject matter taught whenever possible.

12. Formal evaluation does not need to be made at the end of each lesson. However, the assessment of students' progress and performance should be made frequently.

13. Students' growth and development can be assessed by the teacher during each part of the lesson through the use of oral questions.

14. A formal teaching plan is not required for each lesson.

15. Students should leave each class as enthusiastic as when they entered the class. They should leave the class with at least one new knowledge, skill or attitude, value, or appreciation.

TEACHING AN OPERATIONAL LESSON

The same component parts of an Informational teaching plan are included in an Operational lesson. However, there are several deviations in the teaching procedures which should be noted.

COMPONENT PART OF AN OPERATIONAL LESSON	SUGGESTED TEACHING PROCEDURE
INTRODUCTION	1. Handle routine details. 2. Review key points and concepts taught in the last lesson. 3. Explain what is to be achieved in today's lesson. 4. Discuss reason *why* lesson is being presented. 5. Ask leading questions to find out what students already know about the lesson. 6. Show realia, if appropriate. 7. Present the teaching situation or problem.

DEMONSTRATION	8. Demonstrate how to perform the skill or operation or job as outlined on the Operation Sheet.
	  • Teacher does and tells
	  • Student does and teacher tells, or
	  • Student does and tells
	  • Teacher distributes Operation Sheets
	9. Students practice under supervision of the teacher.

SUPERVISED PRACTICE	10. During Supervised Practice teacher circulates to observe and assist all students. 11. Ample Supervised Practice time is provided so students can master the skill or operation.
APPLICATION	12. The teacher assigns specific activities or problems or projects for students to complete either in class or outside class time.
EVALUATION	13. Those assigned activities are evaluated in accordance with approved standards of performance.

14. Formal evaluation of new skills learned is determined by examinations.
15. Complementary concepts evolving from the lesson are highlighted by the teacher.

A COMPARISON BETWEEN TEACHING AN OPERATIONAL AND AN INFORMATIONAL LESSON

A comparison between teaching procedures of an Informational lesson and an Operational lesson reveals both familiar and unfamiliar aspects. Some of the more salient are:

1. The Introduction portion of the Operational lesson is usually shorter. Students' interest is usually stimulated when there is activity involved.

2. In an Operational lesson there are *no* Questions for Study. All functional information necessary to perform the skill or operation or job should have been taught previously.

3. For the Operational lesson, ways in which to perform the skill or operation or job are outlined on the Operation Sheet. The "What to Do" (Steps) and "How to Do It" (Key Points), along with materials, tools, and equipment required are listed on the Operation Sheet.

4. There is Supervised Practice in an Operational lesson but no Supervised Study.

5. Concluding statements are not usually developed for Operational lessons. However, there is a conclusion to an Operational lesson. This could be done by a quick review of the steps and key points involved.

TEACHING A MANAGERIAL LESSON

Listed below are suggested teaching procedures that a teacher might follow to teach a Managerial type lesson:

COMPONENT PART OF A MANAGERIAL LESSON	SUGGESTED TEACHING PROCEDURE
INTRODUCTION	1. Handle beginning of class chores.
	2. Review the situation. Refer to the Situation portion of lesson plan.
STATEMENT OF THE PROBLEM	3. Formulate a statement of the problem with assistance of students.
	4. Show realia, if appropriate.
	5. Ask leading questions to draw out factors to be considered in order to solve the problem.
	6. Continue oral questioning until all essential factors have been identified. Ask "what other factors need to be considered?" It may be necessary for the teacher to suggest some of the factors which cannot be drawn from students.
	7. Place problem statement on chalkboard or overhead.
IDENTIFICATION OF FACTORS	8. List all factors to be considered, in proper sequence, on chalkboard or overhead.
	9. After all factors have been identified, the teachers should formulate a question or questions for each factor. This practice will assist students to locate information needed to arrive at a decision.
SUPERVISED STUDY	10. Distribute necessary realia (reference materials, etc.)
	11. Assign each student one or more factors to research. This may be in class or out of class.
DISCUSSION	12. At the completion of Supervised Study, the teacher directs a discussion to establish basic facts and to evaluate factors.

DECISION MAKING   13. Based upon a complete discussion of the factors to be considered, the class makes a decision relative to the problem statement.

APPLICATION   14. The teacher assigns specific activities or problems to be completed by either an individual student or groups of students.

EVALUATION   15. Both formal and nonformal evaluations are made as appropriate.

     16. Complementary concepts stressed in the lesson are pointed out by the teacher.

UNIQUE ASPECTS IN TEACHING A MANAGERIAL LESSON

1. Although educational objectives are developed for the Managerial lesson, they are usually not written out on the chalkboard or overhead. These serve a valuable purpose in formulating the problem statement and also for preparing additional lessons of this nature.

2. The Situation portion of lessons of this type must be fully developed and contain the essential components.

3. An adequate Introduction will usually evolve from a complete review of the Situation and the development of the problem statement with assistance of the students.

4. Due to the time required to teach a Managerial lesson in class, it is acceptable procedure to formulate the problem statement, identify the factors, and make assignments one class period, and complete the Discussion and Application portions of the lesson the following class period.

5. It is desirable for students to utilize outside study (community resources, etc.) to seek information needed to analyze factors and to arrive at a decision.

6. Students should be taught how to utilize a systematic approach to ar-

rive at an intelligent decision. Making the actual decision is *not* the major function of managerial lessons.

7. The teacher must identify *all* essential factors at the time a managerial lesson is being planned.

8. Before teaching the first Managerial lesson, the teacher should review the steps involved in the decision making process with the students. It might be necessary for the teacher to present a lesson on the decision making process.

TIMING, BALANCE, AND SEQUENCE OF A LESSON

How an educational experience is delivered is critical if positive learning is to occur. The difference between an effective teacher and one not so effective can usually be found in the manner in which each teaches a lesson. Certain teachers can adequately plan for instruction, but, when it comes to delivery, they fail miserably. Oftentimes it is due to the fact that they have not paid attention to one or more of the *essentials* for an effective delivery.

Delivery of a positive educational experience requires

• Proper Timing
• Adequate Balance
• Logical Sequence

Timing

When a teacher considers the *timing* of the lesson, both "when to teach it" and "how long to teach it" must be considered. The lesson should be taught when it is the best pedagogical activity to perform at a particular point in time. It is important that the lesson be taught when the students are ready (motivated and interested) to receive the instruction. There is little or no value in delivering a lesson until students are receptive to learning.

Relative to "how long to teach," two points should be considered: total length of time and time to spend upon *each* part of the lesson. Most informational and operational lessons can be taught in one class period (forty-five to fifty-five minutes). It stands to reason that less subject matter can be covered adequately in shorter forty-five minute class periods than in longer fifty-five minute class periods. Teachers will need to shorten or expand the content contained in their teaching plans according to time available to teach. Student interest, the difficulty of the subject matter presented, and the degree of student participation in the experience are other conditions influencing how much new subject matter material can be taught in a class period.

Managerial lessons will usually require two class periods to complete. Again, the degree of detail presented will have an impact upon how much time will be required for completion of a managerial lesson.

Ideally, a lesson should be completed each class period in order to utilize the O.P.E. concept of putting a complete lesson together.

Balance and Sequence

When referring to the *balance* in a lesson, reference is made to the relative emphasis placed upon the various parts of the lesson. Within each lesson, there is an optimum amount of time to spend on each component part. It should be pointed out that in the lesson below the time allotted to each part of a lesson is only suggestive. One can note the relative balance inherent in a lesson by referring to the time allocated to each part of that lesson.

Sequence of a lesson plan means the order in which the component parts of a lesson are presented in the lesson. An appropriate sequence is illustrated in the lesson cited below.

PART OF THE LESSON	TIME TO SPEND
Introduction	ten to fifteen minutes
Questions for Study written on chalkboard or overhead	five minutes
Supervised Study	fifteen minutes
Discussion	fifteen to twenty minutes
Summary/Conclusion	five minutes
	fifty to sixty minutes

In reviewing the above time schedule, several points warrant discussion. One of the critical moments of teaching is time spent in building a case for learning. Providing a stimulating introduction is a challenging responsibility of the teacher. Unless students can be stimulated and motivated to learn, which is the role of the introduction of a lesson, maximum learning will not be realized. Therefore, an introduction must be of sufficient length (and intensity) to build a case for learning.

Depending upon the subject matter being presented and students' prior experiences, the actual time spent to complete the introduction may require more or less time than indicated above. If students buy into the lesson quickly, the introduction should be shortened. On the other hand, if students' interest is difficult to stimulate, the introduction should be lengthened. It may be necessary, in these situations, to provide additional teaching situations and/or utilize more interest approaches. Remember that it is difficult for an individual to learn if that individual does not want to learn. If the teacher believes that student interest will be difficult to arouse, that teacher should be prepared to provide a longer and more intense introduction. This condition should be noted in the written situation portion of the lesson plan as follows: "Student interest will be low!"

A second point pertains to interrupting students' concentration as they work to discover the unknown. If students develop and maintain a high degree of interest during supervised study, the teacher should allow the students to study, even if that study continues to the end of the class period. As long as students are learning, they should be afforded the opportunity to learn even if the time budgeted for supervised study has run out. On the other hand, if student interest wanes, the time allocated for supervised study should be shortened. It is essential that teachers build in flexibility as they prepare their teaching plans.

Optimum learning usually occurs during the supervised study and discussion portions of the lesson. It is the discussion that "fixes" students' learning. Therefore, an enthusiastic discussion should follow the study period. If students' participation in the discussion is active and productive, the teacher should allow sufficient time for this teaching procedure. Conversely, if student involvement is minimum, the teacher should move forward with answers for the study questions.

There should always be a closure to the lesson. Even if the discussion of all study questions has not been completed, there should be a summary of the key points covered in the lesson up to that point and a conclusion should be drawn. Ample time must be planned for this important activity.

Assuming a discussion of study questions was not completed in a class period, it would be necessary to complete the discussion the next class period. If this happened, the teacher would need to readjust the teaching plan. However, the O.P.E. concept can still be utilized. On the second day of a lesson not completed as planned, the teacher would review the previous lesson, re-introduce the lesson, restate the objectives, and continue with the discussion of the questions not answered in the previous day's lesson. If the discussion of the remaining study questions will not require all the time available in the class period, the teacher will need to adjust the teaching plan to include additional teaching-learning activities. These should be placed on the "Daily Plan" discussed in Chapter 6. Based upon the above points, it is obvious that teaching plans must be made flexible!

The beginning and ending of a lesson are considered the two most critical parts of a lesson. Effective teachers present a stimulating introduction and conduct a thought-provoking conclusion. This is where teachers earn their salaries—at the beginning and at the end of the lesson. Most anyone can take roll, make assignments, monitor study periods, collect papers, and dismiss class. It takes time, talent and effort to introduce and conclude a lesson effectively. This is one quality that distinguishes the effective from the less effective teacher.

SUMMARY

Delivery of a positive educational experience does not just happen. It requires planning, timing, sequencing, and teaching. The utilization of the O.P.E. concept will help assure that students are afforded the most effective delivery system.

Suggested teaching procedures were presented in this chapter for Informational, Operational, and Managerial teaching plans. Some of the more important approved teaching practices were also presented along with a discussion of the uniqueness inherent in the teaching procedures of the various types of plans.

Delivering positive educational experiences is both an art and a science. Effective teachers know *how to* and *what to* do to deliver this type of learning on a day-in and day-out basis. These teachers realize the power of positive teaching.

CHAPTER 8

Evaluating Learning to Assure a Positive Educational Experience

A discussion on evaluating learning to assure a positive educational experience impacts both the process (procedure and teaching methods) and the product (the student). All too often, evaluation is perceived as something evil or something which should be avoided at all costs. To the contrary, the evaluation process should be viewed as a valuable and effective teaching tool at the disposal of the teacher. If viewed in this vein, meaningful evaluation promotes positive teaching. At the same time, it can become a powerful motivating force for students, especially if these students have been exposed to a positive educational environment which stresses achievement and recognition for performance.

The phobia or fear held by students against evaluation is due, in part, to the fact that students have often been threatened with grades by a teacher. Remarks like "If you don't behave, I'll give you a test" or "I'll flunk you if you don't do this or that" contribute to this fear on the part of the students. Teachers who resort to this type of motivation usually cause more harm than good. These teachers are creating frightening images of evaluation.

WHY EVALUATE

At its best, evaluation of learning is still a form of criticism. Very few people like to be criticized. Why then evaluate students? Students should be evaluated for two very distinct reasons: *First*, it provides an indication to students of progress being made; and *second*, it is an indicator to the teacher of teaching effectiveness. Thus, if approached from the positive point of view, evaluation assists both the teacher and the student.

VALUES OF EVALUATION

What are the values of evaluation? For the teacher, it provides motivation for students. One of the developmental needs of people is to receive recognition for accomplishments and achievements. This need for recognition is also one of the factors of motivation. If teachers provide recognition for achievement and performance, students will become more motivated. Evaluation also serves useful purposes for the teacher in the revision of course content, in modification of teaching-learning activities employed, and in the assessment of teaching methods.

For the student, evaluation assists in the identification of strong and weak points relative to individual growth and development, in the establishment of effective work habits, in the development and clarification of individual goals, and as an aid in choosing a vocation or career.

THE EVALUATION PROCESS

Evaluation is a systematic process, a deliberate act, in contrast to a "happening." It is the process used to assess the degree of achievement of educational objectives. In this regard, it is important to point out that *how* we evaluate is as important as *what* we evaluate! The evaluation process can be visually illustrated as follows:

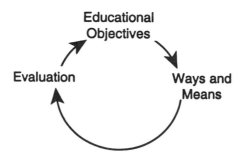

Evaluation is a cyclic process which addresses the achievement of educational objectives expressed as changes in student behavior; those changes are considered to be the "product" and the ways and means used to achieve the educational objectives are the "process." Evaluation is more than giving grades!

PRINCIPLES OF EVALUATION

Several principles, if correctly applied, can provide a basis by which evaluation of learning becomes a positive process.
Evaluation should

1. *Be directed toward educational objectives*
   - In the educational process, one major concern is whether students' behavior has been changed as stated in the teaching objective and also whether the change was in a positive manner. Assuming quality educational objectives have been formulated, one key indicator of desired behavior change is whether students can do or perform those terminal behaviors communicated and described in the educational objective. Thus, evaluation should be based upon the achievement of the educational objectives sought.

2. *Be continuous*
   - Evaluation is not a one time occurrence, but it is an ongoing process. An assessment or appraisal made at any particular point in time will not necessarily be valid at a later point in time. Education is not static; it does not "hold still." It is dynamic and, thus, constantly changes. Evaluation must likewise be a changing and continuing process.

3. *Be concerned with all aspects of the educational process*
   - To be effective and fair to both the students and the teacher, all educational activities must be considered in the evaluation process. For example, a student's attitude might be just as important to appraise as is how well that student performs on a paper and pencil test. All aspects of learning should be used in evaluating student growth, development, and performance. As an example, a student might be able to answer correctly all questions about power tools on a safety examination but, due to poor work habits

or attitude, be a serious safety hazard in a laboratory requiring the use of those same power tools.

4. *Be subjective as well as objective*
   - All too often teachers believe that the only valuable and useful evaluation must be in the form of examinations, either oral or written. Granted, this type of evaluation is probably more objective in nature than most others, but it is not the only method to evaluate student performance.
   - In addition to oral and written expressions casual observations, along with verbal and non-verbal clues, can provide valuable indications of a student's attitude, enthusiasm, perceptions, etc.. The neatness of a student's work can serve as valuable evidence of that individual's potential work habits. These are all subjective evaluations, since they are difficult to measure in a quantitative manner.

5. *Provide the primary basis for future improvement*
   - Evaluation, if properly perceived and conducted, should assist in the identification of the strengths and weaknesses in teaching and learning. Building upon the identified strengths and teaching again to the "soft spots," plans and strategies may be launched to correct the existing weaknesses in teaching and learning.

6. *Be oriented toward positive goals*
   - The evaluation process should be utilized to determine what is happening; it should identify the strengths as well as the weaknesses. It should serve as a basis for making improvements. Utilized in this manner, evaluation can be oriented toward positive goals. If the main purpose of evaluation is perceived as to strengthen and to improve, this emphasis will be positive, not negative.

7. *Be concerned with both the product and the process*
   - As previously mentioned, evaluation should address both students' growth and development and the teachers' teaching effectiveness. It is just as important to assess how well teachers teach as it is to determine how well students learn. In the educational process, the instructional methodology can affect the degree of behavior modification of students. Too often, only the students (the product) are evaluated. To evaluate to assure a positive educational experience,

both the teaching (the process) and the students should be subjected to evaluation.

8. *Be more a means than an end*
   • Evaluation for the sake of evaluation is like the clock without hands. It occurs but nothing positive or constructive happens. Evaluation should serve as a means to determine what, if any, changes, adjustments, or corrections need to be made in the educational process; it also serves to provide an indication of how well students are progressing toward established goals. The results of evaluation should help provide direction. It should be used as a means to improve and strengthen the educational process.

9. *Be valid*
   • Evaluation should reveal the *truth* about what is occurring in the educational process. If it is based upon false data or fabricated biases, the results of evaluation will not be valid. To be of maximum value in determining the performance of students and in suggesting the improvement of the educational process, evaluation must reflect truthfully, completely, and accurately what is *actually* occurring! If evaluation does not reveal the complete and real truth, it should not be considered as valid.

10. *Be subjected to evaluation*
   • "How we evaluate is as important as what we evaluate." The procedures utilized, including the instrumentation, will determine, to a large extent, the quality, reliability, and validity, of the evaluation. Therefore, the evaluation process being used should be reviewed periodically to ascertain whether it is achieving what it is supposed to achieve.

MEASUREMENT

Evaluation by itself does not necessarily provide an indication of how well an objective was achieved. To make evaluation more meaningful, objective measurement should be employed.

What is meant by measurement as it pertains to evaluation? *Measurement* is the process of using standards to determine the degree of achievement in a specific area. In the educational process, measurement is supplied by the criteria or standards specified in the educational objectives. The criteria of an objective specifies how well the terminal behavior is to be performed. Since evaluation is both objective and subjective, measurement (the use of standards) tends to make evaluation more objective.

The following analogy is presented to illustrate how the more objective quality of the measurement component of evaluation can improve the quality of that evaluation.

---

1. Assume the objective is "to draw a straight line, 18 inches long on the chalkboard."
2. A line is drawn on the chalkboard.
3. Evaluation occurs when these questions are addressed:
   - Is it a straight line?
   - Was it drawn on the chalkboard?
   - Was the line 18" long?

   Evaluation was employed to determine if the objective was achieved.
   — The line drawn on the chalkboard was determined to be more straight than curved.
   — The line appeared as if it were in the vicinity of 18 inches. It was longer than a pencil and not as long as a desk.

   Therefore, evaluation occurred. But what was the quality of the evaluation?
4. To improve the quality of this evaluation, it is necessary to determine *how straight* was the line drawn and *how long* was the line.
5. To determine these, measurement must be applied. Some type of acceptable measuring device must be utilized.

   By placing a yardstick on or near the line, both the straightness and length of the line can be measured relatively accurately.
6. The use of objective standards, in this case a yardstick, can assist to make evaluation more accurate.

PRINCIPLES OF INDIVIDUAL EVALUATION

Several principles, if applied, can make the evaluation of individual students more effective and more meaningful and thus more positive.

1. *Evaluation should recognize individual differences.*
   - Individuals differ in all sorts of ways. In reality, there is no such thing as an average student. The average student is largely a myth. Each student grows and develops at a different rate. For evaluation of students to be most positive, the teacher must identify these differences and take them into account as the relative degree of change in behavior is assessed. Any class of students will possess a vast range of differences. No two individuals change at the exact same pace; therefore, the teacher must consider this principle when assessing the relative change in students' behavior.

2. *Evaluation should consider both the beginning status and growth.*
   - As pointed out above, individuals do not change at the same rate and at the same pace. The behavioral changes occurring within a class of students will be as diverse as are the students themselves. It is *not* the rate and pace of growth and development in students' behavior that is really important; it is the *amount of growth and development* occurring that is important in the final analysis. Thus, both the beginning and ending status must be considered by the teacher when evaluating an individual student's growth and development. This approach promotes positive teaching!

     Using the illustration below, which student exhibits the greatest amount of growth?

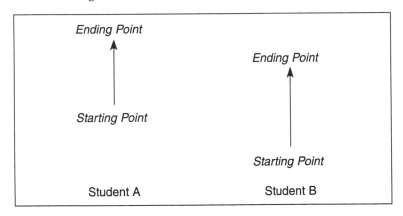

   - Which student started at the higher level?
   - Which student ended at the higher level?
   - Which student exhibited the greatest overall growth?

3. *The primary function of evaluation is to aid in guidance.*
   - One of the principles of evaluation points out that evaluation should provide the primary basis for future improvement. Evaluation should assist to identify the strengths and weaknesses of an individual student's behavior modification so teachers can use this information to plan and direct the future teaching-learning process. Evaluation should help teachers guide the learning process of students.

4. *Evaluation is an integral part of the teaching-learning process.*
   - Evaluation procedures used should contribute to the behavior modification of the student. Thus, evaluation should have a positive effect upon an individual student's learning. Evaluation must involve the student if positive teaching and learning are to result.
   - Teachers who practice positive teaching perceive evaluation as a teaching tool. They approach it as an educational experience, not as a "job" to be done!

5. *Varied measuring devices should be used.*
   - Students differ in all sorts of ways. Furthermore, these differences are augmented as students study and learn and gain more and more experiences. Therefore, no single evaluation tool or technique should be used to assess the growth and development of students in a class. Certainly, the use of paper and pencil tests as the only evaluation instrument could result in inaccurate and inappropriate student assessment.
   - No single evaluation technique can assess objectively the rate and degree of behavioral change occurring in a student as it relates to the cognitive, psychomotor, and affective domains of learning.

6. *One learns to evaluate self through evaluation.*
   - Students are basically what they learn! People are what they have experienced! Since people learn from their own involvement in their learning, people learn how to evaluate by becoming involved in the evaluation process. Before improvements can be made, it is essential to realize and recognize that improvements need to be made. By becoming involved in evaluation, an individual will tend to appreciate more objectively the values and benefits which can result from evaluation.

7. *Comprehensive records are needed.*
 * Evaluation is not a "once-in-a-while" proposition; it must be an on-going process if an accurate and fair assessment of student performance is to be made. Therefore, a record of the results of the continuous formal and informal evaluation techniques employed must be recorded for each student.
 * An analysis of the comprehensive record of each student's performance recorded over time will provide a more objective assessment of the growth and development unique to each student.
 * An accumulation of records on a particular student will assist in making the evaluation process more objective and, thus, more fair to the student. Records of evaluations promote positive teaching!

EVALUATING STUDENT PERFORMANCE

Teachers define, observe and measure, or judge learned behavior. Therefore, the more activities used to evaluate student performance, the greater will be the tendency to provide a more realistic and objective assessment of a student's actual growth and development. As pointed out earlier, if a teacher relies solely upon paper and pencil tests to arrive at a student evaluation or grade, the teacher may not be accurately or fairly assessing student performance.

Although it will vary with every subject matter area and with each educational experience, students' growth and development assessment should include sufficiently varied types of evaluation to determine the relative rate and degree of behavior modification for each domain of learning—cognitive, psychomotor, and affective. Numerous activities can be employed to achieve a more comprehensive evaluation of a student's total growth and development. Some of these are as follows.

 * Class participation
 * Attitude and interest indicators
 * Notes and notebooks, their quality and quantity
 * Oral reports
 * Written reports
 * Application of approved practices learned
 * Oral critiques

- Skills developed
- One-on-one interviews
- Casual observation of daily behavior
- Formal observation of work habits
- Project construction
- Experiments
- Paper and pencil tests
- Oral quizzes
- Individual conferences
- Performance tests
- Competency checklists
- Rating scales

The more types of evaluation used by a teacher to identify students' strengths, weaknesses, and growth and development, the more valid and the more positive will be the evaluation. Thus, the more positive the teaching will be.

Assigning a grade which accurately reflects a student's "true" performance in all three domains of learning for a specific period of time is an awesome responsibility. It is a task which should not be taken lightly by the teacher. An important part of a teacher's job is determining student grades. This is usually accomplished by one or both of the following two methods:

- Curve grading
- Capacity grading

Curve Grading

This method of grading results in each student being graded on how well that student performs and achieves in comparison to other students in the class. Normal curve grading assigns a "normal" number of A's, B's, C's, D's and F's to students in the class. This is illustrated in Figure 8.1.

It is felt by those who advocate this form of determining student grades that curve grading *forces* students to apply themselves. Likewise, parents feel they know where their children really "stand." However, curve grading my force slow learners to give up and bright students may achieve "top" grades without exerting themselves.

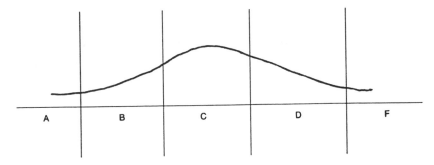

Figure 8.1   Normal "Bell-shaped" Curve

Capacity or Ability Grading

This method of grading places major emphasis upon determining whether or not a student is working up to capacity (ability). Each student is graded upon how well that student achieves as measured against the individual's ability to learn. Capacity grading tends to encourage the slow learner. The "average" student will try harder to achieve, and the bright student must apply real effort under this method. The major difficulty with capacity grading is that the teacher may not always know enough about a student's ability to learn to provide valid evaluation.

Determining Student Grades

A combination of curve grading and ability grading yields the most positive method to fairly determine students' grades. This method requires that all evidence about students be carefully weighed and evaluated. Student achievements are then ranked. Rank is considered in determining grades, but the accomplishments of all students are weighed against some standard of expectancy. Students not working up to capacity are advised of this fact.

Adjustments in grading may be made to encourage the slow learner; however, the teacher must not mislead students to believe that they are performing at a higher level than they actually are.

An adaptation of the capacity grading system is referred to as *contract grading*. Students are evaluated in the light of their achievement of predetermined educational objectives (educational activities) which the student and the teacher agreed upon prior to the start of the educational experience(s). Those students who achieve at higher levels of performance are, likewise, evaluated at higher levels. Contract grading does assist teachers to provide for individual differences between students.

There is no perfect method for determining student grades. However, the student should always be given the "benefit of the doubt!" The student must be graded in a fair manner and as objectively as possible. Remember, there is no such thing as pure objectivity in evaluation. At best, grades are judgments. Somewhere and somehow, personal biases creep into the evaluation process. Who formulated the educational objectives to be achieved? Who decided upon the type of evaluation instrument to be employed? Who framed the questions?

In addition, under any circumstance, grades should not be used as a "reward" or as a "punishment."

EVALUATING LEARNING DOMAINS

Since learning occurs in three main domains, student progress should likewise be measured in the cognitive, psychomotor, and affective domains. One of the common errors made by teachers as they attempt to assess student growth and development is that they measure the cognitive domain to a greater extent than they do the psychomotor. And most teachers usually do not attempt to assess probably the most important aspect of learning—students' attitudes, values, interests, and appreciations. Evaluation of each of the three learning domains is discussed later in this chapter.

FUNCTIONS OF AN EXAMINATION

For several reasons examinations are used to evaluate student performance. Well prepared examinations are designed to help both the student and the teacher.

For the student, examinations help the learner to

1. focus upon the important points in the unit of instruction

2. identify where more study is required

3. gain confidence by showing that progress is being made towards the achievement of educational objectives

For the teacher, examinations help the instructor to

1. determine whether the students have learned what they were supposed to have learned

2. identify what portion of the subject matter should be reviewed

3. determine the individual differences existing among students

4. evaluate the students' progress

5. determine the effectiveness of the teaching: is the instructor teaching the proper material and teaching it in such a manner that it is retained in the students' minds

QUALITIES OF A GOOD EXAMINATION

A well written examination should possess the qualities listed below. It should

1. *Measure what it is supposed to measure*—the students' knowledge of the subject matter in question. The examination should be valid.
   - In measuring knowledge that the student possesses, it is important not to confuse *memory* (rote recall) with *understanding* (use of knowledge). It is important for teachers to design examinations to measure understanding rather than just memory.

2. *Measure the students' knowledge as accurately as possible.* It should be reliable. It should measure learned behavior consistently.
   - To design a reliable examination, the test items should require answers that are definite. The acceptable answer should not be left to the interpretation or opinion of the teacher.
   - The examination should cover all parts of the unit of instruction taught up to the time the examination is given so a broad sample of the students' knowledge can be obtained.
   - Questions should vary in degree of difficulty. If all the high achieving students answer the questions one hundred percent correctly and all the low achieving students cannot answer correctly any of

the questions, the degree of ability and the amount of learning of individual students will not be determined.

3. *Be easy to give, easy to take, and easy to score.*
    - In constructing the examination, the teacher should do everything possible to save students' time and effort in writing answers to the evaluation items. Also, the amount of time and effort for the teacher to score the examination should be considered.

4. *Be well balanced using a variety of evaluation items*
    - The examination should contain several different types of evaluation items. In addition, the more items used, the more valuable will be the results.

5. *Serve as a positive teaching tool*
    - The examination should be considered as a vital part of the lesson.

In the final analysis, a good examination should be reliable; it should yield consistent results. It should be valid: it should measure what it is supposed to measure. It should be objective, be comprehensive and cover all objectives, and be designed to detect the difference between levels of student performance.

KINDS OF EXAMINATIONS

Two main kinds of paper and pencil examinations are used to evaluate student performance.

- Objective examinations
- Essay and problem solving examinations

The objective examination can be further divided into two types of evaluation instruments.

1. Recognition item tests
    a. True—False questions
    b. Multiple choice questions
    c. Matching questions

2. Recall item tests
    a. Single answer questions
    b. Completion questions

TYPES OF EVALUATION ITEMS

Evaluation items are commonly referred to as "test" or "examination" questions. A well constructed test or examination should consist of a variety of evaluation items. Each item possesses certain characteristics which aid in assessing student performance. If the educational intent is to test students' ability to recall knowledge, there are evaluation items which are more appropriate for assessing this level of mental activity. On the other hand, if a teacher desires to determine a student's ability to analyze relationships, other specific kinds of test items should be used.

OBJECTIVE EXAMINATIONS

Recognition Questions: True-False Evaluation Items

One of the best known recognition type items are true-false questions. They are constructed by writing a series of true statements, in complete sentences, covering the subject matter to be tested. Each statement should contain only one thought. Some true statements should then be changed to false ones entirely by chance, as if by throwing a pair of dice. If an odd number comes up, change the statement to false. But if an even number comes up, leave the statement as written. There should be about the same number of true and false items.

Since each individual item measures knowledge of only one specific point, several true-false items should be utilized on a unit examination. It is, likewise, essential that the statements cover the important points studied in the unit.

Advantages of Using True-False Evaluation Items

True-false evaluation items have several distinct advantages. Some of these are as follows:

1. They can be adapted to most subject matter areas and are well known to students.

2. They are easy to construct.

3. They can be scored easily in an objective manner.

4. They can be answered in a short amount of time.

5. They are effective for use in daily quizzes.

6. They can be used to measure facts, understanding, or knowledge requiring reasoning. They can effectively assess the cognitive domain of learning.

7. They are useful as the first questions on a unit examination.

Disadvantages of Using True-False Items

True-false type evaluation items possess these disadvantages:

1. They are of doubtful value for measuring achievement (performance) of students.

2. Guessing and memorization are encouraged by true-false questions.

3. They are difficult to construct so that they are either entirely true or entirely false.

4. They tend to be constructed from textbook statements.

5. They have low reliability since each item deals with only one point. Reliability can be improved, however, by using a large number of items.

6. Items dealing with minor points receive as much credit as items pertaining to significant points.

Suggestions for Preparing True-False Items

There should be as many false items as there are true items on a unit examination. Do not make the statement false by simply using a negative word. Also, do not let the grammatical construction of the statement provide a clue that the answer is false such as "always," "never," "no," "should," "all," or "only."

The use of double negatives should be carefully avoided. Do not use "trick" or "catch" questions. Also, do not use items which are part true and part false. Do not have an item which suggests an answer to another item even if the items are not close together.

When preparing the item(s), space for recording the answer should be provided so scoring can be quickly and easily completed with a check strip as indicated below.

	Directions:	Place the symbol (+) in front of the true statement and the symbol (-) in front of the false statement.
1. -	_____	1. Maintenance of teaching supplies should be assigned to the janitor.
2. -	_____	2. Students should be charged for the instructional materials used in the class.
3. +	_____	3. An inventory of teaching supplies should be kept.
Check Strip	Etc.	

Always provide clear directions so students know exactly what is expected of them, including the type of answer sought such as "+ or -," "+ or 0," "T or F," etc.

Recognition Questions: Multiple Choice Evaluation Items

When only one evaluation item is utilized on an examination, many educators believe multiple choice items provide the best single indicator of student performance of all of the objective forms of questions. It is one of the most valuable of the various types of objective test items. This kind of item is harder to prepare than the true-false type, but tests containing these evaluation items are easy to give and students usually prefer them.

A multiple choice item consists of a question or an incomplete statement followed by several possible answers. Research indicates that four possible answers provide the most satisfactory measurement, although some test designers claim five choices will make it harder for students to guess the correct answer. However, it takes time and effort to construct incorrect answers, called distractors, so that they appear correct.

Advantage of Using Multiple Choice Evaluation Items

Multiple choice evaluation items possess several advantages.

1. They can measure effectively a student's ability to interpret, to discriminate, to select, and to make application of subject matter learned. They can measure understanding, judgment, and reasoning ability.

2. They can measure understanding more effectively than can simple recall items such as single answer and completion questions.

3. They can be scored objectively.

4. Guessing is kept to a minimum by using multiple choice items.

5. Students usually understand how to complete this type of test item.

Disadvantages of Using Multiple Choice Items

1. Much time and effort is required to construct multiple choice items which measure application of subject matter taught rather than memorization. They are time consuming to construct.

2. It is difficult to construct four distractors of equal consistence or discrimination ability.

3. It is sometimes difficult to construct one completely correct answer.

4. Questions require more space on the test paper. They are space consuming!

Suggestions for Preparing Multiple Choice Items

A series of multiple choice items consisting of a "stem" or a direct statement and four or five possible answers, one of which is the most correct, provides an effective way to assess student understanding of the subject matter in question.

It requires much ingenuity to develop multiple choice distractors which appear correct. Part of the secret is to avoid leaving clues. For example, avoid one answer being longer than the others. Or, avoid having one or more distractors which do not pertain to the same subject matter.

Sometimes grammatical constructions are clues, such as mixed singulars or plurals.

```
The result of addition is the:
_____ a.   Products
_____ b.   Sum
_____ c.   Factors
_____ d.   Quotient
```

Distractors "a" and "c" are plurals. For the stem to be grammatically correct, the verb should be "are" for these two distractors.

For the same reason, avoid using "a" or "an" as the last word in the stem.

The location of the correct answer in the list of choices (a, b, c, d) should vary at random. There should be as many "a" correct answers as "b," "c," or "d."

As with true-false items, specific directions should be provided so students know precisely what is required of them. Likewise, provisions should be made for recording the answer quickly and easily by the student. The samples of multiple choice items shown in Figures 8.2 and 8.3 illustrate two different but easy methods for student response.

Recognition Questions: Matching Evaluation Items

This type of item requires the students to match two sets of materials in accordance with directions provided. The most common matching items consist of two columns of words or phrases. Students are required to match each item in one list with the most clearly related item provided in the other list. Although they are adaptable to numerous situations and subject matter areas, they are inferior to multiple choice items when judgment and/or application of subject matter taught are to be measured.

Advantages of Using Matching Evaluation Items

1. They can be used for testing various outcomes.

Directions: Check (√) the one answer for each question which you
               think is most nearly correct. Check only one answer for each
               question. Answer all questions.

- -

Question: When the change in price is equal to the relative change in
               quantity taken or available, a commodity is said to be

               _____ a. inelastic
               _____ b. elastic
               ___√___ c. unitary elastic
               _____ d. perfectly inelastic

Question: The diagram shown below represents which one of the fol-
               lowing curves?

               ___√___ a. a supply curve
               _____ b. an equilibrium curve
               _____ c. a demand curve
               _____ d. a unit elasticity curve

Question: When the change in price is *less* than the relative change in
               quantity taken or available, a commodity is said to be

               _____ a. inelastic
               ___√___ b. elastic
               _____ c. unitary elastic
               _____ d. perfectly inelastic

Figure 8.2   Sample A: Multiple Choice Format

2. They are especially applicable for measuring students' abilities to recognize relationships.

3. They are easy to construct.

4. They are space conserving.

5. They nearly eliminate guessing on the part of the students.

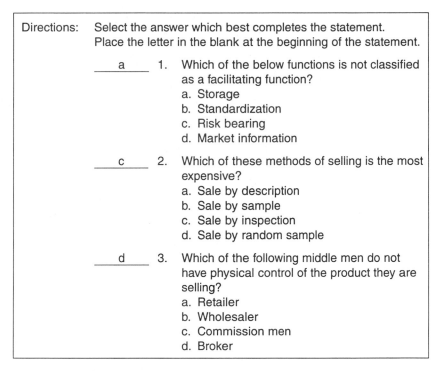

Figure 8.3 Sample B: Multiple Choice Format

6. They can be scored objectively.

7. They are easy to score.

8. They are easy to answer by students.

Disadvantages of Using Matching Items

1. Since the set of words or phrases must be short, matching items provide a poor measure of comprehensive understanding or interpretation on the part of the student.

2. They are not as effective in measuring judgment or application of subject matter as are multiple choice items.

3. They emphasize the memorization of facts.

4. In constructing these items, unintentional clues to the correct response are often difficult to eliminate.

Suggestions for Preparing Matching Items

To construct matching items, the teacher should write a set of complete statements which cover the content taught. The subject is divided from the predicate to form the two columns. The subject parts are numbered and arranged in one column. The predicate parts make up the other column. The arrangement of the predicate parts are divided by chance.

Between ten and twenty matching items should be constructed to eliminate guessing. More than twenty items wastes the student's time. If less than ten items are used, there should be an excess in one column or the other.

The same suggestions for avoiding clues in constructing multiple choice items apply to matching type items; use only related materials in any one set of matching items. In addition, be sure that every predicate used will match grammatically with the subject of every sentence.

Directions provided to the students should be as specific as possible. Use capital letters to designate the two columns "A" or "B." Arrange the "answer" column in a logical sequence. Figure 8.4 is a sample of matching type evaluation items with directions.

Recall Questions: Single Answer Evaluation Items

Evaluation items with a single answer require the students to supply the answer with a single word. Recall type items have high discrimination value since students either know the correct answer or they do not.

Advantage of Using Single Answer Items

1. They effectively eliminate guessing.

2. They are really easy to construct.

3. Most students are familiar with single answer questions.

4. They are space conserving.

> *Directions:* Place the letter in Column B which best describes the item in Column A.
>
> | | Column A | | Column B |
> |---|---|---|---|
> | d | 1. Exchange function | a. | Distribution of goods |
> | f | 2. Marketing process | b. | Assembly of goods |
> | a | 3. Dispersion | c. | Flow of goods |
> | b | 4. Concentration | d. | Selling of goods |
> | c | 5. Equalization | e. | Grading of goods |
> | | 6. Etc. | f. | Movement of goods |
> | | 7. Etc. | g. | Etc. |
> | | | h. | Etc. |
> | | | i. | Etc. |
> | | | j. | Etc. |

Figure 8.4   Sample of Matching Evaluation Items

Disadvantages of Using Single Answer Items

1. They require more time to score than recognition items.

2. They tend to promote memorization.

3. They measure factual knowledge more effectively than judgments and/or reasoning ability.

Suggestions for Preparing Single Answer Evaluation Items

The teacher writes a series of statements which cover the subject matter taught. In phrasing statements, be sure the sought answer appears as part of the statement. For example:

> *Transpiration* is the process by which a plant loses moisture.

The sought answer is transpiration, not "moisture."
Thus, the item can be written in a better manner as follows:

> The process by which a plant loses moisture is *transpiration*.

The statements are then rewritten in the form of a question. For example:

> What is the process called by which a plant loses moisture?

It is important that each item have only *one* correct answer. If there is the possibility of more than one acceptable answer, make it center around a single point or idea. For example:

> How is mail moved long distances at high speed?

The sought answer was airplane; however, train or truck would also be plausible answers.

A better way to construct this item would be as follows:

> What is the fastest way to move mail long distances?

The most appropriate answer would be "by air" or "by airplane."

As with other evaluation items, avoid using "a" or "an" before the blank as a clue to the answer.

Recall Questions: Completion Evaluation Items

Completion items are similar to single answer questions but are more difficult to construct.

Advantages of Using Completion Type Evaluation Items

1. They effectively measure retention of specific points.

2. They are relatively easy to construct.

3. They have wide application.

4. They have a high discriminatory value.

Disadvantages of Using This Type of Item

1. They tend to emphasize memorization.

2. It is somewhat difficult to avoid subjectivity in scoring.

3. They are not effective in measuring understanding.

4. Students cannot always recall the exact wording required to answer the item correctly.

Suggestions for Preparing Completion Type Evaluation Items

The first step is to prepare a list of questions with their answers. The answers, with key words omitted, are the basis for the completion item. For example:

Question: Which kinds of reproduction allow plants to develop from seeds?
Answer: Sexual reproduction allows plants to develop from seeds.

In omitting key words, be sure that only the correct word, or possibly one expressing the same idea can be filled in by the student.

Sexual reproduction allows plants to develop from seeds.

It is *best* to not have too many blanks in one sentence; otherwise, the meaning of the sentence might not be clear. For example:

_____ reproduction allows _____ to develop from _____

Omit only those words which test students' knowledge. It should be kept in mind that completion items should be used to assess information, not become a puzzle for students' entertainment.

Make all blanks for recording the answers the same length. Blanks of different lengths can serve as clues to the answers expected.

Do not use textbook sentences or paragraphs as completion type statements. This procedure will tend to encourage students to answer the item from memory.

Provide specific directions explaining how students are to answer each item. Build in provisions for the student to supply the answer in a simple manner and to provide the teacher ease in scoring.

ESSAY AND PROBLEM SOLVING EXAMINATIONS

Essay Evaluation Items

The essay examination item is a long established evaluation item which requires answers of one or two sentences, several paragraphs, or several pages. It is fairly easy to prepare. It is adaptable to most subject matter areas and most educational activities. However, it is difficult to score fairly since the answer depends upon opinion which may be influenced by neatness or by writing ability rather than depending upon knowledge of subject matter. Often the student who knows the least writes the most. The student tries to bury ignorance under a mountain of words.

Advantages of Using Essay Evaluation Items

Essay type evaluation items have these distinct advantages [1]:

1. They can assess higher mental processes than can objective type items. They can measure the ability to
   a. outline or organize
   b. evaluate
   c. make decisions
   d. discriminate
   e. communicate in written form
   f. synthesize and analyze

2. They provide for a more comprehensive evaluation of student performance if included in a unit examination.

3. They can measure attitudes.

4. They are adaptable to most subject matter areas.

5. They promote effective study habits.

6. They encourage creativity on the part of the students.

7. They require the use of correct English.

8. They are easy to construct.

9. They minimize guessing on the part of the student.

10. They promote the application of subject matter taught.

11. They can be used to assess the affective domain of learning better than objective type items can.

12. They can "cross" subject matter areas (English, history, etc.).

Disadvantages of Using This Type of Item

1. They have low reliability (consistency) due to difficulty in maintaining grading (scoring) uniformity.

2. They are difficult to score objectively and require a great amount of time to evaluate.

3. They tend to measure a student's ability to organize and outline rather than measure understanding of subject matter.

4. Questions of this type can be easily misinterpreted.

Suggestions for Preparing This Type of Evaluation Item

Any evaluation item should measure students' performance. However, teachers must decide what they want the answer to tell about the student. Items of this type can measure (1) general information, (2) knowledge evolving from the unit of instruction, (3) understanding of basic principles, or (4) ability to apply principles to unfamiliar situations.

Emphasis should be placed upon essay question items which begin with words like

- Classify
- Compare
- Criticize
- Discuss
- Why
- How
- Explain
- Define
- Show the significance of
- Interpret
- Trace
- Justify

The teacher should guard against essay question evaluation items which can be answered with memorized textbook or lecture information. Items prepared in this manner will not measure understanding.

Questions should be as specific as possible. Students must know clearly and precisely what answer is expected. Moreover, it may be necessary to provide students direct help in answering the item. The kind and amount of help depends upon what the item is designed to test. For example, giving the student the mathematical formula required to answer the item would be the right kind of assistance if the intent of the item were to measure the student's ability to apply the formula to certain situations and/or problems. However, too much help should not be provided. Be aware that the use of words like "not," "always," etc., give clues to the answer sought.

Essay items should be brief and concise. All unnecessary words and phrases should be omitted. The intent of the item must be absolutely clear. For example, consider the correct answer to this question: "What do the people of Hawaii do?" "They grow pineapples," or "they surf," or "they play the ukulele" could all be correct responses depending upon what the teacher intended the question to measure.

Avoid using negative words when phrasing items, especially double negatives such as "not unknown." They are confusing.

All items should be written in correct English, adhering to the rules of grammar, punctuation, and spelling.

Illustrated below are examples of poor and better essay evaluation items.

Poor

> Explain, in detail, why nuclear reactors are one of the most important developments in electrical energy generation replacing hydrocarbon type electric generators?

Better

> Why are nuclear power stations replacing hydrocarbon type power stations?

Problem-Solving Items

Every unit examination should contain at least one problem-solving question. Evaluation items of this nature serve at least two important functions. *First*, they assess students' ability to analyze factual information and/or data as they arrive at intelligent decisions. *Second*, problem-solving questions, if used consistently on unit examinations, communicate to students that they must do more than memorize facts; they must be able to apply knowledge to solve problems.

Examples of problem-solving questions are shown in Figure 8.5.

GENERAL GUIDELINES FOR CONSTRUCTING UNIT EXAMINATIONS

The following guidelines are offered to assist teachers to design unit examinations which will more objectively measure student understanding and also provide for a positive learning experience for the student.

Guideline   1. *Construct all evaluation items around the educational objectives*
- One of the principles of evaluation is that "evaluation must be made in the light of educational objectives."
- Never make an examination a "guessing" game for the students.

Guideline   2. *Utilize several types of evaluation items*
- Each type of evaluation item possesses certain advantages, as well as limitations. By using several types in constructing unit examinations, the teacher is providing a variety of items which will tend to better meet the diverse needs of students.

Guideline   3. *Design evaluation items with an appropriate degree of difficulty*
- An examination should serve as a positive learning experience, not as a means to show students the teacher is smarter than they, or to provide a way for the teacher to "get back" at the students.

Example A

A commodity broker purchases 1,000 troy ounces of gold. The broker intends to hold the metal and sell later. He is interested in protecting himself from a fall in gold prices and he decides to hedge. Show how he might do this.

Answer: Sell a 1,000 troy ounce gold contract on the future's market on the day of the cash purchase and buy a 1,000 troy ounce gold contract on the day of cash transactions.

Example B

A business woman has an opportunity to invest $10,000 of extra capital in her business. She has four choices. She wants to select the best use of the money to achieve the greatest net profit.

Below is a summary of the four choices available.

Use of Funds	Returns	Expenses	Net
Choice A	$ 2,472	$ 2,090	$ 382
Choice B	3,600	2,200	1,400
Choice C	960	775	185
Choice D	11,000	10,000	1,000

1. What use of the $10,000 will yield the greatest net profit?
2. If she had an additional $10,000 to invest, where should she invest it?
3. What is the percent return to investment for each of the four choices?

Answers:
1. She would invest the $10,000 in Choice B.
2. She would invest an additional $10,000 in Choice D.
3. Choice A would yield 3.82% on investment.
   Choice B would yield 14%.
   Choice C would yield 1.85%.
   Choice D would yield 10%.

Figure 8.5   Examples of Problem-Solving Questions

• The examination should measure what students have been taught. Evaluation items should be constructed to assess students' understanding at the same level of mental activity as students were taught, not at a higher or lower level. For example, if the students have been expected to "list" the parts of a sentence, the examination should measure students' ability to "list," not to "analyze" or to "interpret."

Guideline 4. *Base evaluation items upon the same references or materials used when teaching the lesson*
- The examination should test what the students have learned as a result of instruction. It should not measure something superficial or unknown to the students.
- The information contained in the students' notes should provide the primary basis for constructing evaluation items to be used on an examination.

Guideline 5. *Group the evaluation items by type*
- An examination should be easy to give, easy to take, and easy to score. Grouping items by type on a unit examination provides the optimum use of time and effort for students to complete and for the teacher to grade.
- Also, this allows students to maintain optimum mental focus since they would have to change their line of thought as each new type of evaluation item appeared on the examination.

Guideline 6. *Arrange items in order of increasing difficulty*
- As previously discussed, the thought of completing an examination creates a fear for some students. This natural fear can be minimized if students experience success in "taking an exam." Since there are evaluation items which require a lower level of mental activity and which are easier for the students to complete, these types should be included as the first set of items on the unit examination. For example, true-false items are more appropriate to begin an exam than are essay or problem solving items.

Guideline 7. *Include clear directions for each group of items*
- Examinations should measure student performance, not how well they can guess what the teacher expects. Thus, the students should be informed as specifically as possible what they are to do to answer the evaluation items contained on the examination.

• Illustrated below are samples of how *not* to provide directions to students.

Directions: Answer each question to the best of your ability.

Directions: Answer each question by writing true or false or by placing a + or - by each correct statement.

• The sample directions provided below provide more specific directions for students to follow.

General Instructions: This unit examination includes 50 items of various types on Human Nutrition. Directions for each group of questions are included at the start of each section.

Section I.   True-False

Directions: Answer the following questions true or false. Place the symbol (+) in front of the true statements and the symbol (-) in front of the false statements. Answer all questions.

Guideline   8. *Devise items so they require the students to make application of subject matter learned rather than merely recalling or recognizing facts.*

• This item requires recall only:

Write the formula for calculating the volume of a cylinder.

• This item requires student to apply knowledge:

How much liquid would be contained in a cylinder 18" high with a 12" diameter? Give answer in cubic inches.

Guideline   9. *Include a large number of items in the unit examination.*
- This tends to increase the reliability of the examination.

Guideline   10. *Design each item independent of the other items included in the examination.*
- Do not have the correct answer to one item dependent upon the answer to another item. Nor should one question answer another.

The use of the above ten general guidelines will assist teachers to design unit examinations which should help to promote positive learning experiences for students.

STEPS IN UNIT EXAMINATION CONSTRUCTION

The following steps suggest a logical sequence teachers can utilize as they construct examinations for a unit of instruction.

Step 1.   List the educational objectives for the unit or subject matter area.

Step 2.   Construct evaluation items of one or more types for each objective listed in Step 1.

Step 3.   Assemble the items by type for the examination.

Step 4.   Write clear and concise directions for each type of evaluation item.

Step 5.   Review examination for "face validity."
- It is suggested that other teachers be utilized to read through the examination to identify ambiguous items and to help maximize clarity of the items.
- The examination could also be administered to other students to determine those items lacking clarity or to discover which items are likely to be misinterpreted.

Step 6.   Construct a key—a "Desk Copy" of the examination.
- A complete examination with correct answers recorded should be kept by the teacher. This key should be maintained in a place unknown to students.

Step 7.   Conduct a pre-test.
   - Give the test to other teachers or individuals so that they can further assist the teacher to eliminate ambiguous, vague, and/or misleading items. It will also assist to determine those items which can be answered by common knowledge or experience.

Step 8.   Complete an "Item Analysis" to determine the discrimination power of each item.
   - Figure 8.6 is an example of an item analysis for a test item.
   - Those items which tend to discriminate between those students who know and those who do not know the correct response should be kept and utilized on future examinations. This is assuming the items measure what they are supposed to measure.
   - It is evident that the multiple choice question shown in Figure 8.6 has a high discrimination value. This question would discriminate between high and low achievers.

The evaluation portion of instruction is just as important as the planning or delivery component. However, it is probably the most neglected and the poorest planned, conceived, and administered part of the teaching-learning process. The importance of well constructed paper and pencil examinations cannot be overemphasized.

Positive teaching requires that evaluation of students' performance, of their educational growth and development, be planned and administered in such a manner that it will be oriented toward positive goals and serve as a valuable teaching tool.

EVALUATING THE
COGNITIVE DOMAIN OF LEARNING

As noted in an earlier chapter, various degrees of mental activity are associated with the cognitive domain of learning [2]. These range from the level of acquisition of knowledge to the levels of evaluation and judgment making. A brief review of these mental activity levels is appropriate at this point since the degree of mental activity required for successfully achieving stated educational objectives has a direct impact upon the type of evaluation employed.

ITEM 12.   With limited capital, a business owner would tend to invest
his available capital in:

_____ a. long-term improvements.
_____ b. quick turnover operations.
_____ c. new equipment.
_____ d. labor saving devices.

ITEM STATISTICS
Multiple Choice Responses and Percentages
Correct Answer = 2(b)

Upper 27%	1(a)	2(b)	3(c)	4(d)	5*
N = 33	1	33	0	2	0
PCT = 91.67	2.78	91.67	0.00	5.56	0.00
Lower 27%					
N = 8	10	8	6	12	2
PCT = 21.05	26.32	21.05	15.79	31.58	5.26
Total Correct					
N = 59	29	59	8	24	2
PCT = .48	23.77	48.36	6.56	19.67	1.64

Discrimination Index = .71

* Nonresponse

Figure 8.6   Example of an Item Analysis Test Item

The lowest degree of mental activity involves "remembering." At this level, students are required to demonstrate mastery of their learning by defining, by writing, by listing, by identifying, by naming, etc., the knowledge learned.

"Understanding" of subject matter taught is the next degree of mental activity in the cognitive domain. Included in this level of cognition are the ability to comprehend and the ability to apply learning. For students to demonstrate their mastery of subject matter learned, they must be able to translate, to conclude, to differentiate, to explain, to summarize, to apply, to operate, to build, to use, etc., the subject matter they were taught.

The highest degree of mental activity is associated with "thinking." The abilities to analyze, to synthesize, and/or to evaluate subject matter taught are required by students in order for them to demonstrate their mastery of their learning at this level.

Evaluation Depends Upon Objectives

Based upon the above review, it stands to reason that the type and quality of evaluation items used to assess mastery of learning in the cognitive domain as well as in the two other domains depends upon the quality of the educational objectives. If the educational objective calls for students to recall subject matter taught, the students should not be expected to demonstrate their ability to analyze or to make application of what was taught. One of the principles of evaluation states that "evaluation should be in the light of educational objectives." In essence, the same level of mental activity as expressed in the educational objectives should be used to measure students' performance on an examination. Of more consequence, when students prepare to be tested for facts, they learn to memorize; when they prepare to be tested for understanding, they learn to think. One of the greatest sins of test construction is to teach at the "remembering" level and then test at the "synthesis" level.

Evaluation Techniques to Use

Evaluation techniques, as used in this book, connote specific methods useful to assess student performance.

In order to provide the most positive educational experience, a variety of evaluation techniques should be used. The more activities used to evaluate student performance, the more objective will be the assessment of student growth and development. Evaluation should be a positive learning experience for students; therefore, the effective teacher utilizes those evaluation techniques which assess the "knowing behaviors" of students as accurately as possible.

The cognitive domain of learning can be evaluated by various techniques. Some of the more common include evaluation of the following.

- Class notes
- Oral quizzes
- Written quizzes
- Comprehensive paper and pencil examinations
- Work habits
- Daily behavior

- Oral critiques
- Written reports
- Problem solving skills
- Performance in one-on-one interviews
- Performance in individual conferences

EVALUATING THE PSYCHOMOTOR DOMAIN OF LEARNING

The psychomotor domain of learning deals with acquiring manipulative skills requiring dexterity, coordination, and muscular activity. Evaluation of the psychomotor domain will depend again upon the learning intent stated in the educational objective(s). The same principles of evaluation apply to the psychomotor domain as they do to the cognitive domain. Since "doing behaviors" are to be assessed, the teacher should employ those techniques which assess these types of student performance.

Evaluation Techniques to Use

Again, a variety of evaluative techniques should be used to assess students' performance in the psychomotor domain. Those techniques selected and utilized should include an acceptable *standard* of performance by which to assess students' growth and development. Many of the techniques utilized to assess the cognitive domain can also be used in the psychomotor domain, especially the use of class notes, quizzes, paper and pencil examinations, and observations. However, there are several specific evaluation techniques which are valuable to assess students' performance in the psychomotor domain. Some of the more appropriate are

- *Psychomotor tests*
  These are actual manipulative tests which measure motor performance. They assess students' ability to assemble/construct/operate specific designs, simulations, models, etc., within predetermined "time" and "number" criteria or weights. These are also referred to as "talent assessment programs."

- *Performance Evaluation Scales*
  These are designed to assess students' ability to follow proper procedures (or processes) in demonstrating mastery of a skill, job, or operation (task). The standard of performance is usually based upon an operation or skill sheet.
- *Observations*
  Teachers can observe how well students perform a specific task based upon a set of acceptable procedures or weighted values.
- *Project Design and Construction*
  Teachers can assess students' ability to design and/or construct a specified project in the light of acceptable standards or criteria. Both the process employed by the student and the final product completed by the student can be assessed.
- *Competency checklists*
  Teachers can evaluate students' degree of competency regarding specific competencies taught utilizing a checklist similar to the scale in Figure 8.7.

EVALUATING THE
AFFECTIVE DOMAIN OF LEARNING

"Feeling behaviors" such as attitudes, interests, values, and appreciations are associated with the affective domain. As with the cognitive domain, there are various degrees of mental activity associated with this domain of learning [3]. The lower levels involve "Receiving" and "Responding." For students to demonstrate mastery at the "receiving" level, they must show they are aware "that a value, attitude, appreciation, or interest exists." At the "responding" level, students must demonstrate their *reaction* to the attitude, interest, value, or appreciation.

The higher levels consist of "valuing," "organization," and "characterization by a value." The worth or value a student places upon a value, attitude, interest, or appreciation must be demonstrated for mastery at the "valuing" level. Students are required to demonstrate mastery at the "organization" level by arranging, combining, and/or organizing values, interests, and/or appreciations. At the "characterization" level, students must demonstrate mastery by behaving based upon interests, attitudes,

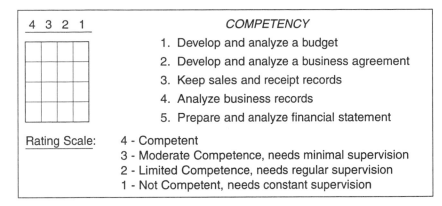

4 3 2 1	COMPETENCY
	1. Develop and analyze a budget
	2. Develop and analyze a business agreement
	3. Keep sales and receipt records
	4. Analyze business records
	5. Prepare and analyze financial statement

Rating Scale: 4 - Competent
3 - Moderate Competence, needs minimal supervision
2 - Limited Competence, needs regular supervision
1 - Not Competent, needs constant supervision

Figure 8.7   Sample of a Competency Checklist

appreciations, or values acquired. These students "practice what they believe!" Their behavior is predictable on a consistent basis.

Evaluation is Based on
Subjective as well as Objective Factors

Due to the nature of the behaviors assessed in this learning domain, it is somewhat more difficult to arrive at an objective assessment of student performance. One of the principles of evaluation states that "evaluation should be both subjective and objective." Therefore, teachers should not be overly concerned if the evaluation techniques used to assess student performance in this domain are not always objective in nature. Although these behaviors are more difficult to evaluate objectively, they are not any less important in the teaching-learning process.

Evaluation Techniques to Use

Several techniques may be employed to assess student performance in the cognitive and psychomotor domains which are useful also in the affective domain. Teacher observations, conferences, interviews, and cri-

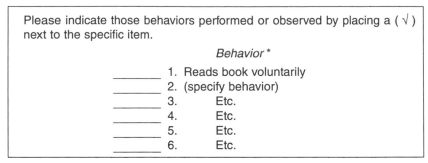

*This could also address interests, values, attitudes, and appreciations.

Figure 8.8   A Sample Checklist

tiques can serve as valuable evaluation techniques. However, the use of quizzes and paper and pencil examinations are valuable only to indicate student knowledge and/or understanding of subject matter associated with "feeling behaviors." With the exception of essay questions, it is extremely difficult to use recognition or recall type questions to assess objectively student performance and/or growth and development in this domain.

At least three specific techniques are recommended for teachers' use in assessing students' growth and development in the affective domain.

- *Checklists*
  Teachers can utilize checklists to assess students' behavior pertaining to their interests, values, attitudes, and appreciations. Checklists employ the "either-or" format, as shown in Figure 8.8. A list of desirable behaviors is used to design checklists. Those behaviors performed or observed are checked by the teacher. Checklists provide only whether or not a behavior was observed or performed. It does not indicate how well the behavior was performed.
- *Rating Scales*
  Rating scales are designed to provide teachers with a quantitative value for observed or performed behaviors associated with the affective domain. A Likert-type scale is usually employed, as shown in Figure 8.9.

Rating scales can also employ the use of Bi-Polar Scales. These instru-

Indicate by circling the appropriate number for each item listed below.

Rating Scale

5 - Excellent
4 - Above Average
3 - Average
2 - Below Average
1 - Poor
0 - Not Observed

Ability (Behavior)*	Rating					
1. Dresses appropriately	5	4	3	2	1	0
2. (Specify Activity)	5	4	3	2	1	0
3. Etc.	5	4	3	2	1	0
4. Etc.	5	4	3	2	1	0
5. Etc.	5	4	3	2	1	0
6. Etc.	5	4	3	2	1	0

*This could also address interests, values, attitudes and appreciations.

Figure 8.9   A Sample Rating Scale

ments are used to determine "feeling about certain concepts." Judgments are made relative to a series of descriptive scales. An example of a Bi-Polar Scale is shown in Figure 8.10.

- *Self-Assessment Instruments*
  Self-assessment instruments are adaptations of rating scales. They are designed to solicit students' own assessment of their ability to perform. See Figure 8.11.

GRADING POLICY

Most educational agencies (schools and universities) have an adopted grading policy in operation. It is essential that teachers understand how this policy operates. They, likewise, need to adhere to this policy as they assign grades to individual students.

Directions:
       Please indicate your feelings about each set of adjectives by placing a mark (x) to indicate how you feel about the concept.

Good	- - - - - - - - - - - - - - - -	Bad
Clean	- - - - - - - - - - - - - - - -	Dirty
Worthless	- - - - - - - - - - - - - - - -	Valuable

Figure 8.10   A Bi-Polar Scale

Assigning a grade to an individual student is an important part of the evaluation process. Grades communicate to students how well they have achieved within a certain time period. Parents and others have become accustomed to relying upon the grade(s) a student receives as an indication of that student's growth and development. In the final analysis, it is imperative that teachers are able to justify objectively why a certain grade was assigned to a certain student. Teachers must keep accurate and complete records of all information influencing evaluations on each student.

Grades are usually based upon one of three methods: percentage grades, letter grades, and number grades. Percentage grades are usually based upon a percentage of 100, while letter grades are A, B, C, D, and E or F. Number grades are 4, 3, 2, 1, 0.

In order to arrive at a relative composite grade for all academic work completed, many educational agencies utilize the G.P.A., or grade point average. The value is calculated by summing the numerical value of all grades and dividing by the number of individual grades or units of instruction completed. If the number grading method is used, this is a simple calculation. However, if letter grading systems are employed, these values must be converted to a numerical grade before the G.P.A. can be determined.

Effective teachers adhere to the principles and approved practices of evaluation as discussed in this chapter. Because of this their individual assessment of an individual student's performance is accurate, fair, and meaningful. They follow the concept "I do not give grades; I only report how individual students perform within established and maintained standards."

Indicate by circling the appropriate number by each item below the degree
to which you feel you can perform each ability.

Rating Scale:

4 - Very Well
3 - Adequate
2 - Some
1 - Very little
0 - Cannot perform

Ability:	Rating
1. Attentiveness	4 3 2 1 0
2. (Specify Ability)	4 3 2 1 0
3. Etc.	4 3 2 1 0
4. Etc.	4 3 2 1 0
5. Etc.	4 3 2 1 0

Figure 8.11   A Self-Assessment Instrument

SUMMARY

Evaluation of learning is a vital component of the teaching-learning process. It should result in both a fair and realistic assessment of student performance. Evaluation should be considered as a teaching tool.

Throughout this chapter, principles of evaluation have been discussed in an attempt to provide teachers with a means to make evaluation of learning a positive, useful, and meaningful teaching and learning component.

The educational function and quality of effective examinations were presented along with a thorough explanation of the various types of evaluation items which should be included in a comprehensive examination.

The evaluation of the three domains of learning with appropriate techniques was presented.

Students should be taught broadly defined values. As such, these values (including attitudes, interests, and appreciations) should be reflected in both the educational objectives sought as a result of the teaching-learning process and in the evaluation process. In the final analysis, the teaching and evaluation of "feeling" behaviors may be the most important aspects of the educational process. The author knows of few people who failed for lack of knowledge, but knows of many who failed because they possessed and/or demonstrated attitudes, values, etc., of a questionable or unacceptable nature.

Positive teaching requires that evaluation of students' performance, which is reflective of their intellectual growth and development, be planned and administered in such a manner that it will be positive-oriented, accurate, reliable, and valuable.

ENDNOTES

1. Adapted from a monograph prepared by John F. Thompson, Department of Agricultural and Extension Education, University of Wisconsin, Madison.
2. Bloom, Benjamin S., ed. *Taxonomy of Educational Objectives; The Classification of Educational Goals, Handbook I: Cognitive Domain.* New York: David McKay, 1956.
3. Krathwahl, David R. and others. *Taxonomy of Educational Objectives: the Classification of Educational Goals, Handbook II: Affective Domain.* New York: David McKay, 1964.

CHAPTER 9

Applying Learning to Assure a Positive Educational Experience

Application of learning, as used in this book, refers to any educational activity, project, or procedure which promotes the use of the subject matter taught. Application helps "fix" the learned competencies so students can better utilize them when they leave the educational environment.

Many educators believe that they teach for the future! If this is true, the implications for students who are able to apply their learned competencies in future encounters are significant. For a truly positive learning experience, teachers must ensure that their students possess the ability to make application of the newly acquired knowledges, skills, attitudes, appreciations, etc. Effective teachers strive continuously and consistently to assure that new competencies acquired by their students are carried to the *application* stage. It has been said that learning is not permanent until it can be used. Thus, application of learning should be the goal of every teacher.

Knowledge and understanding are of primary importance for students, but the ability to utilize and apply these in a productive and useful way is the epitome of a positive educational experience. Several psychological laws of learning suggest the need for teachers to create opportunities for application of what students are learning. For example, the law of exercise ("The more often an act is repeated, the more quickly a habit is established") and the law of disuse ("A skill not practiced or a knowledge not used will be largely lost or forgotten") are two examples that underscore the need for the application of learning. In essence, as stated earlier, it is the application of what students have been taught that "fixes" learning. Application augments learning effectiveness. Application of learning leads to permanence.

WHY UTILIZE APPLICATION AS A PART OF THE TEACHING-LEARNING PROCESS?

Why is it important that teachers strive to have students make application of those competencies taught them? Some of the more important educational functions served by the application stage of the teaching-learning process are identified below.

- Application of learning promotes the use of what has been taught. Simply mastering a few skills or facts does not guarantee that students can put understanding to use. Application helps insure the future use of learning. Of more consequence, the application and use of knowledge assists students to learn to make sound decisions and to solve real problems.
- It makes instruction more relevant by demonstrating to students the utility and value of the subject matter learned. Understanding is not synonymous with performance.
- It provides lifelike educational experiences improving both the quantity and quality of learning.
- It allows for the utilization of learning in various situations. It focuses upon the concept of "transfer of learning."
- It promotes the use of decision making and problem solving.
- It promotes the concept of "hands-on" learning. There is a vast difference between "know how" and "knowing how to do." Learning "about" is not as effective as learning "how to do" something!
- It reinforces the development of those competencies being taught. Repetition of competencies taught is provided when learning is applied.
- It helps to integrate the "theory of learning" with the "practice of learning."
- It promotes within students the development of quality work habits along with subject matter competence.

- It provides the teacher with an opportunity to evaluate how well students understand what is or has been taught.

It must be noted that some subject matter areas are easier to make application of than those of other disciplines. Not all subjects lend themselves to immediate and practical application. Music teachers, for example, through the use of instruments and recordings, can integrate theory and application with relative ease. On the other hand, teachers of ancient history might find it more difficult to identify activities and projects whereby application of learning can be made. However, the effective teacher is creative and resourceful in locating ways to apply what has been taught.

WHERE CAN APPLICATION OF LEARNING BE MADE?

Many teachers believe that application of subject matter taught can only be made in special laboratories. While this may hold true for some disciplines, wholesale application of learning can occur in numerous educational environments. It stands to reason that the type of learning being applied will affect where it can be best made.

Like learning, application of learning can occur in various educational environments.

- In the classroom students are provided with a confined learning environment under the supervision of the teacher with provisions for student seating and for student reading and writing accommodations. The teacher is usually provided with realia such as chalkboard, overhead projector, bulletin board, reference materials, computers, etc.

- In the laboratory students find a specially designed and equipped learning environment wherein they can demonstrate or practice the use of the subject matter taught under the supervision of the teacher.

- In the field field trips provide an open learning environment, usually away from the school facility, where students can observe firsthand the real life relationships, processes, situations, and/or surroundings asso-

ciated with the subject matter area being taught. Teacher supervision
is essential.

- In the community are found learning environments where students
  can observe and participate in actual, real life learning experiences
  which reinforce subject matter taught. Students can use the knowledge, do the skill, or apply the attitude. Supervision is provided by the
  teacher and by persons associated with the community resource.

- At home a true-to-life learning environment exists where students
  participate in the actual activities associated with life and living. Supervision is usually provided by parents or guardians.

Regardless of where application of learning occurs, it should be
planned and conducted in an organized and systematic manner.

Application of the cognitive domain of learning (knowledge) could
occur most anywhere. Application of the psychomotor domain of learning (skill development) could also occur in several learning environments. However, when specific physical facilities such as wet labs, spe-
cialized performance settings, and technical equipment are required to
make application of the skills learned, application is usually facilitated in
laboratories, in the field, or in the community.

The affective domain of learning, like the cognitive domain, can occur
in most of the learning environments identified earlier.

MAKING APPLICATION OF LEARNING

Any educational activity which promotes the use of what has been
learned can be considered to be "application." Obviously, the application
stage of the teaching-learning process is not the easiest to achieve. Most
teaching stops with the acquisition of information. Not all teachers are
concerned with the application of learning because, in all probability,
they were not involved in the application of their own learnings. However, there should be, in most cases, some degree of application of learning if positive educational experiences are to be afforded students. It
must be pointed out that "practice" is not synonymous with application
of learning. As pointed out in Chapter 16, practice of learning is to assist

students to, among other things, form a habit. Application of learning implies the use of that habit in productive pursuits.

To help teachers identify how they can proceed to make application of learning a vital part of the teaching-learning process, two types of educational activities are suggested. These are individual and group activities.

Individual Activities

Educational activities which promote application of learning for individual students include:

— Independent Study: Study of a topic by a student outside of class

— Homework: Specific assignment made by a teacher for students to complete at home and usually turned in the following class period

— Recitals: Presentations, usually in public, made by a student to demonstrate competencies learned

— Term Papers: Planning, organization, and preparation of a written paper of some length on a specific topic

— Assigned Study: Study of material assigned by a teacher

— Supervised Study: Study under the supervision of a teacher

— Individual Projects: Planning and completion of a specific piece of work

— Note taking/Notebooks: Organization and recording of significant information from classroom presentations or from assigned reading material

— Role Playing: Prepared presentation by a student which represents a specific character (individual) associated with what has been taught

— Individual Experience Programs: Planned program designed to provide participatory learning experience to reinforce competencies taught

— Individual Exhibits: Planning, assembling, and displaying of an idea or concept

— Written Reports: Organized and written presentation on a specific topic or subject

— Oral Reports: Organized and spoken presentation on a specific topic or subject

— Workbooks/Worksheets: Completion of assignments in a pre-prepared exercise book

— Experiments: Planning, conducting, and evaluation of actual experiments associated with the subject matter taught

Group Activities

Many educational activities involving a number of students in a specific learning environment can assist teachers in making application of learning.

— Supervised Study: Group study of a topic or subject under the supervision of a teacher

— Group Project: Cooperative planning and completion of a specific piece of work

— Committee Work: Group responsibility for study of an item and for arriving at a decision and/or recommendation

— Contests: Organized activity designed to promote competition between students who demonstrate acquired competencies

— Demonstrations: Planned and organized presentations designed to display specific competencies learned

— Student Organizations: Formal and functional structure formed to achieve specific application of learning for a group of individuals

— Education Fair: Competitive exhibit of students' work reflecting what was learned

It should be noted that several of the individual activities such as role playing, exhibits, oral and written reports, term papers, and experiments are also applicable for group use.

APPROVED PRACTICES
ON APPLYING LEARNING

Certain practices have proven effective for teachers to use as they make application of learning.

Application of learning should

- not be used as busy work for students
- not become a time filler for teachers
- be planned and conducted for every lesson presented, if possible
- involve worthwhile and relevant educational activities
- stress the actual use of those competencies taught
- include those educational activities which have utility and value
- include provisions for evaluation and follow up

SUMMARY

Application of learning is a vital component of the teaching-learning process. Several educational functions are served by the application stage of the lesson.

Suggestions on where and how application can be made are presented in this chapter. Effective teachers stress the application of what was taught because they realize that application promotes learning effectiveness, and provides a more positive educational experience for their students.

In the final analysis, knowledge does not become *power* until it is applied.

SECTION IV

COMPONENTS OF A
POSITIVE DELIVERY SYSTEM

Planning, delivering, evaluating, and applying learning have been discussed in the preceding section of this book. Section IV is devoted to a detailed discussion of the *Critical Incidents of Teaching*. These are referred to as components of a positive delivery system. These components are, in reality, methods for teaching. Each component presented in the eleven chapters contained in this section addresses three questions:

- What is it? What is its purpose?
- Why is it important?
- How to use it?

The "How to Use" portion of each chapter cites approved teaching practices and, when appropriate, outlines common errors to avoid.

Section IV examines the following *Critical Incidents of Teaching*:

- *Analyzing Subject Matter*
- *Teaching for Problem Solving*
- *Formulating Educational Objectives*
- *Building a Case for Learning*
- *Involving Students Through Questioning*
- *Using Supervised Study Effectively*
- *Providing Relevant Practice*
- *Conducting Demonstrations*

- *Utilizing Field Oriented Learning*
- *Utilizing Realia to Visualize Learning*
- *Concluding a Lesson*

The eleven components of a positive delivery system described in this section are all designed to assist teachers to utilize the O.P.E. concept. The content in most chapters is applicable to all levels of education and suited to most subject matter areas.

Furthermore, the eleven *Critical Incidents of Teaching* contained in this section are presented in a logical sequence similar to the way in which they would be used by a teacher to deliver a complete lesson in the three domains of learning.

CHAPTER 10

Analyzing Subject Matter

Determining what students should be taught becomes one of the challenging responsibilities of the teacher. Too often, teachers let the content of the textbook chosen for the course determine what is covered in the class. However, few textbooks are written to provide all the learning activities essential for students to experience in a particular course. Thus, the teacher must plan those teaching-learning activities which will result in the desired behavior changes sought. Oftentimes it is a difficult task to distinguish between the "must know" and "nice to know" knowledges, skills, and/or attitudes students should learn. Students are often taught much trivial information in the form of facts and figures which are soon forgotten because teachers have failed to think through what is really important for students to learn in a specific discipline at the level of education being taught. Effective teachers complete an analysis of what subject matter *must* be taught to help them plan and provide a positive delivery system.

Planning the most appropriate subject matter which should be taught students in any specific area, unit, or course of instruction requires the teacher to answer these three questions:

- What to teach?
- When to teach it?
- How long to spend on it?

In order to answer these questions, the teacher must determine the educational purpose of the course or unit of instruction. Is it to teach students factual information; to teach students skills, techniques, practices, and/or procedures; to teach students concepts or principles; or to teach students values and appreciations? Most teachers would answer, "*It depends upon what is to be taught!*" This would be followed by "It depends on *why* the subject matter is to be taught!" or by "It depends on what educational objectives are sought!"

Teaching to objectives helps create an atmosphere of positive teaching. However, before educational objectives can be formulated, the teacher must have made an *analysis of the subject matter to be taught.* This analysis would also include when it is to be taught (sequence of instruction) and how long it will be taught (magnitude and depth of the subject matter to be covered). It must be remembered that the intent of any educational endeavor is to achieve the "desired learnings." The purpose of the *analysis of subject matter* is to identify the learning desired and the essential elements of the subject matter to be taught.

WHY IS A SUBJECT MATTER ANALYSIS IMPORTANT?

It is not possible for a teacher to teach students everything about a particular subject in one course or unit of instruction. Therefore, a decision must be made to ascertain what specific subject matter will be presented in the unit or course. Until an analysis of subject matter to be taught has been made, a teacher is more or less uncertain regarding what should be taught!

There are several reasons why a subject matter analysis should be conducted. It assists the teacher

- to determine the educational objectives
- to identify the desired educational outcomes
- to satisfy the contemporary needs of students
- to make the subject matter taught more relevant to the student
- to eliminate obsolete information, and unnecessary skills, techniques, practices, and procedures
- to increase retention of subject matter taught by minimizing trivial information and rote memorization
- to reduce abstractness of subject matter covered

- to concentrate subject matter content on "must know" knowledges, skills and attitudes, values, etc.
- to reduce the amount of content overlap occurring between courses or units of instruction in a particular discipline
- to promote the acquisition of essential competencies
- to assure that optimum "time on task" is placed upon the acquisition of essential subject matter
- to promote articulation between courses or units of instruction in a specific discipline

There is no simple formula or absolute set of rules to be followed in conducting a subject matter analysis. In some educational settings, there are lists of state approved or local board approved competencies or educational outcomes to help guide this process.

Determining what students should be taught is an important task of the teacher. However, the task becomes more simple as teachers study and learn more about the school, the community, the students, and themselves.

CONDUCTING AN ANALYSIS
OF SUBJECT MATTER

An analysis of subject matter to be taught in a particular course involves the following four steps.

Step I.	Assemble Primary Information and Facts Regarding the Subject to be Taught.

The first step in completing an analysis of subject matter is to collect as much data as possible about the school, the students, the community, and the teacher. All available local resources, including personal contacts with key people, should be utilized to determine what is important. In addition, the teacher will want to review textbooks, bulletins, and other pertinent literature to gather important content information pertaining to the subject matter area in question. After all data have been collected, the teacher should analyze the data and draw some basic conclusions. The conclusions drawn should assist the teacher to make decisions on what essential elements of the subject matter should be considered.

Step II.	Differentiate Between "Must Know" and "Nice to Know" Subject Matter Content

As mentioned earlier, it is not possible to expose students in one course to all the facts, information, concepts, or principles associated with a specific subject matter area or discipline. Therefore, the teacher must decide between the essential (must know) subject matter content and the non essential (nice to know) content. Thus, Step II involves the listing of *all* subject matter content which could be taught students in a specific course or unit of instruction.

A simple topic with which most people should be familiar illustrates how a teacher might complete Step II. In this example a teacher desires to identify the subject matter content which should be taught if the educational intent were "to build a dog house." The following list of subject matter could be taught.

Subject Matter Categories

- Advantages and disadvantages of owning a dog
- Breeds of dogs
- Size of dogs
- Selecting dogs
- Feeding dogs
- Grooming dogs
- Plans for dog houses
- Caring for dogs
- Materials to use in building a dog house
- Controlling external parasites
- Ordering materials
- Training dogs
- Constructing a dog house
- Types of paint
- Sawing and fastening wood
- Finishing dog houses
- Etc.
- Etc.

After a list of subject matter categories has been completed, the teacher then divides the categories into "must know" and "nice to know" columns. This task is largely judgmental. At this point, effective teachers involve other parties such as advisory committees, etc., to assist them make the final decision about "what to teach?"

Must Know	Nice to Know
• Size of dog (will determine size of house to build)	• Owning a dog
• Plans for dog houses	• Breeds of dogs
• Material to use (metal, wood, etc.)	• Selecting dogs
• Ordering materials	• Feeding dogs
• Constructing dog houses	• Grooming dogs
• Finishing dog houses (painting, etc.)	• Caring for dogs
	• Controlling external parasites
	• Training dogs
	• Types of paint
	• Sawing and fastening wood

The categories listed in the "nice to know" column would be interesting to study, but are *not* essential competencies needed to build a dog house.

The items listed in the "must know" column would be used by the teacher to plan for instruction on building a dog house. It is assumed that "types of paint" would have been taught as an information lesson and "sawing and fastening wood" would have been taught as an operational lesson. Thus, the teacher can now concentrate upon "how to build a dog house."

Step III.	Using "Must Know" Subject Matter, Identify the Educational Objectives to be Achieved.

Once the "must know" subject matter content has been determined, the next step in the analysis process would be to formulate those measurable and observable educational objectives to be achieved. Refer to Chapter 12 on "Formulating Educational Objectives" for more detail.

Using the "must know" subject matter content on "building a dog house," the teacher could then formulate a list of desired educational objectives to be addressed. For example, some of the desired educational objectives would be as follows:

Students will be able to

- identify the size of the dog house to build
- draw plans for the dog house based upon size of dog
- select building materials to be used to build a dog house
- calculate the amount of material needed to build a dog house
- order the building materials needed to build a dog house
- construct the dog house
- finish (paint) the dog house

It should be noted that there is at least one educational objective for each "must know" item identified. They have been arranged in a logical sequence.

Step IV.   Determine the "Must Know" Subject Matter Content Necessary to Achieve the Educational Objectives.

With the educational objectives formulated, the teacher must then decide what subject matter content must be covered (competencies taught) if the students are to achieve the objectives sought. The content to be addressed can be stated in the form of

- Questions for Study/Discussion
- Skills to be learned
- Problems to be solved
- Attitudes, values, etc., to be achieved

The following points warrant serious critical consideration as Step IV is completed.

1. Make certain competencies (knowledges/skills/values) sought are at the students' level of ability.

2. Be sure questions of basic information and fact can be answered from reference or realia available.

3. Develop separate "questions and/or problems" for each educational objective.

4. Arrange "questions/problems" from most simple to more complex.

5. After all questions/problems have been identified, arrange in sequence. *NOTE*: This may necessitate reordering (sequencing) the educational objectives identified in Step III.

Referring to the objectives for "to build a dog house," the student should be able to demonstrate mastery of the following "must know" subject matter and skill content:

1. Determine the necessary dimensions of a dog house to accommodate a ____ pound dog.
   (size)

2. Using dimensions found in question #1, draw to scale the floor, front, back, and side views of the dog house.

3. Determine the building materials to be used to build the dog house, including fasteners, finish, and roofing materials?

4. Calculate the actual amount of building materials needed to build the dog house based upon information found in question 3 above.

5. Prepare an order form (bill of material) for actual building materials needed to build the dog house and place the order.

6. Construct the dog house as outlined on the demonstrated operation sheet.

7. Finish the dog house as outlined on the operation sheet.

Subject matter items 1, 2, 3, 4, and 5 could be handled in the classroom. It is assumed students had been taught how to determine the size of the various breeds of dogs; how to make an isometric and orthographic drawing; how to choose the correct type of building materials including fasteners and finishing materials; how to prepare a bill of material and order form; how to square, measure, saw, and fasten building materials; and how to finish a project such as a dog house. This information would need to have been taught students before the actual project "to build a dog house" was undertaken.

Subject matter items 6 and 7 could be handled as operational lessons under the supervision of the teacher.

Once the "must know" subject matter has been determined, the teacher can then decide when the subject matter material should be taught based upon a logical sequence of events. Likewise, the necessary

Course or Unit of Instruction _____

Step I.   Assemble Primary Information and Facts Regarding the Subject to be
          Taught.

Step II. Differentiate Between "Must Know" and "Nice to Know" Subject
          Matter Content

          MUST KNOW   NICE TO KNOW
          _____

Step III. Using "Must Know" Subject Matter, Identify the Educational
          Objectives to be Achieved.

          Educational Objectives

          1.

          2.

          3.

          4.

Step IV. Determine the "Must Know" Subject Matter Content Necessary to
          Achieve the Educational Objective(s)

          Questions for Study or Skills to be Learned or Problems to be Solved.

          1.

          2.

          3.

          4.

Figure 10.1   Analysis of Subject Matter

amount of factual instructional and supervised practice time, including evaluation activities, required to effectively teach the material can be determined.

To assist teachers to conduct a subject matter analysis, the form shown in Figure 10.1 might be beneficial.

SUMMARY

It is obvious that some type of systematic process must be employed if teachers are to be better able to identify what subject matter should be taught students in a given unit of instruction or course of study. Effective teachers utilize the steps outlined in this chapter to help them answer the questions of

- What to teach?
- When to teach it?
- How long to spend on it?

It should be pointed out that there will be some frustration and anxiety on the part of the teacher the first few times the process outlined is used. However, with experience, the process becomes easier and more objective over time.

Although there is a great deal of judgment inherent in the process outlined, it will still provide a more systematic means to answer the above three questions so more positive teaching will occur.

CHAPTER 11

Teaching for Problem Solving

The highest level of mental ability associated with the cognitive domain of learning is *thinking*. One of the principles of learning, stressed in an earlier chapter, notes that students learn more and better when thinking is stimulated. Teaching students how to think is one of the prime purposes of education. "There is only one reason why a human being ever thinks—because he wants to solve a problem" [1].

If students are to learn how to think and make intelligent decisions, they must be taught the skill of thinking. As pointed out in Chapter 6, "Planning a Positive Educational Experience," managerial teaching plans are useful to develop high order thinking and decision-making ability on the part of students.

What is meant by teaching for problem solving? It is nothing more than *building teaching upon real life problems* and then actively involving students in seeking intelligent answers to these problems. Effective teachers use the process of "solving the problem" to teach students how to think, how to reason, and how to make decisions.

WHY IS TEACHING FOR PROBLEM SOLVING IMPORTANT?

Teaching for problem solving promotes positive learning by:

- providing participating experience in the problem-solving process
- promoting the concept of cooperative learning whereby students col-

lectively pool and utilize their resources and faculties to arrive at intelligent decisions
- promoting thinking on the part of students
- preparing students to cope with and to solve real life problems they will be confronted with when they leave the educational setting
- assisting students to learn to analyze essential data (information and facts) in order to arrive at a decision
- exposing students to the concept of risk and uncertainty in a supportive environment
- increasing learning effectiveness by reinforcing the use of the decision-making process

COMPARISON OF LEARNING AND DECISION MAKING

It has been said that an individual does not really learn until there is frustration! Or, stated in another way, learning does not take place until there is frustration! When people experience frustration, it is usually because of problems which need to be solved. If this is the case, could there be a parallel between problem solving and learning?

The learning process as expressed by John Dewey's Steps in Reflective Thinking is illustrated as follows [2]:

Step 1.   Experiencing a difficult situation.

Step 2.   Describing the problem to resolve and determining question(s) to be answered.

Step 3.   Securing information to answer the questions.

Step 4.   Deciding upon possible solutions.

Step 5.   Applying the plausible solutions.

Step 6.   Evaluating the results.

The steps in the decision-making process as presented in Chapter 6 are presented below.

Step 1.   Experience a provoking situation which needs to be resolved.

Step 2.   Identify the problem by stating the decision which needs to be made.

Step 3.   Determine the factors (elements of the problem) which need to be considered before a decision can be made.

Step 4.   Arrive at a decision by evaluating all factors in Step 3.

Step 5.   Take action by implementing the decision.

Step 6.   Accept the results by reaping the benefits of making the correct decision or suffering the losses of an incorrect decision.

A review of Dewey's Steps in Reflective Thinking and the steps in the decision-making process shows a definite correlation. A close relationship does exist between thinking, decision making, and learning. This comparison is probably the most significant reason *why* the effective teacher utilizes teaching for problem solving to deliver positive learning experiences for students.

PROPER TIMING ESSENTIAL

To ensure that the maximum benefit is derived from teaching for problem solving, the teacher must not confuse students by intermingling factual information with decision making. If a great deal of factual information is required to solve a problem, it should be taught first. For example, if students have not been taught the factual information needed for the steps involved in the decision-making process before they are involved in problem-solving teaching, they could become quite confused. They would be required in this situation to learn this factual information at the same time they were learning how to apply the process. Effective teachers remember to teach facts first and problem solving second.

AN ILLUSTRATION OF
PROBLEM-SOLVING TEACHING

Figure 11.1 illustrates how teaching for problem solving might work in a typical teaching situation.

As illustrated, teaching for problem solving is a cyclic process; when one difficulty is overcome, when one problem is solved, another difficulty arises, etc., etc.

Circle 1 indicates that a difficulty exists which prevents the attainment of a goal. As discussed in Chapter 6, this difficulty could be ex-

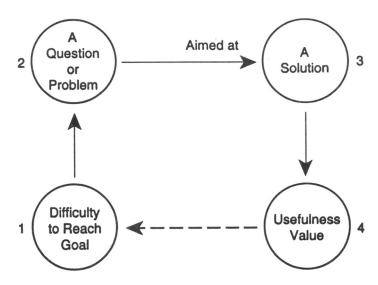

Figure 11.1   Teaching for Problem Solving

pressed as a "teaching situation." A teaching situation is described as "an experience, a condition, an example, an incident, a problem which focuses upon or illustrates or demonstrates the problem in question." The most effective teaching situation is one based upon student and/or community needs.

Once the difficulty has been experienced, the next step in problem solving involves the identification of questions which must be answered or a statement of the problem which must be solved. Circle 2 illustrates this phase of problem-solving teaching. At this stage, there are significant implications to the teacher for the type of educational objectives sought.

The questions or problems identified in Circle 2 should serve a useful purpose in solving the problem (or answering the questions for study).

Circle 3 represents the solution to the problem. This stage of the problem-solving process would parallel the "drawing of conclusions" in the teaching-learning process. Unfortunately, most teaching stops at this point.

Circle 4 indicates usefulness, value, utility. This is the point of actual decision making. Evaluating the results is reflected by this circle. In teaching and learning this circle represents the "application of learning."

The broken line from Circle 4 back to Circle 1 illustrates the cyclic nature of problem-solving teaching.

In essence, for problem-solving teaching to occur, there must be a *difficulty* which leads to a *problem* to be solved which necessitates the formulation of *questions* to be answered which requires the assembly of factual information if a conclusion (solution to difficulty) is to be reached. When the decision has been made, the benefits (or losses) are realized. The process then repeats itself.

CONDUCTING TEACHING FOR PROBLEM SOLVING

As pointed out in Chapter 6, managerial lessons are utilized by teachers to help students learn how to make intelligent decisions and also to provide students training in decision making. The author wishes to caution the readers that teaching for problem solving can be utilized whenever there is a difficulty which prevents students from reaching their goal(s). Finding the answers to study questions or learning how to perform a task involve just as much problem solving as does the use of a managerial teaching plan. In essence, the use of a managerial teaching plan is not the *only* way that teaching for problem solving can be conducted. However, managerial lessons provide a logical sequence for students to follow as they learn how to make decisions.

To illustrate how a teacher could conduct this type of teaching, we will use a simple hypothetical situation: whether or not to purchase a new automobile. Figure 11.2 outlines the teaching plan.

Using the six steps in the decision-making process, the teacher could conduct problem-solving teaching in the following manner.

Step 1.   Experience a provoking situation.

- Using the situation outlined on the teaching plan, the teacher can explain why the lesson is important. The use of leading questions will further draw out student knowledge of the topic. And finally, a review of the educational objectives should provide ample insight so a statement of the difficulty can be made. It may be necessary to build the teaching situation around one individual student's experience or situation. Also, realia (visual aids) in the form of pictures of the various makes and models of cars could further build a case for learning.

AREA: Free Enterprise

UNIT: Car Ownership

LESSON: #20 Costs of Car Ownership

COMPETENCY(S) TO BE TAUGHT:

1. Capital resources are required to own a car.
2. Both variable and fixed costs must be considered when deciding to own a car.

SITUATION:

1. Students are developing plans to determine the economic feasibility of ownership of various makes and models of cars.
2. Students will need to make a decision on whether to own or lease their own cars.
3. Students have limited capital resources.
4. Several students will be purchasing cars in the future.
5. Interest should be high.
6. The lesson will require two class periods to complete.

OBJECTIVES:

1. Given the cost, useful life, interest, taxes and insurance rate, to calculate the annual fixed costs of owning a new car.
2. Given the fuel, lubrication and repair costs, to calculate the cost per mile to operate a new car.

INTRODUCTION:

1. Review the situation(s) cited above.
2. Ask leading questions
   - How much does a new car cost?
   - What does insurance cost?
   - How long will it last?
   - What are the property taxes?
   - What is the interest cost?
   - What is the cost of maintenance?
   - What is fuel consumption?
3. What other factors do we need to consider if a sound decision is to be made?

PROBLEM:

1. Formulate a statement of the problem: "To determine whether to purchase a new car which costs $9000 with a useful life of 10 years."

FACTORS TO BE CONSIDERED:

1. *Annual fixed costs*
   a. Depreciation   1a. What would be annual depreciation?
   b. Interest   1b. How much would the interest be?

Figure 11.2   A Lesson in Problem Solving

c. Taxes	1c. How much would license and property taxes amount to?
d. Insurance	1d. What would be the insurance costs?
2. *Estimated miles driven per year.*	2. How many miles will the car be driven each year?
3. *Variable or Operating Costs*	
a. Fuel per mile	3a. What would be the fuel cost per mile driven?
b. Oil & lubrication per mile	3b. What would be the oil and lubrication costs per mile?
c. Repairs per mile	3c. How much would repairs cost per mile driven?
4. *Other Alternatives*	
a. Leasing	4a. What would it cost to lease a car?
b. Purchasing a used car	4b. Could a used car be purchased?
5. *Other Factors to be Considered*	
a. Capital Available	5a. Is capital to purchase a new car available?
b. Repayment Plan	5b. How would car be paid for?

SUPERVISED STUDY:
1. Distribute reference materials.
2. Assign each student one factor to research.
3. Allow remainder of class period for study.

DISCUSSION:
1. Through questioning, have students present their findings on factors assigned.
2. Write findings on chalkboard.
3. When all factors have been evaluated, have class draw conclusions on whether a new car should be purchased.
4. Make a decision.

APPLICATION AND TESTING:
1. Assign students similar problems to complete as individual study.
2. Include ownership problem on unit examination.

REALIA:
1. Current local newspaper(s).
2. Amortization tables from local bank.
3. Current insurance rates.
4. Current tax rates from county assessor's office.
5. Information on fuel consumption, lubrication, and repair costs.
6. Hand calculators.

Figure 11.2 A Lesson in Problem Solving (continued)

The identification portion of the lesson should be placed on the chalk-board or overhead projector.

> **Step 2.**   *Identify the problem by stating the decision to be made.*

- Through the use of oral questions, formulate in cooperation with the students a statement of the problem as outlined on the teaching plan.
- Place the problem statement on the chalkboard or overhead projector.

> **Step 3.**   *Determine the factors which need to be considered before a decision can be made.*

- Ask leading questions to draw out all factors to be considered. Factors are elements of the problem which must be thoroughly examined before a sound decision can be made.
- It may be necessary for the teacher to suggest those essential factors which cannot be drawn from the students.
- List all factors to be considered, in sequence, on chalkboard or overhead.
- After all factors have been identified, the teacher should develop a question(s) for each factor. These questions should be numbered by factor (see Figure 11.2).

> **Step 4.**   *Arrive at a decision by evaluating all factors in Step 3.*

- The procedure of writing out questions for each factor will assist students in researching the factors more effectively.
- Distribute necessary realia. For certain managerial lessons, the teacher may want to take a field trip or bring in a resource person to help evaluate the factors.
- Assign each student one or more factors to research.
- Using oral questions, the teacher directs a discussion to establish factual information and to evaluate each factor.
- In certain situations, it may be desirable for the teacher to develop one or more worksheets for students to use as they evaluate each factor. See Figure 11.3.

Problem or Decision _____	

1. Factor: _____	
1 a. (Question)	1 a. (Answer)
1 b. (Question)	1 b. (Answer)
1 c. (Question)	1 c. (Answer)
2. Factor: _____	
2 a. (Question)	2 a. (Answer)
2 b. (Question)	2 b. (Answer)
3. Factor: _____	
Etc.	Etc.
Etc.	Etc.

Figure 11.3   Sample Worksheet

- Based upon a comprehensive discussion and evaluation of all factors, the students make a decision in the light of the problem statement. (NOTE: This should be cooperative education at its best.) Lessons built upon principles of cooperative education promote several positive learning experiences for students. Some of the more salient are that (1) cooperative education stresses a team approach to solving problems; (2) it encourages the use of students' own experiences in lieu of teachers' experiences in problem solving (students teach each other); (3) it provides more realistic learning activities; and (4) it minimizes students' fears of being called upon for an answer which they may not know. In essence, it reduces the development of an inferiority complex in students.
- The completion of Step 4 would be comparable to the "Conclusion" portion of an informational lesson.

Step 5.   Take action by implementing the decision.

- As pointed out in an earlier chapter, in the classroom the decision-making process is usually carried to the fifth step.

- However, it could be possible for the class to take action by implementing the decision made in Step 4.

Step 6.   Accept the results.

- Whether this step is realized depends upon what happened in Step 5.

After completing the lesson, the teacher would need to follow up with the application and evaluation stages of the teaching plan.

It is relatively easy to teach for problem solving if a complete teaching plan has been developed and the steps in the decision-making process are followed. The task becomes easier as more managerial teaching plans are utilized. By teaching problem solving, the teacher learns how to use problem-solving teaching!

However, it must be pointed out that certain conditions must exist in the teaching-learning environment if problem-solving teaching is to be most effective. Some of these conditions are cited below.

- Teachers must allow students ample input in the delivery of the lesson.
- Teachers must allow greater student freedom in the evolution of the lesson.
- Teachers must make optimum use of oral and written questions to promote maximum student participation.
- Teachers must place primary emphasis upon the process (learning) and less upon the product (results of problem solving).
- Students must be actively involved throughout the lesson.

SUMMARY

Teaching for problem solving serves numerous educational functions which promote positive teaching and learning effectiveness. This method of teaching utilizes *real life* problems to teach students how to think and make decisions. It stresses practical cooperative education since group decision making is advocated. As such, it also helps eliminate students' fear of not knowing the answer to a question or problem. In groups, students usually are less afraid of being embarrassed if they do not know the correct or complete answer.

Why problem-solving teaching should be used and *how* it can be conducted were explained in this chapter. Learning and problem solving are complementary processes. The more the use of problem-solving teaching, the more effective and longer lasting will be the learning. Effective teachers have realized this relationship for a long time.

ENDNOTES

1. Marsell, James L. *Successful Teaching*. McGraw-Hill Book Company, Inc., 1954, p. 314. Reproduced with permission of McGraw-Hill.
2. Adapted from John Dewey. *Democracy and Education*. Macmillan Company. New York, 1916, p. 163.

CHAPTER 12

Formulating Educational Objectives

Perhaps nothing is more distracting than not knowing what one is supposed to do in a given situation. In the educational process, students should be afforded the opportunity to know what the teacher expects them to do as a result of instruction. Students have the right to know the objectives (goals) proposed for their educational experience.

How can teachers teach effectively if they do not know what to teach? One of the first steps in designing strategies to affect the behavior modification of students is to "decide what to teach." In the final analysis, it will be the educational objectives which will serve as ends to guide action.

As Mager points out, an *educational objective* is an intent communicated by a statement describing a proposed behavioral change in a student—a statement of what the learner is to be like when the learning experience has been completed successfully [1]. It is a description of the pattern of behavior as evidenced by performance that the teacher desires the student to be able to demonstrate. The educational objective describes the terminal behavior sought in the student. Such terms as performance objectives, student objectives, outcome-based objectives, performance-based objectives, and instructional objectives are synonymous with the term "educational objectives" as used in this book.

When a teacher has identified what is to be taught and has expressed this intent in terms of educational objectives, a prime portion of the planning has been completed. It is the teacher's job to change the behavior of students as a result of that teacher's direction of the learning process. In order to achieve this task, teachers need to answer these questions:

- What must we teach?
- How will we know when it has been taught?
- What materials and procedures should be used as we teach?

For teachers to provide an effective learning experience for their students, the following essentials of positive teaching must be utilized:
The teacher

1. must decide upon the desired outcomes sought at the end of the instruction

2. must select the teaching plans, procedures, content, and methods essential to reach the desired outcomes as expressed by the educational objectives and/or competencies to be taught

3. must assess the student's achievement of the desired outcomes originally sought

In reference to the above three points, the implementation of the *O.P.E. Concept* takes on additional meaning and importance. The teacher formulates the desired educational *objectives*, selects the most appropriate teaching methods and *procedures*, and *evaluates* student performance in the light of the attainment of educational objectives.

In formulating educational objectives, several terms require definition.

- Behavior — observable activity displayed by an individual which demonstrates how that individual performs

- Terminal Behavior — the observable and measurable behavior the teacher would like the student to be able to demonstrate or perform at the time the teacher's influence on the student ceases

- Criterion — the standard or test by which the terminal behavior will be evaluated

- Condition — those items which students will be allowed to use or those which will be deprived students; in essence, the conditions under which the terminal behavior will be expected to occur.

In describing terminal behavior, it is noted that the words "observable" and "measurable" are used. Why? Educational objectives must be written in such a way that they can become *measurable and observable*. If they are not formulated in this manner, it is impossible for the teacher to determine whether or not the instruction has met the desired outcome. Behavior is both covert and overt. It is not possible for the teacher to objectively assess covert behavior; therefore, educational objectives must be measurable and observable—overt in nature. "To appreciate math" could be a very important behavioral change; however, it cannot be evaluated in an objective manner since it is not measurable nor observable. Since the educational process must impact students, it must be measurable so the teacher can assess the impact upon students. In the final analysis, student performance is measured or evaluated according to the educational objectives originally selected.

WHY ARE CLEARLY DEFINED EDUCATIONAL GOALS IMPORTANT?

When clearly defined educational objectives are lacking, it is nearly impossible to evaluate objectively the outcome of instruction. Of more consequence, there is no sound basis for selecting appropriate materials, content, or teaching methods best suited to achieve the objectives.

Well-developed educational objectives which can be measured will help to

- promote more effective learning by communicating to students what they are expected to learn
- promote more positive teaching by communicating to teachers what they should teach
- provide a basis for positive communication between the students and the teacher
- facilitate the selection of the most appropriate teaching methods, procedures, and subject matter content
- provide a more objective method to assign student grades
- provide a basis for more valuable evaluation of student growth and development

Without clearly defining educational objectives which are measurable and observable

- the teacher will function without direction until a decision is made about what the students are *to be able to do* at the end of the instructional period
- the teacher cannot evaluate effectively the degree to which the students are able to perform unless these "conditions" are specified in the educational objectives
- the students will not be provided a clear indication of their progress toward the attainment of educational goals

Since one of the developmental needs of people is the need to strive for goals that make sense and are within reach, the importance of educational objectives which make sense and are within reach cannot be over stressed. One way to satisfy this basic need is for teachers to state their educational objectives in observable and measurable terms.

Mager further points out that a meaningfully stated educational objective possesses the following three characteristics [2].

1. It succeeds in communicating to the student the teacher's exact instructional intent.

2. It describes specifically the desired terminal behavior or educational outcome strived for.

3. It identified the kind of performance (criterion) acceptable to provide objective evidence the student has achieved the objective sought and taught.

Too often, educational objectives are written in such a manner that they may have many interpretations. It is essential that the "action" desired for students to demonstrate be so clearly stated that both the teacher and the student understand precisely what the educational intent is designed to achieve.

In formulating educational objectives, teachers should avoid those "action" words open to many interpretations, such as:

- to know
- to learn
- to understand
- to really understand
- to like
- to become familiar with
- to value
- to dislike
- to grasp the significance of
- to enjoy

- to believe
- to appreciate
- to suggest

- to have faith in
- to really like
- to have an attitude for

However, teachers should utilize those "action" words which are open to fewer interpretations, such as:

- to write
- to recite
- to differentiate
- to solve
- to build
- to contrast
- to perform
- to calculate
- to outline

- to plan
- to construct
- to design
- to list
- to compare
- to choose
- to demonstrate
- to make
- to describe

HOW TO FORMULATE EDUCATIONAL OBJECTIVES

Until the teacher describes what the students will be *DOING* when demonstrating that they "understand" or "appreciate," very little in the way of measurable or observable educational objectives has been identified. Therefore, the objective which communicates best will be one which describes the terminal behavior of the student sufficiently to preclude misinterpretation.

The three basic steps involved in formulating educational objectives are as follows [3]:

Step 1 – Identify the *terminal behavior* by name: For example, what the student is to be able to demonstrate at the conclusion of the instruction.

Step 2 – Further define the desired terminal behavior by describing the important *conditions* under which the terminal behavior will be expected to occur. For example, define what students will be provided or not provided when they demonstrate the ability to do or perform the terminal behavior.

Step 3 – Specify the *criteria* (standards) of acceptable performance by describing how well the student must perform the terminal behavior to be considered acceptable.

IDENTIFYING THE TERMINAL BEHAVIOR

In the teaching-learning process, an educational objective is effective only to the extent that it communicates what the student(s) will be able to do or perform when demonstrating mastery of the objective. It is not possible to know objectively what another person actually knows, understands, or can perform. Therefore, it is absolutely essential that the teacher utilize some observable or measurable means to determine whether the student actually knows, understands, or can do a skill. In essence, the most important characteristic of a properly formulated educational objective is that it identifies and communicates specifically what the student will be able to do or perform when the student demonstrates mastery of the sought objective.

An Exercise

Evaluate the following educational objectives in behavioral performance terms:

1. To develop an understanding of the process of photosynthesis.
2. To learn the difference between simple and compound leaves.
3. To identify, by name, the parts of a flowering plant.

Objective 1—This might be an important objective for a biotechnology student to achieve; however, the statement does not communicate specifically what the student will do when demonstrating mastery of the educational objective. "Develop an understanding of" is open to numerous interpretations. No two people would agree upon the meaning of "understanding."

Objective 2—What is the student to do when demonstrating mastery of this educational objective? Will the students have achieved the objective when they can distinguish between overall appearance of the two leaves in question, or when they identify and describe the shape of each leaf, or when the students can distinguish which leaf goes with which plant? The "action" word used to describe the terminal behavior in this objective is obviously open to numerous interpretations!

Objective 3—Which words describe what the student will be doing when demonstrating accomplishment of this objective? "To identify, by name, the parts" communicates specifically what the student must do to provide evidence that this objective has been achieved. This terminal behavior can be both observed and measured.

In conclusion, the following points should be utilized when identifying the terminal behavior [4]:

1. An educational objective describes the desired behavior modification (outcome) sought.

2. One of the most important characteristics of a properly formulated educational objective is that it identifies and communicates specifically what the students will be able to do or perform when they demonstrate accomplishment of the sought objectives.

3. The list of educational objectives formulated for an entire unit of instruction will consist of several specific statements. The more objectives the teacher includes, the greater probability the teacher will communicate the desired educational intent to students.

4. The best formulated educational objective communicates the desired instructional intent to the person (teacher or students) selecting the objective.

DEGREE OF MENTAL ACTIVITY

Since the central purpose of education should be to develop within an individual (a) rational reasoning ability, (b) problem-solving ability, and (c) thinking ability, it is essential that the terminal behavior sought promote the development of these three attributes. To have students only "list" or "know" will stress mainly the acquisition of knowledge. This may be appropriate in certain situations. However, educational objectives should be formulated with a hierarchy of mental activities, progressing from "remembering" to "thinking" terminal behaviors in the cognitive domain of learning. Initially students need to possess certain knowledge (facts) before they can develop understanding. Both knowledge and understanding are prerequisite to the development of thinking ability.

A teacher should not attempt to improve the "quality" of his or her educational objectives by merely using "action" words in describing the desired terminal behavior which are of a higher order of mental activity. The teacher should identify exactly and precisely the instructional intent of the educational experience. But all positive instruction should strive to include an array of mental activity within each unit of instruction.

A list of action words useful to teachers as they formulate educational objectives for the cognitive domain of learning is found in Figure 12.1. The reader will note the various levels of mental activity ranging from "knowledge" through "evaluation." Also, attention is called to Figure 12.2 which provides a key for analyzing the degree of mental activity associated with the different levels of cognition.

Some action words useful to teachers as they formulate educational objectives for the psychomotor domain of learning are found in Figure 12.3.

Selected action words appropriate for teachers to utilize as they formulate educational objectives for the affective domain of learning are found in Figure 12.4. As with the cognitive domain, five levels of mental activity are associated with the affective domain ranging from "receiving" through "characterization."

DEFINING THE CONDITIONS

To state an educational objective that communicates precisely what is expected of students when they demonstrate mastery of an objective, the teacher should further define the terminal behavior by describing the *conditions* under which the change in behavior will be expected to occur. To assist in identifying these conditions, the following questions should be asked [5]:

1. What will be provided the students as they demonstrate the sought terminal behavior?

2. What will be denied the students as they demonstrate achievement of the objective?

3. Where, when, and how will the terminal behavior be expected to occur?

4. What knowledges, skills, and abilities are not to be demonstrated as these relate to the sought terminal behavior?

1. KNOWLEDGE
   to define
   to write
   to list
   to recall
   to recognize
   to acquire
   to develop
   to outline
   to identify
   to order
   to name

2. COMPREHENSION
   to translate
   to prepare
   to comprehend
   to interpret
   to conclude
   to predict
   to estimate
   to differentiate
   to explain
   to summarize
   to demonstrate
   to see implications, effects,
      and consequences
   to paraphrase
   to indicate
   to make predictions

3. APPLICATION
   to apply
   to employ
   to relate
   to predict
   to use
   to build or construct
   to make
   to repair
   to operate

4. ANALYSIS
   to distinguish
   to discriminate
   to analyze
   to detect
   to calculate
   to infer
   to categorize
   to choose
   to discover

5. SYNTHESIS
   to create
   to propose
   to integrate
   to plan
   to design
   to synthesize
   to formulate
   to perceive
   to organize
   to prepare
   to make recommendations
   to compile
   to incorporate
   to visualize

6. EVALUATION
   to select
   to judge
   to assess
   to compare
   to appraise
   to evaluate
   to decide
   to determine

Figure 12.1   Action Words (Verbs) Useful in Formulating Educational Objectives for the Cognitive Domain of Learning

REMEMBERING	1.00	KNOWLEDGE
	1.10	Knowledge of specifics
	1.11	Knowledge of terminology
	1.12	Knowledge of specific facts
	1.20	Knowledge of ways and means of dealing with specifics
	1.21	Knowledge of conventions
	1.22	Knowledge of trends and sequences
	1.23	Knowledge of classification and categories
	1.24	Knowledge of criteria
	1.25	Knowledge of methodology
	1.30	Knowledge of universals and abstractions in a field
	1.31	Knowledge of principles and generalizations
	1.32	Knowledge of theories and structure
UNDERSTANDING	2.00	COMPREHENSION
	2.10	Translation
	2.20	Interpretation
	2.30	Extrapolation
	3.00	APPLICATION
THINKING	4.00	ANALYSIS
	4.10	Analysis of elements
	4.20	Analysis of relationships
	4.30	Analysis of organizational principles
	5.00	SYNTHESIS
	5.10	Production of unique communication
	5.20	Production of plan or proposed set of opportunities
	5.30	Production of set of abstract relations
	6.00	EVALUATION
	6.10	Judgments in terms of internal evidence
	6.20	Judgments in terms of external criteria

Figure 12.2   A Key for Analyzing the Degree of Mental Activity Required by Formulated Educational Objectives

to construct	to build
to make	to design
to assemble	to fabricate
to demonstrate	to perform
to draw	to service
to install	to use
to maintain	to operate
to compose	to form
to discover	to lay out

Figure 12.3 Action Words (Verbs) Useful in Formulating Educational Objectives for the Psychomotor Domain of Learning

Assume the educational objective is "to calculate the volume of a "cylinder." To achieve this objective, the students must use this formula: $V = h\,\pi\,r^2$. Is this formula included as a condition in the objective ("Given the formula for finding volume of a cylinder ($V = h\,\pi\,r^2$), the student will be able to calculate the volume of a cylinder")? If the formula is not included in the objective or otherwise provided the students, students may fail to demonstrate achievement of this objective because they forgot to memorize the formula.

Another example to illustrate the importance of defining the condition(s) when formulating educational objectives is as follows:

The teacher wants students in chemistry class to balance chemical equations. Instruction has been provided by the teacher whereby the "periodic table of chemical elements," hanging on one of the walls of the classroom, was referred to as each chemical equation was balanced. Students were also provided a set of sample problems on chemical equations to work in class using the periodic table. On the evaluation to assess students' mastery of the objective, the paper and pencil test was distributed to each student after the periodic table had been removed from the classroom.

It is obvious only those students in the class who had memorized the information on the periodic table could demonstrate they had achieved the educational objective with any degree of success.

Was the teacher's instructional intent to teach students "to balance

1. RECEIVING

    to select
    to choose
    to share
    to separate
    to hold
    to direct
    to accept
    to control

2. RESPONDING

    to answer
    to read
    to practice
    to discuss
    to play
    to approve
    to participate
    to follow

3. VALUING

    to assist
    to debate
    to support
    to specify
    to deny
    to form
    to help

4. ORGANIZATION

    to define
    to organize
    to arrange
    to combine
    to formulate
    to prepare
    to compare
    to discuss

5. CHARACTERIZATION

    to serve
    to display
    to manage
    to act
    to solve
    to verify
    to change
    to complete

Figure 12.4   Action Words Useful in Formulating Educational Objectives for the Affective Domain of Learning, by Level of Mental Activity

chemical equations" or "to recall the valences and weights of chemical elements and then to balance chemical equations"?

In the exercise below, evaluate the effectiveness of the following educational objectives; how well do they describe the conditions under which the terminal behavior will be expected to occur?

---

1. To identify by name the parts of a flowering plant.
2. To identify by name the parts of a flowering plant by placing the "part number" opposite "part listed."
3. Given a checklist with all parts listed, to identify by name the parts of a flowering plant by placing the "part number" opposite the "part listed" on the checklist.

Evaluation: Objective 1—This educational objective identifies the terminal behavior only. There is no reference made to what will or will not be provided the students when they demonstrate the ability to do the terminal behavior.

Evaluation: Objective 2—Again, the terminal behavior sought is identified. How the students will "identify by name the parts" is further defined, but this objective does not describe (define) the key conditions.

Evaluation: Objective 3—This educational objective describes the conditions under which the students are to demonstrate their ability to perform the terminal behavior. "Given a checklist with all parts listed" indicates to the students that they do not have to learn to spell the part or to remember all of the parts, etc. It communicates to the students they are "to identify," nothing else!

In conclusion, oftentimes teachers teach students one thing, yet evaluate them on different things. Positive teaching can be promoted by describing the key conditions which will be provided or denied students and in that way specifying what competencies (knowledges, skills, and/or abilities) the teacher is *not* attempting to develop.

SPECIFYING THE CRITERION

The third step in formulating educational objectives is to state the acceptable level or degree of performance. Once the teacher has described what the students are to be able to do or perform, and has also defined the conditions under which the desired terminal behavior will be demonstrated, the teacher can increase the ability of the educational objective to communicate by specifying to the students HOW WELL they must be able to perform the terminal behavior. For maximum communication and minimum misinterpretation, the teacher should inform the students of at least the minimum acceptable performance for each objective. By specifying the criterion, the teacher and the students will have a performance standard against which to evaluate whether the educational objective was achieved.

Specifying the criterion can be achieved by adding words which describe the criterion (standard or test) for success. The two most common ways that a teacher can specify minimum acceptable performance are (a) setting a time limit or (b) setting a *minimum number* limit.

When using the time limit, the teacher allows students a certain amount of time to complete a pencil and paper examination, to do a job, or to perform a task. With a minimum number of correct responses, the teacher is establishing a minimum performance for all students to achieve. For example, those students who answer more than the minimum number of questions correctly will be evaluated at a higher level of achievement. It is imperative that teachers establish their evaluation (grading) scales at the same time the criterion for each objective is specified. For example, on a one hundred item identification test, if fifty is an acceptable minimum number of correct responses, it can be assumed a score of fifty would be translated to be "average" or a "C" grade. If a student only answered thirty correct, what grade should this student receive? What if a student had ninety correct responses; what grade should this student receive?

As was discussed in the chapter "Evaluating Learning to Assure A Positive Educational Experience," specifying the criterion for each educational objective and communicating this standard to students will improve the quality of the evaluation process. One improvement in the process will be objectivity (fairness) in evaluating student performance. Students should be informed by the teacher of the acceptable minimum performance. Too often, students must "psych out" the teacher to ascertain what the teacher is really attempting to assess, especially on paper and pencil examinations.

In the exercise below, evaluate the following objectives in terms of criterion or standard of minimum acceptable performance.

1. Given a checklist with all parts listed, to identify by name the parts of a flowering plant by placing the "part number" opposite the "part listed" on the checklist.
2. Given a checklist with all parts listed, to identify by name at least eight parts of a flowering plant by placing the "part number" opposite the "part listed" on the checklist.

Evaluation: Objective 1.

This educational objective describes both the terminal behavior desired and the condition under which the students are to demonstrate their ability to perform the terminal behavior. However, the minimum acceptable level of performance is lacking.

Evaluation: Objective 2.

This objective specifies the criterion or standard of minimum acceptable performance that students must perform when demonstrating mastery of the terminal behavior. "To identify by name at least eight parts" communicates to the students how well they must perform to achieve this educational objective.

A QUICK REVIEW

If the information contained in this chapter is adhered to by teachers as they formulate educational objectives, positive teaching will tend to occur and more effective behavior modification of students is likely to result. The more salient points are as follows:

An Educational Objective

1. describes an intended behavior change in students which can be observed, measured, or both.

2. communicates the educational intent of instruction to the teacher.

3. identifies the terminal behavior which describes what the student will

DO or perform when demonstrating his or her achievement of the educational objective.

4. describes the conditions under which the desired terminal behavior will be expected to be performed or occur.

5. describes how the student will be evaluated (how well the student must perform); minimum acceptable performance is specified as a standard.

Finally, an educational objective should possess the following characteristics [6].

1. Objectives should be stated in terms of career or life activities (life outside of school or life on the job).

2. Each objective should represent an observable or measurable change in the behavior of the student.

3. Objectives should be clearly written and definite in description and be stated in sufficient detail to be measurable and to serve as a basis for selection of subject matter content.

4. Objectives should be attainable with the time, resources, and facilities which may be available and used.

5. The lesson objectives should be derived from the unit objectives, just as the unit objectives, in turn, get their sanction from the aims of the subject matter area.

6. The objective specifies standards of performance so the teacher and student know when they have reached the objective.

7. Each objective should definitely imply a corresponding student's goal. It is important that students make the attainment of objectives their goal. This is best done by stating them in terms of the behavior expected of the student.

8. Each lesson objective, when reached, should contribute to attaining a unit objective or an aim of the subject matter area.

9. Objectives should belong to and be identified with the course so that anyone may know what are the objectives of the course and its units of instruction.

SUMMARY

As mentioned at the beginning of this chapter, when a teacher has identified what is to be taught and has expressed this intended educational intent in terms of measurable and desirable educational objectives, a major portion of planning for teaching has been achieved. Positive teaching necessitates that the teacher communicate to students as precisely and accurately as possible the sought outcomes desired as a result of instruction. In essence, the more specific the educational objectives are written, the more effective they will be.

In order to better communicate the educational intent of instruction, the more objectives formulated for a unit of instruction, the more effectively the teacher will communicate the desired educational outcomes to students. Formulating observable and measurable educational objectives is one of the teacher's responsibilities which requires much time and effort; however, once completed, the instructional program will become more effective as well as more positive. Formulating objectives which are observable and measurable will assist in promoting a more positive educational experience for both teachers and students.

ENDNOTES

1. Mager, Robert F. *Preparing Instructional Objectives*. Fearon Publishers, Palo Alto, California, 1962, p. 3.
2. Mager, *op. cit.*
3. Adapted from Mager, R. F. *Preparing Instructional Objectives*. Fearon Publishers, Palo Alto, California, 1962, p. 12.
4. Mager, *op. cit.*
5. Mager, *op. cit.*
6. Adapted from Hammonds, C. (1950). *Teaching Agriculture*. McGraw-Hill, New York, p. 54–55.

CHAPTER 13

Building a Case for Learning

Students can be placed in a learning environment, but they cannot be made to learn! The art and science of teaching can be thoroughly tested in situations where students are not interested in the educational experience being presented. Teaching, at times, taxes the imagination, talent, and patience of the teacher when situations arise where students don't want to learn.

It was pointed out in Chapter 5 that motivation is the most basic element of learning. It is motivation that forces a person to move toward a goal; in the case of education, the goal is the achievement of predetermined educational objectives. No one learns without feeling some urge to learn. It is an awesome responsibility and challenge for a teacher to create a need or desire to learn on the part of the students. However, for positive teaching to occur, the teacher must build a case for learning for each lesson taught.

WHY IS IT IMPORTANT TO BUILD A CASE FOR LEARNING?

Building a case for learning must begin in the opening of a lesson or in the INTRODUCTION to the lesson. *To ignite a spark* of interest on the part of the students, it is essential that they "buy into" the lesson. Students need to be made to realize *what* is being taught, *why* it is being taught, and *how* it is being taught! Students need to realize also the value to be gained by getting involved in the lesson. If the teacher can get the students to buy into the lesson, there will be, in all probability, greater interest demonstrated by the students. Since interest begets motivation, it is essential that students be stimulated and motivated to achieve the desired educational intent of the learning experience being provided.

It is in presenting to the students the Introduction portion of the lesson that the teacher can determine

- whether the students are ready to receive instruction
- how much emphasis must be placed upon building a case for learning
- what to do in today's lesson from a pedagogical point of view
- the general attitude and enthusiasm of the class members
- whether the attention of students is sufficient to move to the body of the lesson

It is in the Introduction of the lesson that the effective teacher draws upon his or her knowledge and understanding of "how people learn" — the psychology of learning—to stimulate student interest. All of the basic principles of learning can be and should be utilized effectively in building a case for learning. For example, students learn more and better when

- student interest is aroused
- student needs are being satisfied
- student thinking is stimulated
- students participate actively
- two or more of each student's senses are used
- teachers maintain a positive climate of success

Case Situations

Each of these six principles can be applied in the Introduction if certain approved practices and pedagogical techniques are utilized. To illustrate this point, reference is made to two case situations.

Case Situation 1

> Students enter the classroom; the teacher is busy at the desk doing paperwork. The bell to start the class rings; the teacher takes roll.
>
> When all students are seated in their chairs, the teacher stands up and makes this announcement: "Open your books to page 143; read the next ten pages quietly and, when you are finished, answer the questions at the end of the chapter."

What type of "case for learning" was provided to the students? Would you expect interest to be high or low? Do students realize the value of the lesson? Are their needs being satisfied? In the above situation, were the six principles of learning utilized or applied?

An Assessment of Situation 1

- Was there interest?
  Maybe; maybe not. The degree of interest would naturally vary with the subject matter being covered and the interest of individual students. However, the teacher did nothing to build a case for learning.

- Were students' needs being satisfied?
  Depends again upon the subject matter and inherent interest of students. The teacher did nothing to relate the lesson to students' needs nor was the value or usefulness of the lesson cited.

- Was thinking stimulated?
  Probably not since students were not involved in the analysis of content or the solution of a problem. The only learning occurring was probably memorization (recall of what was read).

- Did students participate actively?
  Yes; they opened the books, read words, and answered questions. Students did participate, but their participation probably resulted in little or no permanent learning.

- Were two or more senses used?
  Yes; students read (sight) and held (touch) the book. However, the intensity of the learning experience was not strong.

- Did a positive climate of success exist?

  It depends upon the perception of each individual student. From a pedagogical point of view, a positive climate of success could have been presented in a better manner. Students were not told what to read for; there were no objectives cited; the reasons for reading the assignment were not stated; the utility of the reading (lesson) was not revealed, etc.

Case Situation 2

As the students enter the classroom, they are greeted by the teacher in a positive manner. The teacher inquires of certain students how "this or that" is going. A friendly atmosphere exists. The bell rings; the teacher takes roll.

When all students are seated and looking at the teacher, class begins. The teacher takes out from under the desk a one gallon paper container with a big "?" on the side. The teacher makes this statement: "Inside this container, I have the most important thing on earth—without it, we would not survive!" The teacher asks several students "what is it?" As students respond, the teacher places the students' responses on the chalkboard until there are no more!

The teacher goes to the chalk board and circles the word or words which illustrates the lesson topic for today's class.

The teacher asks, "Why is this the most important thing on earth?" Again the student responses are solicited and discussed, if appropriate. On several occasions, the teacher asks the student providing the response, "Why did you say that?" The teacher occasionally challenges the student's response.

When the teacher has the attention of a majority of the students, the educational intent (objective) of the lesson is provided to students along with several reasons why it is important for the students to study the topic at hand!

Were the six principles of learning utilized or applied in this situation?

An Assessment of Situation 2

- Was there interest?
  Probably there was very high interest. Why? Because these motivational skills were used.
    1. The natural impulse of curiosity was present.
    2. The teacher was more interested since the teacher had taken the time to plan for the use of the "mystery container."
    3. Students were challenged to think.
    4. The state of suspense was created and sustained by the teacher and the container.
    5. The novel and unexpected were present.
- Were student needs being satisfied?
  This point cannot be assessed; however, the teacher did stress the importance of the lesson.
- Was thinking stimulated?
  Most certainly.
- Did the students participate actively?
  They saw the container, they heard the teacher ask questions, and they answered questions which required thought.
- Were two or more senses used?
  Yes, the one gallon container and the teacher's questions caused the students to use their natural senses of seeing and hearing. Also, the teacher utilized the chalkboard to record student responses so the sense of sight was again utilized.
- Did a positive climate of success exist?
  This cannot be assessed objectively. But, the teacher did many things to create a positive climate. The teacher greeted the students, the teacher involved students through questioning, the teacher used a visual aid, and the teacher stressed what was to be achieved and why it was important for students to learn this information.

TEACHING SITUATIONS AND VISUAL AIDS

What is the main element in situation 2 which was not present in situation 1? Among other things, in the second situation, the teacher

- developed a teaching situation
    and
- utilized a visual aid (realia)

The use of these two simple techniques can make the opening of a lesson more exciting, interesting, and effective. The teacher in the second situation "built a case for learning," while the teacher in the first situation made no use of the psychology of learning.

Teaching Situations

A teaching situation is created when an *Interest Approach* is used to stimulate, involve, and motivate students. It is a teacher's tool used to ignite that spark of student interest so essential to provide positive teaching. To develop and utilize teaching situations effectively requires imagination, initiative, resourcefulness, and a great deal of creativity on the part of the teacher. It certainly is an acquired ability which any teacher can learn to master. A realistic teaching situation can promote fascination and fascination may lead to real motivation on the part of students.

As defined in this book, a teaching situation (Interest Approach) is developed by utilizing an experience, a case study, an example, an incident (real or fictitious), and/or a problem which focuses upon or illustrates or demonstrates the importance of the lesson in question. It differs from the "Situation" component of a teaching plan. The "Situation" utilized in lesson planning specifies for the teacher the conditions under which instruction will take place such as why, when, where, how, and who, while the "teaching situation" is a feeling developed within the classroom through which students are motivated to learn.

Visual Aids (Realia)

The use of visual aids (realia) in the Introduction of the lesson affords numerous advantages and opportunities to the teacher. They tend to stimulate and involve students as the teacher is establishing in the introduction *what* and *why* instruction is being offered. An appropriate visual aid effectively utilized by a teacher who asks leading questions pertaining to the visual aid(s) being used makes application of several principles of learning. Realia, properly used, does these things:

- Creates interest
- Involves students
- Promotes thinking (if accompanied with oral questions)
- Promotes use of more than one sense
- Promotes more effective learning environments

When a teaching situation (Interest Approach) and a visual aid are used in tandem in the Introduction, most of the principles of learning can be applied.

Although very effective in the Introduction, this is not to infer that realia should not be used throughout the lesson. To the contrary, visual aids should be utilized whenever applicable throughout the lesson. Refer to Chapter 19 for a detailed discussion on using realia to visualize learning.

HOW TO BUILD A CASE FOR LEARNING

An Introduction to a lesson is an important component to promote positive teaching. How should a teacher go about "Building a Case for Learning?" There are probably as many approaches and techniques to achieve this task as there are teachers.

The intensity and magnitude of an Introduction will depend upon such factors as students' general interest in the topic, the difficulty of the subject matter, the degree of mental activity sought in the educational objectives, the relevancy of the lesson, and the experience of the students, to name a few. The Introduction for some lessons will require a minimum of interest approaches; for others, several techniques might be required. Specific techniques are presented below which might be utilized to stimulate student interest.

Technique 1: Apply the "Interest Approaches" useful to motivate students

Interest Approaches were discussed in Chapter 5 under the discussion on principles of learning. They are repeated here in part.

- Interest Approach 1.   Refer to natural impulses, urges, or drives of students.

- Interest Approach 2.   Refer to that which affects us, others about us, and humanity at large; these ideas tend to interest students.

- Interest Approach 3.   Build upon those things students are already interested in.

- Interest Approach 4.   Build upon the knowledges, skills, and attitudes students already possess.

- Interest Approach 5.   Utilize interesting things to create student interest in uninteresting things.

- Interest Approach 6.   Require thinking on the part of students.

- Interest Approach 7.   Use an enthusiastic and interesting teaching delivery.

- Interest Approach 8.   Show students they are progressing toward a goal.

- Interest Approach 9.   Maintain suspense.

- Interest Approach 10.   Use ideas already acceptable to students to create new interest centers.

- Interest Approach 11.   Employ the novel and unexpected.

- Interest Approach 12.   Use humor.

The use of any one or a combination of these interest approaches could assist teachers in building a better case for learning. A variety of approaches is essential.

Technique 2: Satisfy the developmental needs of the students

Not only the Interest Approaches, but the developmental needs of people and the basic needs of students were discussed in Chapter 5 under the discussion on principles of learning.

The Developmental Needs of people are as follows:

- Need to belong
- Need to be a part of something worthwhile
- Need to receive recognition for accomplishments
- Need to select and train for an occupation
- Need to strive for goals that make sense and are within reach
- Need to accept and share responsibility
- Need to do things which have real purpose and value

Any attempt on the part of the teacher to relate to one or more of these basic needs in the Introduction will tend to help students buy into the lesson. In some situations, only one reference will be sufficient while, in other situations, a teacher will need to try to satisfy several of the above cited needs of people.

Satisfaction of the primary needs of students tends to stimulate interest as well. Students must understand that the educational experience being provided will help satisfy one or more of these needs listed below.

1. Making money

2. Securing a job

3. Seeking economic independence

4. Developing self confidence

5. Assuming responsibility

6. Developing self esteem

7. Obtaining job satisfaction

8. Satisfying developmental needs

9. Doing something worthwhile

Alert teachers know the *needs* of students and make use of these *needs* to "sell the lesson" to the student. Effective teachers recognize that students relate to these needs. For example, if a teacher can, in the Introduction, show or demonstrate to students how what is being taught can help them get a job and make money, student interest and motivation to become involved in the educational experience will be stimulated. Remember, people need and want to do those things which have a real purpose and value.

Technique 3: Utilize those techniques
which arouse interest [1]

1. Begin each educational experience (lesson) with a review of the previous day's lesson, if appropriate. Repetition of subject matter in the form of a quick review is an effective teaching technique and can arouse interest by referring to information that students are already familiar with.

2. Show enthusiasm at the very beginning of the lesson. Be sure to involve those students who show an interest early in the introduction. In many cases the interest of these students will flow to disinterested students.

3. Require thinking. Thinking is basically interesting while memorization (recall) is not.

4. Stress the value and usefulness of the lesson being presented. Effective teachers teach for the future. They relate utility of the lesson to the satisfaction of students' needs.

5. Take every opportunity to apply the twelve Interest Approaches presented in Technique 1, especially
   • appealing to or involving the natural impulses, urges or drives
   • moving from interesting things in which students already are interested and of which they possess some understanding to those new less interesting things
   • building upon what students already know, can do, and have appreciation for
   • demonstrating how progress is being made as educational objectives are achieved
   • utilizing humor

6. Arrive at valid conclusions which have application to the satisfaction of students' goals and needs.

Arousing students' interest, lesson-in and lesson-out, requires much skill on the part of the teacher. Only a few of the techniques available have been presented above to illustrate how teachers can stimulate interest and motivate students. The techniques presented are based upon those principles and psychological laws affecting learning which were presented in Chapter 5 of this book. Effective teachers make teaching interesting, challenging, and exciting from the Introduction through the Conclusion of the lesson.

CONTROLLING INTEREST

Arousing students' interest is of prime importance to the teacher if a positive educational experience is to occur. However, once student interest has been stimulated, *that* interest must be reinforced continuously, especially when the teacher can detect that it is becoming less intense. Teachers can control student interest by

1. basing their teaching upon the needs of their students

2. making use of the natural impulses, urges, and drives of their students

3. introducing appropriate illustrations and teaching situations

4. using visual aids frequently and appropriately

5. providing a positive learning environment including satisfactory physical conditions; the teacher should check the lighting, temperature, and ventilation conditions and student seating arrangements at the beginning of each class.

6. basing their teaching upon stimulating thinking, not mere memorization

7. organizing their subject matter by considering it from the standpoint of their students

8. creating doubt, suspense, and curiosity

9. developing and exhibiting a pleasing personality

10. building interest which will endure

To illustrate how a teacher could apply one of these techniques for controlling interest, the following procedures are suggested to help teachers base their teaching upon the needs of students.

1. Make assignments apply to the real life problems/situations of students.

2. Have students indicate how the lesson will benefit them, what is expected from them, or how they can use the educational experience.

3. Stress the economic value of the lesson.

4. Use current events to show utility of the lesson.

5. Plan and deliver instructions on a seasonal sequence basis.

6. Point out who has previously benefitted from mastery of the lesson or who has been successful as a result of the instruction.

7. Stress application of the lesson.

8. Do not teach the lesson until or unless there is a need in the lives of the students. Postpone teaching the lesson until a need is recognized.

Teachers who employ one or more of the techniques suggested above will be able to deliver a more positive educational experience for their students.

SECURING RETENTION
OF ACQUIRED COMPETENCIES

Securing students' attention and maintaining interest in a lesson is hard work. The effective teacher is concerned about maintaining that interest throughout the class. Teachers do not employ skills and techniques to arouse interest just to entertain students. Stimulation of students' interest is undertaken in order to motivate students to study, to learn, and to acquire additional knowledges, skills, and/or attitudes germane to the predetermined educational objectives.

Not only must teachers control student interest, they must develop the kind of interest that will help to insure retention of newly acquired knowledge. It is one thing to stimulate student interest in a lesson through the use of a "quality" introduction and to maintain the quality of interest throughout the lesson. However, it is quite another thing for students to retain the newly acquired knowledge for future use.

It is true that the retention of what has been taught is not directly related to "building a case for learning," but since the amount of retention of newly acquired competence will be dependent upon the degree of student interest in the lesson, there is a need to discuss this most critical dimension of teaching and learning. A direct relationship exists between students' interest and initial desire to acquire new competencies and the amount of subject matter retained. Therefore, since motivation of students and retention of subject matter are directly dependent upon student interest, it appears appropriate at this point to present some suggestions on how teachers can promote the retention of acquired competencies!

Listed below are some suggested procedures which teachers can utilize to secure retention of those competencies taught students.

1. Require much repetition of the material during and after learning.

2. Require that students give close attention during the learning process.

3. Require intense effort and concentration during the supervised study period.

4. Carefully organize the material to be taught.

5. Maintain a high degree of teacher interest.

6. Recall and review material frequently after it has been learned.

7. Require learning to be carried beyond the "threshold of reproduction."

8. Present material in a novel manner.

9. Inspire students to want to master the subject matter when studying.

10. Give to the students the clearest possible understanding of the material to be learned.

11. Present material as vividly as possible.

12. Require laboratory work and supervised practice as a means of fixing all important truths.

13. Require application whenever possible.

14. Stress the formation of many mental associations with the new learning.

15. Require the material learned to be frequently used in the subsequent thinking of the students.

COMPONENTS OF AN INTRODUCTION

Based upon the discussion thus far, what should be included in the *Introduction* part of a teaching plan? An Introduction should include the following:

* 1. Review conclusions derived from the previous day's work

  2. Inform students about what they are expected to do (include directions, if applicable)

* 3. Review situations, if applicable

* 4. Identify educational objectives

  5. Cite present and future value—utility and/or application

* 6. Use real objects and visual aids (realia)

* 7. Use personal (teacher) experiences

* 8. Relate lessons to student problems

* 9. Relate lessons to community situations

*10. Use leading questions—exploratory questions

*11. Ask "questions for study"

*Not all eleven points cited above would or should be included in the same introduction, but a combination of these points should be considered. However, there are several points which should be included as "minimum" for an effective introduction: points 1, 3, 4, 6, 7 or 8 or 9, 10 and 11.

EDUCATIONAL FUNCTIONS OF THE COMPONENTS OF AN INTRODUCTION

What is the rationale for including the parts listed above in the Introduction? What does each contribute in building a case for learning?

Point 1.   *Review*
            This serves at least two vital functions. *First*, the review ties the previous work to the present lesson. It reinforces what

has been learned and extends that information to what is to be learned in the current lesson. It also stresses the fact that progress is being made toward a larger goal. *Second*, it provides a very effective vehicle to repeat what has been taught and learned. Repetition, as already noted, is an effective teaching tool. It also requires students to think about what was previously learned. It reinforces the fact that students have achieved past educational objectives. Furthermore, a review helps to build upon what students already know. It sets in the students' minds the lesson for "today."

Point 2.   *Provide Directions*
Clear and concise directions communicate to students what they are to do or not do. When students know what is expected of them, they are more secure and, thus, more receptive to learning.

Point 3.   *Review Situations*
The situation portion of a teaching plan identifies the conditions under which instruction will take place. It contains valuable information which, if shared with students, will assist students to better understand *where*, *when*, *how*, and *why* the lesson is being taught.

Point 4.   *Identify Educational Objectives*
Identifying the educational objectives sought will communicate the instructional intent of the lesson to the students. It will establish a more favorable learning environment by letting students know exactly what they are to do or to perform. Identifying the objectives in the introduction also assists later in the closure of the lesson and in the evaluation of student growth and development.

Point 5.   *Cite the Value and Utility of the Lesson*
This part, if properly presented, establishes *why* the lesson is important for the student to learn, its value and utility. Through the later application phase of the lesson, the future value can be illustrated.

Point 6.   *Utilize Realia*
The use of real materials and other visual aids tends to "bring the introduction of a lesson to life." Their use creates

interest and involves students. Realia provide for the effective use of leading questions. They provide variety and prevent the pooling of ignorance.

Point 7. *Utilize Personal Experience*

Point 8. *Relate Lessons to Student Problems*

Point 9. *Relate Lessons to Community Situations*
Points 7 or 8 or 9 serve as a basis for formulating the teaching situation based upon real experiences, problems, or incidents. Depending upon student interest, only one of these points may be necessary to build a case for learning. In other cases, it may be necessary for the teacher to employ all three, if applicable. These points can also assist the teacher to identify and describe the importance and usefulness of the lesson. Interest is created when something affects us or people around us.

Point 10. *Use Leading Questions*
It is important that teachers learn what students already know or can do. Through the use of leading questions, the teacher can find out what students know and do not know about the lesson at hand. Leading questions also provide an effective way to involve students in the introduction of the lesson.

Point 11. *Ask "Questions for Study"*
Questions for Study are used only in informational lessons. For these lessons, asking "Questions for Study" is a very effective means to tie the introduction into the body of the lesson. Also, by asking these questions for study, the teacher will learn whether the students already know the answer to specific questions; if they do, it would be superfluous to have the students answer them again. On the other hand, asking these questions will indicate to the students what they do not know. If the teacher has done an adequate job in building a case for learning, asking study questions will help students identify specific subject matter content which they need to know in order to achieve the educational objectives. Asking questions for study provides for a smooth transition between the Introduction and the Body, the new subject matter to be studied, of the lesson.

INTRODUCING A LESSON

To illustrate how a teacher might write out an introduction on a teaching plan, the following example is provided.

INTRODUCTION

1. Review previous lesson. Relate to summary and conclusions of prior lesson.
2. Cite individual student problems, teachers' experience, or community situation related to the lesson.
3. Discuss why lesson is important by reviewing key points cited under "Situation" portion of the plan.
4. Draw objectives from students; explain desired outcome of lesson and write educational objectives on chalkboard.
5. Ask leading questions to find out what students already know about the lesson.
6. Show realia; ask specific questions about each object shown.
7. Draw out "Questions for Study" by asking the questions to students prior to placing on chalkboard.

The procedures and devices used for introducing the lesson should be varied frequently in order to create and maintain interest.

COMMON ERRORS

Several common errors are often made by teachers as they build a case for learning. Some of the more common ones are listed below.

1. Beginning the lesson without an introduction

2. Teaching in the introduction by "covering" or providing lesson information rather than focusing upon the importance of what the students are about to learn; do not provide answers to study questions when asked in the introduction

3. Beginning the lesson with the same type (procedures) of introduction for every lesson

4. Failing to use a "teaching situation" in the introduction

5. Failing to use realia (visual aids) at least once in the introduction

6. Failing to ask leading questions about visual aids used

7. Providing too brief an introduction to properly motivate students to buy into the lesson

8. Extending the introduction after student interest has already been aroused

9. Presenting a poor (weak) transition between the introduction and body of the lesson

10. Writing out all details of the introduction on the teaching plan, for example, which leading questions to ask, etc.

CRITIQUING AN INTRODUCTION

Planning an Introduction and including it in the teaching plan is one thing. Delivering an effective Introduction is quite another. Since it is impossible to show a person how to present a challenging and stimulating Introduction through the use of printed words, this text can only present a critique form (Figure 13.1) with selected criteria to be used in assessing how well a teacher achieves this important pedagogical task which, in reality, is an acquired art and skill [2].

SUMMARY

The *INTRODUCTION* portion of a lesson is designed to set the stage for student participation in the educational activity planned. It should help stimulate interest on the part of the students to achieve the educational objectives of the lesson.

Positive teaching requires teachers to plan and deliver effective *Introductions* essential for stimulating students' interest so they will involve themselves early and enthusiastically in the educational experience at hand. Building a case for learning is an acquired ability which will promote more effective and enjoyable teaching and learning for both the students and the teacher.

Did the teacher in the introduction:	How well accomplished?
1. Relate the lesson to previous day's lesson or work?	_____
2. Relate the lesson to the students' prior knowledge and/or experience?	_____
3. Relate to teacher experiences, community situations, and students' problems?	_____
4. State *why* the lesson was important in terms of student needs?	_____
5. State specifically *what* the objective(s) of the lesson were in terms of students' behavior? Were they stated in measurable and observable terms?	_____
6. State *how* the students might proceed in accomplishing the objectives(s)?	_____
7. State how the students would know when they had achieved the objectives(s)?	_____
8. Point out to the students the future value and usefulness of lesson?	_____
9. Use leading questions?	_____
10. Provide opportunity for students to respond and to participate?	_____
11. Express enthusiasm in the lesson?	_____
12. Use real objects, specimens, and other instructional aids?	_____
13. React favorably toward students' questions, answers, and comments?	_____
14. Ask "Questions for Study" (for informational lessons only)?	_____

Figure 13.1 Selected Criteria for Assessing the Effectiveness of a Teaching Plan Introduction

ENDNOTES

1. Adapted from *Permanent Learning* by W. H. Lancelot. John Wiley and Sons, New York, 1944, P. 197–198.
2. Cameron, Walter A. and Cotrell, Calvin J. *Assessment of Micro-Teaching and Video Recording in Vocational and Technical Education: Phase X — Remote Feedback Techniques for Inservice Education.* Center on Education and Training for Employment, Columbus, Ohio (formerly NCRVE/CVTE, Ohio State University), 1970. Used with permission.

CHAPTER 14

Involving Students Through Questioning

As has been pointed out several times in this book, students learn primarily by their own efforts. The point has been made earlier that the degree of student involvement in the educational process influence, to a great extent, the relative amount of behavioral change resulting in the student. One of the most effective and most easily implemented teaching techniques at a teacher's disposal to involve students in the teaching-learning process is the *use of oral questions*. However, the questions must be of the proper type and stated in the most appropriate terms to meet this charge. Oral questioning can change most learning environments into a positive, active educational experience.

It was stated earlier in this text that if telling were the same as teaching, we would all be so smart we could not stand it! The use of oral questions can help the teacher "ask and not tell!"

WHY IS ORAL QUESTIONING IMPORTANT?

As previously stated, one of the teacher's primary goals is to develop within an individual the ability to reason, to think, and to make decisions. The pedagogy utilized by a teacher will influence *how* and *how well* that teacher will direct the thinking process of students. As a lesson unfolds, oral questions are valuable to

- identify what students already know or do not know about the lesson being taught
- keep the students alert
- solicit students' reaction to teaching situations
- assist the teacher in identifying which student(s) need help
- involve students in the educational process
- set the stage for the lesson
- get the students to think
- review, in the summary, key points covered in the lesson
- reinforce learning
- assess whether educational objectives were achieved

The ability of a teacher to utilize oral questions and oral questioning techniques effectively is an acquired ability which can be perfected through use and practice. The ability to stimulate students' thoughts through oral questions can make the difference between mediocre teaching and positive teaching.

EDUCATIONAL FUNCTIONS

Philip Groisser points out that questions serve many valuable and useful functions [1]; they

1. arouse interest

2. promote understanding

3. develop new insights

4. develop ideals, attitudes, and appreciations

5. strengthen learning

6. stimulate logical or critical thinking

7. test a pupil's preparation for the lesson

8. test for the achievement of objectives

In planning and delivering a complete lesson (which includes an introduction; a presentation of new knowledges, skills, and/or attitudes, values, appreciations, etc.; and a conclusion) Richard H. Wilson states that oral questions serve three major educational functions in individual and group instruction [2]. Oral questions

1. stimulate learning

2. direct learning

3. evaluate learning

The educational functions of oral questions as proposed by Wilson contribute to the O.P.E. concept and substantiate the fact that oral questions can and should be used throughout the lesson starting with the question, "What did we discuss in yesterday's class?" and ending with, "What did we learn today?" in the closure of the lesson.

KINDS OF QUESTIONS

The term "Kinds of Questions" refers to the relative level of mental activity required to answer correctly the question asked—the lowest level being recall (memorization) and the highest level involving thinking and/or judgment decisions.

To accommodate the O.P.E. concept that every lesson should have an opening, an exploration of new knowledges, skills and/or attitudes, and an ending, the kinds of questions discussed herein are leading questions, study or discussion questions, and evaluation questions.

Leading questions, referred to as preliminary or exploratory questions, are used mainly in the Introduction to prepare students for the lesson. Questions of this nature can be answered from the actual or pseudo experience or through recall of specific facts. These questions usually begin with "who," "what," "when," "where," or "have you." Examples of leading questions would be

- "Who has balanced a chemical equation?"
- "What is the valence of the element carbon?"
- "When were radio isotopes discovered?"
- "Where can the theory of relativity be applied?"
- "Have you seen this instrument?"

Study/discussion questions are used mainly in the discussion phase of the lesson. Some sources refer to these as comprehension and analysis questions. Answering questions of this nature requires a higher degree of mental activity than does answering leading questions. Answers to study/discussion questions require understanding on the part of students, not mere recall of facts.

Students must be able to interpret, to summarize, to show by relationships, or to explain through definition in order to answer questions of this nature. These questions begin mainly with "how," "what," or "why." Examples of this kind of question would be

- "How is the volume of a cube determined?"
- "Why is the volume of a cylinder calculated differently than for a cube?"
- "What is the volume, in cubic inches, of a cylinder 20 inches high with a diameter of 6 inches?"

Evaluation questions are utilized to test the results of the instruction and to assess the relative amount of change occurring in students' behavior. Often these are referred to as examination questions. These questions may measure students' abilities to interpret information, to summarize new knowledge gained, to reveal relationships existing, to synthesize new facts into principles or generalizations, and to evaluate new material. Questions of this nature should stress thinking, reasoning (judgment), and decision making. Evaluation questions usually begin with "should," "would," "in your opinion," or "in your judgment." If the question can be answered either "yes" or "no," it should be followed with "why." Examples of evaluation questions are

- "Should the amount of money spent on national defense remain the same? Why?"
- "How would a change in foreign currency affect the import-export balance?"
- "In your opinion, should social security benefits be changed? How?"

Effective oral questioning requires practice. It also requires a good sense of timing! Questions should be asked in a relaxed manner. Asking questions is an acquired ability which any teacher can improve. Since it is one indication of successful teaching ability, the need for and importance of oral questioning competence cannot be over emphasized.

ESSENTIALS OF A QUALITY QUESTION

Lancelot, in *Permanent Learning*, states that there are four essentials of a quality question [3]. Each question should *call for thinking*. If thinking on the part of the students is not required, a question loses much of its effectiveness in developing thinking abilities.

A question must *be interesting*. It should carry a "charge" of new interest. Questions that "prod and pry" tend to make students avoid participation in the discussion.

The third essential is that the questions asked should *lead forward step by step*. Questions should build upon one another, not lead the discussion in numerous directions. Questions should never be asked in a "shotgun" approach or projected in all directions.

The last essential proposed by Lancelot is that the questions asked by the teacher *must not suggest their own answers*. The use of clue words such as "never," "always," "not," "impossible" should be avoided when phrasing oral questions since these types of words provide "hidden" signals to alert students.

To guide the thinking process of the class, teachers should use oral questions which

1. require thinking

2. are interesting and relate to the lesson topic being taught

3. lead the thought process forward step by step to a desired conclusion

4. do not suggest their own answer

In addition, high quality oral questions should

1. be relevant

2. be clearly stated

3. be concise

4. challenge attention

5. require thinking and organizing

6. have a proper sequence

7. be adapted to the class

8. bring forth clear responses

9. bring forth responses readily (not necessarily immediately)
    a. by reference to the known
    b. by being clear and definite
    c. by varying the difficulty with students' age and ability
    d. by asking interesting questions
    e. by using a variety of questions which solicit a variety of responses

The ability of the teacher's questioning techniques will determine the quality and quantity of students' responses. For a quality question to result, it must possess certain essentials. Quality questions require students to "use knowledge," not just "remember knowledge!"

APPROVED ORAL QUESTIONS PRACTICES

Several approved questioning techniques will, if properly utilized, improve a teacher's ability to use oral questions to involve and stimulate students. Some of the most effective practices are as follows.

1. *Ask a question; then call on a student.*
    - calling the name of the student before the question is asked creates two negative effects. *First*, it puts one student "on the spot" with little or no time to think about an answer. *Second*, it alerts other students in the class that they do not need to think about the answer.

2. *Pause after asking a question.*
    - calling for the answer to a question immediately does not allow sufficient time for students to think about the answer. But, pausing after the question is asked provides an opportunity for the question "to burn in" on the minds (thoughts) of all students in the class. Teachers who use this technique in conjunction with good eye contact can get much mileage out of a well phrased question. Pausing causes all students in the class to think until the teacher calls upon one student. Teachers' silence, assuming good eye contact is utilized, is a powerful tool to promote positive teaching and effective student learning.

3. *Call on an interested student first.*
   - Since interest flows from interesting to uninteresting things, effective teachers call on the most interested students first. Teachers learn to note facial expressions of their students which provide an indication of which students appear interested.

4. *Ask thought-provoking questions.*
   - The quality of the question will dictate the quality of mental activity required. Study/discussion questions should be used to the greatest extent in order to develop thinking ability in students.

5. *Utilize "why."*
   - Why ask "why?" The use of the word "why" can make any question into a thought-provoking question since thinking is required to answer questions of this kind. Even a good "prod and pry" question can become a quality question by the use of "why."

6. *Challenge students' responses.*
   - This approved practice must be used with much tact and human understanding. If not, challenging a student's response could "turn that student off," or embarrass the student, or telescope the notion that the teacher either dislikes or disapproves of the student's response.
   - Assuming a positive atmosphere prevails in an educational environment, challenging students' responses is a very effective way to promote thinking. It requires students to justify their responses. Teachers may challenge a student's own responses or they may call upon other students to ascertain these students' reaction to the original student's response.
   - This approach may "start a chain reaction" of student-on-student interaction. Whenever this situation happens, the teacher can "step back" and let the students become the directors of the learning process. Teachers have "arrived" when they can stimulate this degree of interest and interaction so they can step aside and let the students "learn from their learnings." Teachers who have experienced this situation in their classrooms should cherish the moments since they do not occur often.

7. *Have students challenge other students' responses.*
   - At times, the teacher may call upon other students to ascertain their reaction to the original student's response. This is also an effective technique to ask students for more information and/or meaning.

8. *As the lesson unfolds, call on "uninterested" students.*
   - As student interest increases, the teacher should then begin involving those students who were not interested at the beginning of the class. All students should be involved in the lesson at some point in time. Addressing questions to all students is one way to involve all students in the lesson.

9. *Ask questions which build upon each other.*
   - Oral questions, as well as written questions, should lead forward to a desired conclusion. Leading questions should lead to study/ discussion questions which should provide the foundation for evaluation questions. Questions designed to gather facts should be used to lead to answers to thought-provoking questions. As the lesson unfolds, higher level questions should be asked by the teacher.

10. *Ask and use questions which are relevant to the topic being discussed.*
    - The essentials of a quality question should be utilized in asking relevant questions which pertain to the topic at hand.
    - For maximum development of the thinking, reasoning and/or decision-making ability of students, questions asked should provide an indication to students of the utility or value or usefulness of their thinking about (answering) these questions.

The number of questions asked is not the key point, but the *quality* of the questions asked is of utmost importance. Once the ability to phrase (ask) quality questions is mastered, a teacher must then master the skill of using approved questioning techniques.

ASKING QUESTIONS

To illustrate some effective and some ineffective oral questioning techniques, attention is called to the following questions:

Question 1. Is studying interesting?
             (This is a poor question since it can be answered with a "yes" or "no" answer.)

Question 2. Billie, what is meant by the word "interest"?

(Asked in this manner, places one student on the spot and "releases" the other students from thinking about the answer.)

Question 3. Kelly, what is the definition of a professional?

(This question again calls on the student first. It is a poor quality question to develop thinking because the correct answer will require a memorized response.)

Question 4. Why use problem solving in teaching? Do you agree with the answer given? Why? Why not?

(This series of questions asked in this sequence tends to challenge students' responses. They require students to think.)

Question 5. What is Einstein's theory of relativity?

(This question would be too difficult for most students to answer.)

Question 6. How many have used oral questions in teaching? How effective were they? Did they work?

Why ask students questions when it is easier and faster to tell them? What techniques should the teacher use when asking questions?

(This series of questions leads forward since they build upon each other.)

This brief demonstration helps illustrate how teachers could improve their oral questioning techniques if they would utilize the approved oral questioning practices presented earlier. The effective use of oral questions contributes substantially to positive teaching and learning.

COMMON ERRORS IN ORAL QUESTIONING

The use of oral questions is a very effective way to assist teachers to "ask and not tell!" The development of approved questioning techniques on the part of the teacher necessitates the avoidance of common errors. Some of the more common errors in oral questioning are listed below.

1. Repeating students' answers

2. Jumping at student's conclusion without permitting student to finish speaking

3. Adding to student's answer to avoid formulating another question or asking another student which would bring out the information from the class

4. Permitting student to answer a different question than the one asked

5. Use of suggestive questions which suggest or provide an answer to the question asked

6. Use of questions requiring only a "yes" or "no" answer

7. Using "rapid-fire" questions; asking another question before the first one is answered

8. Not asking any questions

9. Asking questions at an inappropriate time in the lesson

10. Asking too difficult or too irrelevant questions

11. Not getting adequate "mileage" out of oral questions because approved practices are not followed

Richard H. Wilson, in his monograph entitled "On Questions and Questioning," provides the following Do's and Don'ts of questioning [4].

1. Do evaluate teaching continuously as the lesson unfolds. Ask questions to test comprehension, understanding, grasp of idea or relationship.

2. Do provoke and direct thinking by a series of questions asked in a logical sequence, each building on the preceding.

3. Do phrase questions precisely and carefully so students understand what the teacher wants answered.

4. Do ask challenging questions. Avoid the trite or ridiculously simple probe question lest the answer be likewise.

5. Do get more "mileage" from questions. Ask several students before acknowledging the right or correct answer.

6. Don't ask questions that students cannot be expected to answer. The teacher must inevitably supply the answer. Students build the lazy habit of quietly waiting for the teacher to answer questions they could answer. Students may come to question the teacher's good sense if he or she persists in asking questions they should not know.

7. Don't name student to respond before asking question. The teacher telegraphs the idea that all other students can relax. Exceptions could be when the teacher has over-participation of students; addressing a question to a particular student aids in controlling the confusion. In certain situations, the teacher may desire a specific student's answer.

8. Don't always reject the first wrong answer. Continue testing it on others who identify it as wrong, rather than the teacher doing so.

9. Don't supply answers to questions students should be able to answer, unless teacher's desire is to demonstrate his or her knowledge.

10. Do ask questions to work the students, not the teacher.

11. Don't identify correct answers by facial expression if the teacher wishes to keep students in doubt.

12. Don't ask questions leading to simple "yes" or "no." They provoke limited thought and little discussion. If asked, follow with "Why?"

13. Don't over-question on one point. Cease when sufficient answers have stimulated thought, directed thought, or tested thought. To continue asking questions exhausts students' patience and interest.

14. Do raise questions, when teaching, which premise the teacher's answer. Phrase questions as though students raised, "Now, you may ask . . . ?" followed by the teacher's answer.

15. Do ask each student in the class at least one question during the lesson.

CRITIQUING ORAL QUESTIONS

It is impossible to provide actual experience required to perfect a teacher's use of oral questions by reading about how to improve one's oral questioning competence. However, a critique form with selected criteria (see Figure 14.1) can be presented to help assess how well a teacher can perform this very important pedagogical task of asking questions effectively [5].

When using questions during the lesson,   How Well Accomplished
did the teacher:

  1. Use questions to draw information
     from the students?   _____

  2. Ask a question, pause to give the students
     time to think about the question,
     then call on one student?   _____

  3. After calling on students, provide an
     opportunity for them to think about
     the question before requiring a response?   _____

  4. Present the questions in a logical order?   _____

  5. Make an effort to keep from repeating the
     students' answers?   _____

  6. Direct the questions so each student was
     given an equal opportunity to participate?   _____

  7. React favorably to answers given by students?   _____

  8. Ask questions which required more than
     "yes" and "no" answers?   _____

  9. Ask questions which the students could
     relate to their past experience?   _____

10. State the question in clear and concise terms?   _____

11. Require the students to expand and/or
     clarify their first answers or the answers
     of other students?   _____

12. Ask several students to answer the question
     before acknowledging the right or
     correct response.   _____

Figure 14.1   Selected Criteria to Allow Teachers to Assess Their Questioning Techniques

SUMMARY

A question is an act of asking. Quality oral questioning promotes mental activity on the part of the student. It provides an opportunity for students to become actively involved in the educational process. The effective use of oral questioning by the teacher augments the freedom of action on the part of students; affords students more opportunity to express their ideas, values, appreciations, etc.; and makes students less dependent upon the teacher. Of more consequence, asking questions helps to make a teacher a better listener.

Involving students through questions can become a powerful tool, if done properly, to provide positive teaching. Oral questions serve several valuable and useful functions in the teaching-learning process. Oral questioning is an acquired act and skill. Those approved questioning techniques and the list of common errors and "Do's and Don'ts" contained in this chapter should be used by those teachers who desire to improve their oral questioning competence. Effective teachers know the value and importance of oral questions to promote positive teaching and effective learning.

ENDNOTES

1. Groisser, Philip. *How to Use the Fine Art of Questioning.* Teachers Practical Press, Inc., New York, 1964, p. 6. Reprinted by permission of the publishers, Lieber-Atherton, Inc., P.O. Box 157, Rockaway Beach, NY 11693. Copyright © 1964. All rights reserved.
2. Adapted from a handout entitled "On Questions and Questioning" prepared by Dr. Richard H. Wilson, Department of Agricultural Education, The Ohio State University.
3. Lancelot, W. H. *Permanent Learning.* John Wiley and Sons, New York, 1944, p. 190.
4. Wilson, *op. cit.*
5. Cameron, Walter A. and Cotrell, Calvin J., *op. cit.*

CHAPTER 15

Using Supervised Study Effectively

"Capture a student's time and you capture a student's mind!" This is a very interesting premise, especially from a teaching and learning point of view. How can teachers capture their students' time? The fact has been pointed out numerous times in this book that students learn primarily through their own action. They learn by what they do.

Involving students in "exploring the unknown" is one of the prime responsibilities of a teacher. For maximum learning to occur, students must discover the answers to questions, discover how to perform a task, or discover the information necessary to solve a problem by their own efforts. As pointed out earlier, telling is not the same as teaching students the answers to questions or the solutions to problems. Assisting students to discover new knowledge is one of the important components of positive teaching. Learning how to learn is the epitome of a real education.

"Teaching students the answer" is much more difficult for a teacher to do than "telling students the answer." But, teaching is the job of the teacher. Telling is the job of the storyteller.

As pointed out in Chapter 13, building a case for learning is essential to initially stimulate students' interest in a lesson. That interest must be controlled and maintained throughout the lesson. Interest is essential if students are to discover new competencies. Just as important, from an interest point of view, is teaching students how to study, how to discover, and how to explore the unknown. This methodology is referred to as "supervised study." It can become a powerful teaching tool to assist students to become their own scholars!

Supervised study is stated simply as directed study under the guidance and direction of the teacher. It is a specific method utilized by teachers to assist students to become involved, in a systematic manner, in learning new knowledge.

WHY IS SUPERVISED STUDY IMPORTANT?

There are several reasons why the use of supervised study is a time proven teaching tool to make teaching more positive and learning more effective.

Supervised Study

- establishes an educational environment which creates favorable conditions for effective learning
- provides an organized and systematic procedure for involving students in their own study under the guidance and supervision of their teacher
- teaches students how to study, how to read, how to evaluate printed materials, and how to arrive at intelligent decisions
- provides for individual one-on-one instruction by the teacher
- develops positive relations between the teacher and students
- involves students in the teaching-learning process
- provides students a procedure for recording their "discoveries" through organized note taking
- promotes the opportunity for students to think as they analyze what has been read or studied
- promotes student-centered instruction

WHEN TO USE SUPERVISED STUDY

Supervised study should only be used when it is the best approach to achieve the educational objectives and to involve students in exploring the unknown. It is most appropriate to use supervised study when there is a need to

- obtain factual information which can be secured from reference materials
- determine the answers to questions or problems
- evaluate materials from several sources

- evaluate and synthesize results of what was learned or performed
- reach intelligent decisions based upon research and exploration
- involve students in the thinking process

Supervised study commands a key position in the delivery of both informational and managerial lessons.

HOW LONG TO USE SUPERVISED STUDY

For supervised study to be effective, students must be interested in finding the answers to study questions or in analyzing factors necessary to make sound decisions. Student interest in studying is the key factor in determining how long supervised study can be employed productively. As a rule, the interest span for most students is *one minute per year of age*. This fact should be used only as a guideline since several factors must be taken into consideration as teachers plan and deliver their lessons. However, if student interest during supervised study is maintained at a high level, the teacher should let the students study as long as learning is occurring. On the other hand, if and when student interest in studying decreases, the period of supervised study should be stopped. As a rule of thumb, the time allotted for supervised study should be approximately fifteen to twenty minutes in a fifty to fifty-five minute class period. However, the intensity of students' involvement in supervised study should dictate how long it should last in any given situation.

TEACHERS' RESPONSIBILITY

Effective supervised study does not just happen. It requires planning and followup attention on the part of the teacher. Effective teachers do the following to make this time for study a valuable and meaningful part of the lesson.

Effective teachers

- have a well developed teaching plan
- have necessary reference and resource materials available prior to class
- work with the students, and provide adequate supervision and direction
- do not do other tasks during supervised study

- maintain proper physical environment such as lighting, work stations, ventilation, and cooling and heating, etc.
- move about the room quietly and speak in a low voice when assisting individual students; distractions are avoided by both teacher and students
- help students learn how to study by skimming materials and analyzing main points; show them how to pick out key points in the readings
- provide for individual differences between students; assist only those students who need assistance
- introduce new materials (realia) when appropriate
- encourage and stimulate students to study in a comfortable, business-like position
- assist students to interpret data, words, and phrases
- show students how to assemble ideas and take concise notes

LEARNING HOW TO STUDY

Most students either do not know how to study or lack the motivation to participate actively in this valuable learning activity. For supervised study to become an effective teaching tool, teachers must teach students how to study. Students must be taught how to skim through resource materials and select out the essential factual information. They must be shown how to read and interpret experimental data. They must learn how to assemble ideas and prepare reading logs. They must be taught how to interpret research data and other pertinent factual information.

Unless students know how to study, there is no need for the teacher to employ supervised study as a teaching method. The end result will be a frustrating experience for both students and teacher. Effective teachers recognize the need to teach their students how to study and how to gather data. Likewise, these teachers have a specific idea of the reading ability of their students. They attempt to match their students' reading ability with the readability level of the reference and resource materials supplied their students.

During the first few days of class, effective teachers spend sufficient time in class to teach students how to study. These teachers employ the law of primacy. The following suggestions are examples of what these teachers do to accomplish this important task.

- They review students' standardized test scores to determine their reading abilities. They identify those with high and low reading competence.
- They select reference and resource materials most appropriate for their students. They decide how they will work with both high and low reading ability students.
- They communicate to their students what is expected regarding supervised study and note taking.
- They teach their students a lesson on how to study and how to record class notes and reading logs. This lesson might require several class periods at the beginning of the course. Included in this lesson are the following or similar educational activities:

  — An assigned reading followed by an oral discussion of the key points contained.
  — Presentation of prepared questions prior to an assigned reading followed by a discussion of the answers to the questions.
  — Demonstration on how class notes should be recorded. Effective teachers provide their students with a prepared note taking format to be used when recording class notes. If notebooks are required, these teachers instruct their students how to organize and use them.
  — Demonstrate how reading logs are to be prepared. These can be recorded on note cards of specific size. It is suggested that they contain these points:

    — Complete bibliography
    — List of key points
    — Conclusions

  — Distribute experimental data; have students read and interpret data and draw conclusions; discuss results at the end of this activity.
  — Present a set of questions and distribute several different references. Have students record their responses within a given period of time; discuss results.
  — Provide students with several similar statements on the same topic; have students draw conclusions germane to the sample statements; discuss outcome.

- These suggestions listed above are only a few ideas on how teachers can teach their students how to study. The time spent at the beginning of a course on this important topic will yield maximum results in the final analysis. Students must be taught to study effectively, to evaluate information, and to draw realistic conclusions. They must become self directional if they are to cope with life's problems and serve as a useful and purposeful citizen.

- Teachers monitor the class notes recorded by their students, both during study and when they are handed in for evaluation. These notes should be evaluated formally by the teacher. Students' performance should be communicated to the students.

- Effective teachers reinforce students' performance when the students do what is expected of them. Teachers provide positive enforcement for proper behavior and performance.

- The use of awards, contests, and other incentives can be utilized appropriately to recognize exemplary behavior.

Teaching students how to study and take notes will assist students in learning how to learn. "Learning how to learn" will be something students can use throughout their lives.

APPROVED PRACTICES

Numerous approved practices will, if properly utilized, make more effective use of supervised study. A list of the more effective practices serves as a quick review for what has been discussed in this chapter so far.
The teacher

1. uses supervised study only when it is the "best teaching tool for the job"

2. makes provisions on the teaching plan for supervised study

3. teaches students early in the course how to study and record notes

4. makes sure all students have paper and pencil prior to the start of the class

5. utilizes only relevant study questions which require thinking

6. informs students where answers can be found in the reference(s). Students should not have to review each and every page in a reference to find the correct answer

7. provides adequate reference materials which are up-to-date and readily available prior to the start of class

8. is well prepared and organized for supervised study

9. prepares the students for supervised study by providing a motivating introduction

10. utilizes a variety of techniques to assist students to obtain factual information such as field trips, resource persons, slides, video-tapes, etc.

11. circulates quietly throughout the classroom and provides assistance individually *only* when needed

12. keeps the classroom comfortable and neat

13. uses supervised study to develop positive student-teacher relations and to encourage the thinking process

14. maintains class control and prevents student distractions

15. provides additional questions or study activities for those students who finish supervised study before other students; this additional work is handled as an honor or award for extra credit.

16. provides adequate time for supervised study; the length of time should relate
    a. to the difficulty of subject matter, and
    b. to students' interest span

17. allows adequate time in the lesson to discuss answers to study questions in class and to draw conclusions

18. reinforces positive behavior of students who perform as expected

19. utilizes supervised study to develop effective and productive work habits in students

NOTE TAKING

One of the effective techniques that teachers employ to help make their teaching more student centered is the use of note taking or note-books. As with teaching the student how to study, teachers must teach students how to take class notes. This would include instruction on how to organize and utilize notes. The way in which notes are to be evaluated by the teacher should also be communicated to students. The task of note taking can be taught in association with teaching students how to study. In this manner, the psychological law of association comes into play since experiences which occur together tend to reoccur together. Supervised study and note taking are associated learning activities.

There are numerous approaches which teachers can employ to accomplish this task. Probably, the most simple system is the use of three hole punched notepaper for students to record class notes. Some teachers prefer their students to maintain a three ring, loose leaf notebook. A similar system would be the use of a spiral bound notebook. Whatever system a teacher decides to use, that system should be utilized consistently by the teacher and it should be considered as a vital part of the lesson delivery and be included in the evaluation.

Approved practices for organizing, utilizing, and evaluating students' notes are as follows:

1. The general format that students are to use to record class notes should be identified by the teacher at the beginning of the course

2. Evaluation standards for class notes should also be determined at the beginning of the course

3. Prior to the beginning of the course the teacher should order all necessary supplies for students to record class notes

4. Students should be taught how to organize their class notes during the first few days of the course

5. The teacher should take class time to instruct students in how to use class notes and reading logs

6. The teacher should require *all* students to record class notes

7. Class notes should be evaluated according to pre-established standards

8. Class notes should be evaluated at regular intervals

9. Students should be informed of their performance regarding class notes

10. Class note evaluations should be used in determining student performance, especially early in the course when students' work habits are being formed

Effective teachers realize that several educational advantages result when they stress note taking by students as part of the teaching-learning process. Note taking promotes more effective learning by providing

- evidence of what has been accomplished in the class or course
- information of value to the students
- a ready reference for students to use at the time of review or preparation for examinations
- an organized system of resources at students' disposal
- a take-home sample of what has been taught in the class or course
- a means for assessing student progress and performance
- a means for actively involving students in their own learning
- a practical approach for exhibiting the importance of note taking

The quality of students' notes will be directly proportionate to the emphasis the teacher places upon them. If students are told to take class notes and the teacher never refers to them again, the chances are that the quality and quantity of students' notes, in the aggregate, will be somewhat lacking. On the other hand, if students' notes are utilized and evaluated frequently and students are appraised of their performance based upon predetermined standards, the quality and quantity of students' notes will, in all probability, be more acceptable.

To illustrate the importance and value of note taking, effective teachers make application of class notes whenever possible and appropriate. Assuming students have been taught to record those key points evolving from each lesson, these teachers occasionally request, for evaluation, that the students, utilizing their own class notes, list or summarize the key points from each lesson for a specific unit of instruction or for a specific period of time. This technique is an excellent exercise to employ to reinforce the need for and value of complete and accurate class notes to be kept by the students.

SUMMARY

Helping students learn how to explore the unknown is one of the satisfactions effective teachers receive from their positive teaching. Teaching students how to study will help them discover new knowledges, skills and attitudes, values, and appreciations long after the teacher's influence over them has ceased. It is a teacher's obligation and responsibility to assist students to become their own scholars.

Supervised study, as pointed out in this chapter, serves many educational functions to make teaching more positive and learning more effective.

Suggestions and approved practices are offered whereby teachers can more effectively use supervised study to assist students to explore the unknown. Effective teachers employ many of the suggestions and practices contained in this chapter.

The need for and value of note taking as part of the teaching-learning process has been discussed in this chapter along with a list of approved practices for organizing, utilizing, and evaluating students' notes.

CHAPTER 16

Providing Relevant Practice

"Practice makes perfect" is an expression that is familiar to most people, especially those in the field of education. The statement implies that activity is essential if something is to be done or performed according to established standards.

The word "practice" has different meanings to different people. From an educational point of view, the term *practice* connotes the following:

- to do or perform frequently
- to form a habit
- to repeat to learn
- to put into practice
- to use a person's knowledge

Based upon the above connotations of practice, it is obvious that practice is a vital part of learning. In essence, the concept of practice implies "action to learn." It also implies drill. Drilling, as used in education, means repeated mental or physical exercise aimed at perfection through regular practice. Practice promotes the formation of habits. Once formed, the application of these habits results in the use of what has been learned. In the teaching-learning process, practice should not be confused with application of learning. Practice precedes application. Some educators believe practice is a form of application, however.

WHY IS PRACTICE IMPORTANT?

The concept of practice in learning is not new to educators. In fact, practice has been used as a learning technique from the beginning of recorded time.

Using practice in teaching and learning, the teacher applies some of the psychological laws and principles of learning. Specifically, the Law of Exercise ("The more often an act is repeated, the more quickly a habit is established") and the principle of learning ("Students learn more and better when they participate actively") are applied whenever practice is employed by the teacher.

The planned use of practice can lead to more effective learning on the part of students. People learn from what they do. For their learning to be longer lasting, practice is usually prerequisite to retention. Practice encourages repetition which promotes more permanent learning. Proper utilization of practice contributes to more effective learning.

Finally, the purpose of practice is to establish or formulate in the student correct habits which can be utilized in future endeavors.

HOW TO UTILIZE PRACTICE

Practice should be utilized by teachers for all three domains of learning. Likewise, practice, as used in this book, is as much a teaching technique as it is a learning activity. The teacher must control the content, timing, length, and distribution of the practice sessions. For practice to be effective, the teacher must skillfully control that practice.

Proper utilization of practice implies that practice is more than simple repetition. Indeed, practice, on the part of the students, must meet at least four criteria to be effective. These criteria are

1. Students must be actively involved in practice

2. Practice must be appropriate to meet the educational objectives

3. Practice must be timed so that it occurs immediately after instruction

4. Practice must be incremental over time

Active Practice

Effective teachers make certain that students are actively involved in practice. One does not learn to drive a car by reading about how to drive a car. For students to learn any subject, they must actively practice the content of the subject. Such practice must not only be active, but it must also be as realistic (similar) as possible to the actual setting in which learning is to be used. Since learning results in a behavioral change, students must practice the activity in order to learn. Practice is a part of learning and is critical to habit formation. Students must practice the behavior in order to form a habit; then they must continue to practice the behavior to *perfect* the habit.

Examples of ways to keep students actively involved in practice abound. The following few suggestions are listed as ideas and may stimulate others.

- Ask students questions
- Require responses to questions
- Assign written work
- Require sample problems to be solved
- Have students read and respond in writing or orally
- Set up laboratory exercises
- Use models, simulations, trainers, etc.
- Utilize computer simulations
- Review completed work to reinforce habit

Appropriate Practice

Student practice must not only be active but the practice must also help students to achieve the desired educational objectives of the instruction. Students must learn to utilize what they have learned if they are to use that new knowledge to make decisions or solve problems.

Effective teachers design practice sessions that deal with subject matter content and provide student activities which are appropriate to meeting the educational objectives of the lesson. For example, if the objective is for the students to determine the pH of a liquid by titration, students must actually perform the titration with appropriate equipment and materials. Listening to a lecture and taking notes while watching the teacher perform the titration does not constitute practice appropriate to determining pH of a liquid—it only constitutes practice appropriate to watching someone determining pH of a liquid! Similarly, a teacher may distribute various types of essays to a class and then ask students to determine the type of essay they were assigned. Students must determine the type of essay and write the reasons to justify their answer. These two activities, on the part of both teacher and students, could be followed by a discussion of type of essays used after the papers were evaluated. But the best form of practice would be for the students to write their own essay of the type that they had just evaluated.

Examples to illustrate appropriate practice are

- solving algebraic problems
- collecting and identifying types of biological specimens
- debating political alternatives
- balancing chemical equations
- reading and explaining literature
- acting out a drama
- utilizing laboratory exercises
- operating a piece of equipment

Practice which is appropriate to meet educational objectives must lead the student to improvement in the subject being practiced. Practice implies that the student gets better with practice, not simply repeats an activity over and over. Repetition implies performance exactly the same way time after time. It is critical that the student be taught correctly to avoid learning incorrectly a habit. Since learning results in behavioral changes, improvement must occur or positive learning has not resulted. To merely repeat an activity results in no vast improvement in student performance. Improved accuracy, speed, agility, competence, etc., must be the result of practice. As students practice, standards of acceptable performance usually increase. As students practice and their performance improves, they tend to better enjoy the activity they practice. As enjoyment increases, so does time devoted to practice, resulting in further practice and continued improvement. Hence, correct practice makes perfect.

Timing of Practice

Timing of practice does not mean forcing students to perform tasks within a time limit. Rather, the concept of timing of practice means the proximity of student practice sessions to the actual time of instruction. Ideally, practice should occur immediately after instruction. In fact, teachers should consider practice to be an integral part of instruction, rather than a separate activity. Practice should be used by teachers so that students practice to learn rather than simply practicing that which has been learned. It is in the application stage that what has been learned is put to use for both personal enjoyment and constructive purposes.

Effective teachers plan practice sessions as a regular part of instruction. By utilizing the appropriate combination of informational lessons and operational lessons which include sufficient practice time, these teachers have students practice in order to learn. Student practice should occur as closely as possible to the time the teacher explains and/or demonstrates the subject matter which is to practiced.

A few examples to illustrate how timing of practice can be used include the following.

- Working sample problems on the chalkboard; assigning a problem set due at the end of the class period
- Demonstrating how to boot up a computer program; then assigning students to boot up specific programs
- Demonstrating techniques used to dissect a specimen; then having students individually dissect the assigned specimen

Incremental Practice

Effective teachers, when planning practice sessions, spread these practice sessions over a period of time. A series of relatively short practice sessions are preferable to and are more effective than a single extended practice session. A series of class periods can be ideal for practice sessions to develop or formulate desired habits of students.

For example, it is more effective for students to practice a foreign language for a portion of a class period over a period of weeks than to practice for a two or three hour block of time once per week. Likewise, it is preferable for math students to practice a series of problems which illustrate a concept over a sequence of time, rather than an extensive number of problems in a single large block of time.

It must be pointed out that a scheduled sequence of practice sessions avoids "burn out" in students which can lead to errors in procedure, discontent with subject matter, and avoidance of further practice. In addition, a scheduled sequence of practice sessions also allows for teacher supervision of practice on an individual basis.

Examples for implementation include

- Planning for "laboratory exercise" in which practice sessions are spread over time
- Having students recite what is to be learned at the beginning of class each day
- Using a daily twenty minute "spell down" technique for learning correct verb tenses
- Allowing time to develop "key boarding skills," instead of concentrating all of it into the first few days of class

SUPERVISION OF PRACTICE

In order for a teacher to ensure that the four criteria of effective practice are implemented and utilized, supervision of student practice is essential. It is the teacher's duty to see that the conditions which lead to *correct practice* are in place. It is just as easy for students to practice and develop *incorrect* habits as it is for them to practice and develop correct ones. Effective teachers supervise students before those errors become habitual. Supervision of practice allows the teacher to maintain a positive learning environment, to be sensitive to active involvement of students in practice, to assess the appropriateness of practice in meeting educational objectives, to monitor the timing of practice, and to schedule the spacing of practice over time.

SUMMARY

To ensure that teachers provide experiences for students to obtain correct practice, they must remember that practice requires students to be actively engaged in the task; that practice must be appropriate for the attainment of the educational objectives; that practice must be timed in such a fashion that it occurs subsequent to, or is part of, instruction; and that practice sessions are designed to be of a duration to maximize learning and minimize fatigue and other distracting influences. Finally, student practice must be supervised by the teacher so that errors are minimized and efficiency of performance is improved.

CHAPTER 17

Conducting Demonstrations

Teachers need to be effective in using demonstrations. Anyone who desires to develop psychomotor skills in students should employ this instructional methodology. Many teachers attempt to teach skills to students such as keyboarding, laboratory techniques, athletic moves, welding, playing a musical instrument, auto repair, using a sophisticated analytical instrument, operating machinery, or using a microscope by just "telling students how to."

The demonstration is a teaching method which utilizes the operational teaching plan described previously in this book, along with operation sheets, plans, drawings, or models to teach students how to perform specific skills and techniques. The demonstration consists of a specific sequence of teacher activities, not just simply showing students how to perform a skill. Hence, the demonstration method can be replicated in a variety of settings and situations to accomplish specific educational objectives.

It is not sufficient for the teacher to simply "show and tell" students how to perform a certain task, skill, or operation and then assume the students can satisfactorily perform the technique. "Showing and telling" do not constitute teaching any more than "watching and listening" constitutes learning. Yet, if done correctly, showing—watching and telling—and listening can be a part of the method used to bring about learning.

WHY IS DEMONSTRATING IMPORTANT?

Most teachers actually teach a number of skills; certainly, some more than others. Whenever the teacher plans to have students learn to perform motor skills, techniques, manipulations, etc., the demonstration method is the most effective method to be used.

This method of teaching is the method of choice in teaching motor skills. The reason is clear, because these skills involve movement of muscles in the feet, legs, fingers, hands, and/or arms. In addition, coordination with the eyes is usually required for successful performance. The ultimate development of competence in performance results in the formation of habit. And the formation of those habits in students as identified in the educational objectives becomes the goal of the teacher. So the first step in the development of that habit is the demonstration, where the task may be seen to be correctly done.

In order to develop motor skills, the student must be actively involved in the practice (performance) of those motor skills. Following observation of the demonstration, motor skill development progresses from deliberate "first attempts" to efficient performance habit through instruction by the teacher and practice by the student. Clearly, the term "practice" does not simply mean repetition. Since the goal of the teacher is to help students to develop those habits as efficiently as possible, the demonstration teaching method should be utilized.

The demonstration method of teaching is the procedural part of the operational teaching plan as discussed in Chapter 6. The actual demonstration occurs immediately after the introduction to the lesson. Good teaching practice includes the introduction followed by the instructional procedures:

- Demonstration by the teacher
- Practice by the students; supervision by the teacher
- Application of motor skills
- Evaluation of students' level of competence in performance

A quality demonstration requires both preparation and presentation in order to be effective. The actual demonstration method is so clear and straightforward that it may seem simplistic and impossible to make errors. Even so, veteran teachers often fail in presenting demonstrations because they omit certain details in the preparation and/or presentation of a demonstration.

PREPARING DEMONSTRATIONS

The preparation phase of this teaching method is equally as important as the presentation phase of the demonstration. Prior to presenting the demonstration, the teacher must prepare for the demonstration. Preparation for a demonstration includes

- Identifying educational objectives of an operational nature
- Placing the demonstration in a setting which approximates the real setting
- Determining the correct length of time needed
- Organizing the steps of procedure
- Developing an operation sheet (list of steps and procedures)
- Matching the complexity of the motor skill to the capability of the students
- Arranging at least *two* sets of all necessary materials/consumable supplies
- Arranging correct tools, equipment, instruments, etc., within convenient reach
- Reviewing safety precautions including safety suggestions for clothing where appropriate
- Rehearsing required techniques and steps of procedure
- Locating seats/student stations where students can see and hear clearly
- Arranging an adequate number of equipped student stations for practice

The preparation phase of the demonstration is crucial and must be completed prior to the class period in which the presentation phase of the demonstration occurs.

PRESENTING DEMONSTRATIONS

The presentation phase of this method occurs in an educational setting with students in a class observing and participating. The introduction part of the lesson should occur as discussed previously. The introduction of an operational lesson should be used to accomplish the following:

- Develop interest and motivate students
- Identify the educational objectives
- Point out the importance of the motor skill to be learned
- Explain important points to be observed
- Relate the motor skill to all appropriate prior informational lessons
- Relate the motor skill to uses in subsequent lessons

STEPS IN CONDUCTING DEMONSTRATION

The procedure for conducting the actual demonstration occurs in three steps which were identified elsewhere in this book. These steps are

Step 1.   Teacher does and tells.

Step 2.   Teacher does and student tells,

OR

Student does and teacher tells,

OR

Student does and tells.

(NOTE: At the conclusion of this step, the teacher distributes an operation sheet or set of instructions. A sample operation sheet is shown on the next page).

Step 2 provides the teacher with several choices in the demonstration procedure. The teacher may choose one of the three options: teacher does and tells, student does and teacher tells, or student does and student tells. Whichever option the teacher selects will increase the student's ability to acquire the habit or learn the skill. However, one choice may serve the teacher's needs better than the other two. Each option may be best suited for particular situations giving it a competitive advantage for selection.

Step 3.   Students practice under supervision.

First Step

The first step of the demonstration requires the teacher to perform (demonstrate) the motor skill while explaining the important steps in-

OPERATION SHEET

UNIT:

JOB OR EXERCISE: _____

TOOLS AND EQUIPMENT   MATERIALS REQUIRED

                             REFERENCES

WHAT TO DO (STEPS)	HOW TO DO IT (KEY POINTS)

volved. This allows students to see as well as hear the technique performed at its normal speed. During Step One of the demonstration (Teacher Does and Tells), the following approved practices should be observed and employed.

- Face and address the students
- Speak clearly and distinctly
- Perform steps at correct pace (speed)
- Perform steps in proper sequence
- Perform steps accurately
- Perform the motor skill at least to the same standard that students will be held (required to perform)
- Ask questions to check understanding
- Stress safety precautions
- Stay on the subject at hand
- Dress appropriately for the task
- Wear appropriate safety gear
- Stress details/key points
- Use realia to supplement the demonstration
- Answer questions from students after the teacher "does and tells"

Second Step

The second step of the demonstration allows the students to see and hear the technique performed again, this time with some variation of personnel and usually at a slightly slower pace. Step two of the demonstration method may be accomplished by using a combination of the teacher and a carefully selected student demonstrator. Hence, a second set of consumable supplies will be required as pointed out earlier in the discussion of the preparation phase of the demonstration. During Step two (teacher does—student tells, *OR* student does—teacher tells, *OR* student does and tells) of the demonstration, the following details must be observed and employed.

- Select and call on (assign) a student demonstrator with at least average ability.
- Explain to student demonstrator exactly what the teacher expects the student to do.

- Instruct the class members to observe and call to the teacher's attention any errors in procedure.
- Stay close to student demonstrator in case it becomes necessary to intervene.
- Be certain that all steps are performed accurately.
- Be certain that as steps are performed, the teacher or the student demonstrator verbalizes the actions.
- Upon completion of the action, ask questions to check understanding.
- Summarize key points of the demonstration.
- Solicit questions from students.
- Distribute operation sheets prior to individual student practice.

Third Step

The third step of the demonstration provides for individual student practice of the motor skill to be learned. This part of the demonstration employs those learning principles incorporated in the discussion of "Providing Relevant Practice (see Chapter 16).

During Step three of the demonstration students practice under supervision of the teacher. The following details must be observed and employed:

- Provide for student practice immediately after the demonstration
- Provide sufficient student stations in appropriate learning centers to accommodate all students
- Refrain from holding up progress of the entire class for a few who may not understand
- Circulate to each student in a rotation to individualize teacher's supervision
- Give individualized instruction to those students not progressing satisfactorily
- Check accuracy of performance of each student
- Require each student to submit a completed exercise or job where applicable, *or*
- Require each student to demonstrate mastery of performance where applicable

EXAMPLE 1

Examples to illustrate both the preparation and presentation stages of a demonstration of laboratory technique are outlined below. It must be remembered that the preparation stage is a teacher activity which occurs without student participation and prior to the presentation of the presentation stage.

Preparation Stage

Objective: To dissect a complete perfect flower

Class: Freshman Biology—twenty-five students

Location: High School Biology Laboratory

Estimated Time: Ten to fifteen minutes

Materials needed for demonstration:

28 rose blossoms	12 microscopes
26 forceps	26 labeling pens
26 scalpels	26 operation/assign-
27 microscope slides	ment sheets

Safety precautions: Proper handling and use of scalpels
                      Safe learning environment

Set up: Arrange student seats in a semicircle around a portable laboratory station or table with visibility to all materials and equipment.

Set up correct number of work stations (25) with the following materials and equipment: one forceps, one scalpel, one slide, and a labeling pen. These work stations may be located in another classroom or laboratory.

Rehearsing: Arrange one set of materials and equipment prior to the presentation stage of the demonstration. The teacher should use one blossom to rehearse the technique to be sure that the teacher is proficient in demonstrating the task at hand.

Presentation Stage

Teacher does
and tells:
The teacher performs each step correctly and accurately in proper sequence while explaining clearly and distinctly the key points to each step and then stressing safety precautions associated with the skill being developed.

NOTE: Use the second rose blossom for this step.

Student does and
Teacher tells:

- One student of average ability is called upon to perform the technique using the same equipment that the teacher used. NOTE: A third blossom is used.
- Give directions to the student on precisely what the teacher wants the student to do.
- Instruct the observing class members to point out steps, safety precautions, and key points.
- The "selected" student performs each step correctly and accurately in proper sequence as the teacher explains clearly and distinctly the steps and key points along with stressing the safety precautions associated with the skill being developed.
- Observing students monitor the demonstrating student's steps, key points, and safety precautions and add to explanation, if applicable.
- Teacher then asks for questions and distributes the Operation sheets and assigns students to specific work stations which have been previously arranged with proper materials and equipment.

Students practice
under supervision:

- Students then practice the skill while teacher circulates and supervises each student in rotation to individualize instruction.
- Teacher evaluates accuracy and mastery of performance.
- Teacher collects completed Operation sheets for grading, if applicable.

EXAMPLE 2

Another example is outlined below to illustrate the preparation and presentation stages of a demonstration designed to teach performance of an athletic skill.

Preparation Stage

Objective: To properly and legally execute an underhand bad-
                   minton serve.

Class: Elementary School Physical Education—twenty stu-
                   dents

Location: Elementary School Gym

Time: ten minutes

Materials needed for demonstration:
                   22 official badminton rackets
                   11 shuttlecocks
                   Official badminton courts with regulation nets

Safety precautions: Provide enough room for all students to practice
                   safely, free of hazardous situations.

Set up: Set up enough courts with nets and provide enough
                   rackets and shuttlecocks for each student to practice
                   the activity.

Rehearsing: The teacher should practice the serve so it can be per-
                   formed skillfully during the demonstration.

Presentation Stage

Teacher does   The teacher performs each step correctly and accu-
and tells: rately in proper sequence while explaining clearly
                   and distinctly the key points to each step and stress-
                   ing safety precautions associated with the skill being
                   developed.

Student does and
Teacher tells:

- One student of average ability is called upon to perform the skill.
- Give directions to the student on precisely what the teacher wants the student to do.
- Instruct the observing class members to point out steps, safety precautions, and key points.
- The "selected" student performs each step correctly and accurately in proper sequence as the teacher explains clearly and distinctly the steps and key points along with stressing the safety precautions associated with the skill being developed.
- Observing students monitor the demonstrating student's steps, key points, and safety precautions and add to explanation, if applicable.
- Teacher then asks for questions.
- Teacher assigns students two per court. These courts have been set up with proper materials and equipment prior to the demonstration.

Students practice
under supervision:

- Students then practice the skill while the teacher circulates and supervises each student in a rotation to individualize instruction.
- Teacher evaluates accuracy of performance and mastery of performance.

SELF TEST

The checksheet shown in Figure 17.1 can be used by a teacher as a self test to analyze how well certain criteria are incorporated into a teaching demonstration.

SUMMARY

The demonstration is the predominate methodology used in lessons which employ the Operational Teaching Plan in an effort to help students learn motor skills. The demonstration, when used subsequent to a stimulating introduction, allows students to both see and hear how to perform

DEMONSTRATION EVALUATION CHECKSHEET

Date: _____   Teacher: _____

Title of Demonstration: _____

CRITERIA	Excellent	Very Good	Good	Fair	Poor	None
1. State the problem and identify importance of skills						
2. Obtain interest of students						
3. All necessary materials ready						
4. Use questions to draw upon informational lesson						
5. Know the subject						
6. Stress the key points						
7. Performed skillfully						
8. Apply the 3-step demonstration technique						
9. Stress safety						
10. Time required						

Figure 17.1   Teacher's Self Test Checksheet

the selected motor skill, job, and/or operation. The demonstration method incorporates the aspects of practice so that students practice in order to learn to perform the motor skill. Effective teachers utilize the demonstration method of teaching to provide more effective learning for their students.

CHAPTER 18

Using Field Oriented Learning

Teaching and learning are not confined to a classroom or the school laboratory situation. The teaching-learning process can occur whenever there is interaction between a teacher and a learner. Instruction which takes place in the community often results in more effective learning.

Throughout this book, it has been stressed that student and community needs should be satisfied. It has also been emphasized that the most effective learning environment is the one which yields the greatest amount of behavior modification. The value in providing true to life educational experiences for students has also been advocated. Oftentimes the best learning environment exists outside the school setting.

Field-oriented learning connotes the use of community resources to provide more suitable learning environments than can be afforded at the school. Many educators would refer to field-oriented learning as "community based" instruction. The concept of "community" encompasses both the use of community resources to promote learning and the need for education to address community concerns if positive educational experiences are to be provided students. Without a doubt, the use of "community" adds utility and substance to students' educational experiences.

COMMUNITY BASED INSTRUCTION

Community based instruction provides numerous educational opportunities for both students and teachers. The quality of educational experiences is augmented because real life teaching situations are employed. Whenever these types of situations are utilized by teachers, the educational experiences become more relevant, more interesting, and longer lasting for students. On-site observations, actual experiences, experiments, and field trips are some of the more common and readily available field oriented learning opportunities for use by teachers to promote the most suitable educational experiences for their students.

On-Site Observations

The community, broadly defined, provides many opportunities for students to observe firsthand actual procedures and processes employed in public and private enterprises. Community businesses and government offices can provide students opportunity for direct observations on how these function. Opportunities to observe selected cultural, artistic, social, and civic activities inherent in the community are afforded those students whose teachers utilize field oriented learning. What better way to expose students to art than have them visit an art museum? Teachers of drama, theater, history, music, science, etc., have unlimited opportunities to provide their students actual on-site observations.

Needless to say, on-site observations should only be utilized when this technique is the best means to achieve the educational intent of the lesson. While observing, students should be required to become actively involved by answering specific questions, by solving problems, by noting relationships, by comparing and evaluating, by drawing conclusions, etc., as a result of the observation. If the students are to receive maximum benefits from on-site observations, they must become involved to a greater extent than just "viewing" what is being performed. Students must be responsible for completing educational activities associated with on-site observations.

Student Experiences

As with on-site observations, numerous opportunities exist in the community for students to gain actual experiences. Resourceful teachers identify those experiential opportunities available which complement their discipline and then involve their students whenever appropriate to promote the most positive learning experiences.

The opportunities teachers have to provide actual student experiences in the community are only limited to the teachers' own resourcefulness. As has been pointed out in this book, students learn by their own activity. There is no better way for students to learn actual practices, operations, and processes than to participate first hand.

Placement of students in actual businesses, stores, and offices in the community requires ample planning on the part of the teacher. Placement agreements and placement experience plans must be developed cooperatively between the businessess, the students, their parents or guardians, and the teacher. Safety regulations and labor laws must be discussed and understood. The actual experiences to be gained as a result of the student experience program must be identified and agreed upon by all parties concerned.

Experiments

Due to the limited resources available in most school settings, adequate facilities and resources may not exist to provide students the opportunity to conduct large scale experiments such as actual field trials. Those teachers who are aware of what is happening in their community can oftentimes locate opportunities whereby their students can become actively involved in the planning, conducting, and/or evaluation of experiments and experiences in industry settings.

This type of community based instruction should, however, be approached with caution by the teacher. While these opportunities can serve a very beneficial educational purpose, they can also become the "tail wagging the dog." They can become extremely time consuming. It may not always be possible for the teacher to have access to the students when actual experimental events occur since students may be committed to other activities or just not available to participate in the experiment at the actual time it is being conducted.

The health and safety of the students must be of prime consideration. The opportunity to participate in community based experiments may occur; however, each situation must be assessed to ascertain whether it would be in the best interest of the students to participate.

PARENTAL INVOLVEMENT

Although not directly related to community oriented education, it seems appropriate at this point to discuss briefly parental involvement in the educational process.

The value of involving parents (or guardians) in the education of their students cannot be over stressed. Education should be a cooperative venture. The student, the parents, and the school, through the teacher, all play a critical role if the student is to receive the best education possible. Effective teachers resort to every opportunity available to involve the students' parents in the education of their children.

Why is parental involvement in the student's education so critical? Reflect for a moment on the actual number of hours per week or month the typical student spends at school and the number of hours away from school. It is obvious why it is important to a student's education that those people who influence the student's learning "away from school" be aware of and involved with the student's "at school" educational pursuits. It could be possible for peoples' influence upon a student's "away from school" time to wipe out (void) everything that student might have learned "at school," particularly those elements associated with the affective domain of learning. As a point of illustration, parents must reinforce the standards of performance expected at school. Failure to do so results in conflict and dissention when students are in school.

Parent-teacher conferences, open houses, parent volunteer projects, school fairs, and parent-teacher organizations are some programs used by teachers to involve parents in the education of their children. Even colleges and universities sponsor "Parent Days" to encourage parents to visit their campuses.

In essence, whenever parents develop a pride in and a concern for their student's education and assume an active responsibility for providing the most positive support possible, students benefit and their education flourishes.

FIELD TRIPS (Field Classes)

Probably the most widely used field oriented learning is the field trip, referred to as "field classes" by some educators. If properly planned and conducted, a field trip can be a very effective teaching tool. However, field trips should be used by teachers only when they provide the best learning environment to achieve the educational objective(s) sought. Teachers should never take a field trip for the sake of "taking a field trip."

Educational Functions of Field Trips

Field trips serve several educational functions. They

- add variety to teaching and learning, thus relieving the monotony of strictly classroom instruction
- stimulate student interest by increasing involvement and use of senses
- provide opportunities for gaining new experiences not possible elsewhere
- provide participating experiences which help increase retention of learning
- promote the effective use of teacher and students' time
- help develop more thorough understanding on the part of the student

Approved Practices

In order for a field trip to serve as an effective teaching method to achieve predetermined educational objectives, teachers should follow specific guidelines when planning, conducting, and following up or evaluating such learning activities. Referring to the following situation, consider what approved practices should have been followed to make this field trip a positive learning experience for students, assuming the teacher had decided that a field trip was the best method to use for the predetermined learning objectives?

Case Situation

The teacher rushes into a class a few minutes late without any evidence of plans for teaching. The teacher states "We are going to start a new unit of instruction." The students are hurried out of the classroom without directions. Students have no time to collect paper, pencils, coats, etc. The group of students arrives at the field trip site before the resource person arrives. The teacher says to the resource person, "Well, here we are!" It is obvious that the resource person is unprepared for the group. The explanation of the resource person is out of the realm of the students' comprehension. Some students begin to misbehave. The teacher cuts the field trip short, allowing the students no time to ask questions or to thank the resource person. The students return to the classroom where the teacher gives the students an assignment to write up what they learned. A school administrator is waiting at the classroom door for an explanation of where the class has been!

Would the above described field trip have been more effective if the following approved practices had been adhered to?

- *In planning a field trip the teacher should*
    1. determine what educational objectives are to be achieved
    2. make prior arrangements with school administrators relative to
        - leaving school grounds
        - transportation
        - adhering to school policies
    3. contact the resource person well in advance to establish the date and time the field trip will occur
    4. prepare a "field trip outline" which details the educational objectives and what students are expected to do at the time of the field trip; the outline could contain a list of questions to be answered or specific procedures to observe
    5. explain what is expected to the resource person a few days in advance of the field trip; a copy of the "field trip outline" should be left with the resource person

- *In conducting a field trip the teacher should*

    1. prepare the students for the field trip by reviewing the regulations

and procedures to be followed on the field trip; if safety is a concern, safety precautions must be reviewed

recognize that student behavior reflects upon the school and the teacher; students should be reminded at the time of each field trip that they are
- to stay in a group
- to listen to the resource person
- to be polite
- to have neccesary materials
- to ask pertinent questions
- to thank the resource person
2. make certain students have pencil, clipboard, field trip outline, proper clothing, and safety protection.
3. use school transportation; using school transportation keeps students together, lessens the teacher's risk, provides an opportunity for last minute instructions and allows the teacher to summarize the field trip with the students on the return back to school
4. assure that a businesslike manner is used during the field trip
5. make certain that all students can hear and see the resource person or the process or procedure(s) being shown
6. thank the resource person before leaving the field trip site

- *In following up and evaluating a field trip the teacher should*

1. have each student prepare a report based upon the field trip outline; these reports should be turned in and graded
2. evaluate the effectiveness of the field trip with the students
3. give an oral report on the field trip to the school administration
4. write a "thank you" note to the resource person

If properly planned and conducted, field trips can be valuable teaching tools for teachers to provide positive educational experiences for their students.

Since it is not possible to demonstrate how to plan, conduct, and evaluate an effective field trip through the printed page, only a form can be provided which teachers may use to evaluate those field trips they take. Through evaluation, they can discover weaknesses, if any, and then employ those approved practices necessary to improve their future field trips. Figure 18.1 shows a form for the evaluation of a field trip.

EVALUATION OF A FIELD TRIP IN _____

Problem _____ Date _____

Teacher _____ Observer _____

(Use back of sheet for evaluation of class as a whole)

1. Was the aim or purpose clear and educationally sound?
2. Was the aim accomplished?
3. Was the trip well planned so that all arrangements for observation were complete before the trip began?
4. Were plans for the trip made sufficiently in advance to permit proper class preparation for the trip?
5. Was the class instructed about what to observe and what questions to ask?
6. Did the students help to decide what was to be looked for?
7. Were proper directions given about the procedure for making the observation?
8. Was the observation procedure carried out by the students?
9. Were the students well organized for the observation trip?
10. How well were the students directed and supervised when making their observations?
11. Was opportunity given for actual practice?
12. Could such a trip be organized better for practice?
13. What use was made of questions while on the trip?
14. To what extent did students use notebooks to retain facts?
15. Was the class discussion held in the most effective time and place?
16. Were conclusions drawn? _____. If so, were the students required to bring all their observations into use when drawing conclusions?
17. What precautions were taken to avoid accidents in traveling?
18. Was the conduct of the class members above reproach at all times?
19. Was proper courtesy and appreciation shown toward the party who supplied facilities for the field class?
20. Could the problem have been taught more effectively by some other type of class activity? _____. If so, what activity would you suggest?

Figure 18.1   Field Trip Evaluation Form

SUMMARY

Field oriented learning has a definite role to play in the delivery of positive educational experiences for students. The use of this type of learning promotes active involvement on the part of students, adds variety to teaching and learning, stimulates students' interest, improves retention of what was learned, and contributes to real life teaching-learning situations.

Field oriented learning should only be used when it is the best means to achieve the sought educational objectives. It should *never* be used to "get out of going to school." The teacher must thoroughly prepare if learning activities of this nature are to be employed. The health and safety of the students must be carefully considered prior to involving students in this type of activity.

Since students spend considerably more time away from school than they spend at school, their parents and/or guardians must be actively involved in the students' education.

Finally, the approved practices for planning, conducting, and evaluating field classes (trips) are highlighted in this chapter. Field classes can be very effective in promoting positive teaching and effective learning.

CHAPTER 19

Using Realia to Visualize Learning

The concept that people learn with their own involvement has been a common theme throughout this book. Effective teachers employ "anything and everything" at their disposal to assist people to learn more and better. They encourage student learning through the use of instructional realia whenever possible.

To help illustrate the above point, reference is made to two case situations.

Case Situation #1

A teacher is teaching a lesson on "Leaf Types" to thirty-one freshman biology students. His interest approach is to state that the lesson for today is "Leaf Types." He instructs the students to open the textbook to page 114, the chapter which deals with leaves, and read the first six pages. He then distributes two handouts, one with a list of terms to be defined and another with drawings of a simple and a compound leaf with instructions for students to identify the parts.

Case Situation #2

The teacher in the neighboring classroom is also teaching a lesson on "Leaf Types" to thirty-one freshmen biology students. The teacher walks into the room carrying branches cut from an oak tree and a willow tree. She also has a corn plant and a bean plant. She places the various plant materials in front of the classroom, begins to pluck leaves from the oak branch and distributes them to students about the classroom. She then asks questions about the shape and structure of the leaf. Next, she asks questions which require the students to compare and contrast the various types of leaves she brought to class. After such discussion, she points out that the lesson today focuses on "Leaf Types."

Think about these two situations! In which situation would the students be more likely to have a greater interest in learning the subject? Which situation provides a more vivid learning experience? Which one probably creates more enthusiasm to learn? Which scenario involved the students' senses of touch and perhaps smell in addition to their senses of sight and hearing? Obviously, the second situation is designed to be the answer to all the above. The difference between the two cases is extreme but certainly not unrealistic. Such differences occur daily in classrooms across the country. It is obvious that the use of realia was the main difference between the two situations described above. The effective use of instructional realia to visualize learning is the central focus of this chapter.

Instructional realia, as used in this book, are the *sum total* of all resource materials including real situations, direct experiences, and activities used by teachers to relate instruction to real life. Realia are teaching tools in the teacher's "tool chest" which, if used correctly, enable the teacher to teach more effectively and the learner to learn more permanently. Realia are real things and/or real activities employed by the teacher to relate learning experiences to the real world.

The use of the term "realia" goes beyond, yet includes, the traditional concept of audiovisual aids. A quick list of what is referred to as realia includes transparencies, pictures, filmstrips, audio tapes, field trips, videotapes, bulletin and flannel boards, models, slides, cut-aways, mock-ups, real materials, resource people, specimens, CAD programs, real experiences, laboratory apparatus, etc., etc.

Motivation makes students want to interact and learn. Teachers can activate motivation by relying on some of the basic human needs, desires, and impulses. For example, curiosity is present in nearly every student, as is a desire to participate in something new. The need for new experiences is an important factor affecting motivation. If a teacher can capture and guide the basic needs, desires, and impulses of students and use any and all instructional tools available, motivation can be exhibited on the part of the students. When teachers bring instruction to life by using audio, visual and real materials and experiences, they are employing tactics to take advantage of those basic needs, desires, and impulses. Audio, visual, tactile, real, and resource materials can all be utilized to provide new experiences for students.

It has been continually pointed out in this book that learning is an active process. The effective teacher, thus, plans a series and a variety of participatory experiences for the students. The more participation, action, and use of senses on the part of the students, the more residual learning will take place. Realia are the aggregate of all resources available to promote the use of more senses, more involvement, and more action.

WHY IS THE USE OF REALIA IMPORTANT?

Why use realia in instruction? It takes valuable time and effort to collect, develop, prepare, and use realia! Is it worth it? For several reasons realia should be utilized to make teaching more positive and learning more effective. If properly used, realia can

- enable the teacher to focus the attention of students upon the lesson
- stimulate student interest in the topics to be taught
- assist the teacher to apply the principles of learning
- minimize abstractness of the learning experience
- promote the retention of competencies taught
- involve actively students in the participation in their own learning
- promote more interaction in the teaching-learning process
- make the teacher more effective in delivering positive learning experiences for students

EDUCATIONAL FUNCTIONS SERVED BY REALIA

Instructional realia serve many useful functions in the teaching-learning process.

- Realia enable the teacher to provide a variety of learning experiences for students, thereby adding interest to the instruction and thus increasing learning effectiveness
- Realia help speed up the learning process and make it more pleasant for the students
- Realia, if properly used, prevent the "pooling of ignorance" where incorrect or false information is learned
- Realia arouse interest, provide the concept of physical characteristics, show detail, develop appreciation and understanding, span time and distance, add variety to teaching, save time, and present related information, among other things.

The end results of using realia in teaching include

- greater student interest
- more thorough understanding
- increased retention
- more effective use of both the teacher's and the student's time

In essence, realia, when used by an effective teacher, contribute to positive learning.

HOW TO USE REALIA

Chapter 5 of this book discussed six principles of learning.

> Students learn more and better when
> - there is interest,
> - needs are being satisfied,
> - thinking is stimulated,
> - there is active participation,
> - two or more senses are used, and
> - a favorable climate of success is maintained.

Realia can be used by the teacher to implement all six principles of learning.

How can a teacher use realia to create interest? Does showing students real specimens arouse interest? How much interest is created when a new bulletin board or a new exhibit is placed in the classroom? How does the use of realia help a teacher satisfy student needs? Does helping students earn money, letting them actually perform a technique or use judgment help fulfill their needs? Can teachers stimulate thinking by posing a problem or by showing an item that does not work and letting the students figure the solution? How can students participate? If they touch, handle, do, disassemble, assemble, design, debate, question, calculate, seek, or operate are they not participating and are not many senses involved? The use of a variety of realia contributes to maintaining a positive climate of success by involving students. It should be obvious that realia can be used effectively to apply the principles of learning.

Further evidence which supports the use of realia to make teaching more positive can be gleaned from Dale's Cone of Educational Experiences [1], shown in Figure 19.1. Learning effectiveness decreases with an

Figure 19.1   The Cone of Educational Experiences

increase in abstractness. Conversely, the more participating experiences (action) focused upon the student, the greater the learning effectiveness, all things considered. A teacher, therefore, can realize the role of realia in enhancing the teaching-learning process.

The use of realia can help teachers apply, among other things, the six basic principles of learning by minimizing the degree of abstractness of educational experiences and promoting the retention of information and development of skills.

EXAMPLES OF USE

The O.P.E. Concept was discussed in Chapter 7 as it related to putting a complete lesson together. This concept stresses the fact that every lesson has an "opening," a "procedure," and an "ending." The Introduction to the lesson is the opening, the delivery of the lesson refers to the procedures used, and the conclusion is the ending of the lesson. These constitute the three main phases (parts) of a lesson.

These are illustrated as follows:

- Introduction (Building a Case for Learning)
     focusing attention
     stimulating interest

- Procedure
     answering questions
     analyzing problems
     demonstrating techniques

- Conclusion
     reviewing key points
     summarizing the lesson
     applying content to reality

Realia which are effective for use in each part of the lesson are shown below. Flexibility and creativity can and should be employed to meet the needs, desires, interests, and impulses of students while meeting the educational objectives.

Introduction	Procedure	Conclusion
Real materials	Demonstrations	Field trips
Models	Video recorder	Overhead trans-
Exhibits	Field trips	parencies
Overhead trans-	Motion pictures	Slides
parencies	Resource people	Chalkboard
Slides	Overhead trans-	Graphs and charts
Filmstrips	parencies	Real experiences
Chalkboard	Slides	Flannel board
Bulletin board	Still pictures	
Charts and graphs	Audio tape recorder	
Still pictures	Radio	
Video tapes	Chalkboard	
	Charts and graphs	
	Books	
	Bulletins, magazines	
	Real experiences	
	Computer simulations	
	Flannel board	
	Laboratory	

Since the interest span of students is approximately one minute per year of age, several different realia should be used in a fifty to fifty-five minute class period.

APPROVED PRACTICES

Several approved practices will, if properly utilized, improve the teacher's ability to effectively use realia to help students visualize learning. Some of the more valuable practices to be considered are listed below.

1. Plan in advance to use realia.

2. Select appropriate realia to use.

3. Understand and adhere to policies governing the use of realia, including budgeting for and using and operating equipment.

4. Review all realia before using.

5. Establish a coding and storage system so realia can be easily located and used in subsequent classes.

6. Provide an adequate number of realia for all students in the class.

7. If only one or two realia are to be used, be sure objects are large enough to be seen by all students.

8. Use a variety of realia.

9. Use appropriate up-to-date realia.

10. Use realia in every lesson.

11. Do not expect realia alone to do the complete job of teaching.

12. Do not use realia at an inappropriate time in lesson.

13. Do not allow realia, e.g., bulletin boards, to be left up too long in the classroom.

14. Get "mileage" out of realia. Ask at least three oral questions before setting the object aside.

15. Do not over use realia.

16. Do not leave realia laying around classroom or laboratory. Store realia in proper place after using.

17. Establish an inventory of necessary realia for each unit of instruction.

Use the form found in Figure 19.2 as an effective means to establish and maintain an inventory of all realia for teaching a specific unit of instruction.

SOME FINAL CHECKS

When evaluating realia for use in instruction, a teacher needs to appraise many aspects. Simply because an item is readily available does not constitute sufficient reason to use it if the item does not help to meet objectives. The list of questions below are presented to assist a teacher in appraising the utility of realia.

• Does the content match my lesson objective(s)?
• Will the material fit with the instructional method(s) I plan to use?

REALIA
FOR TEACHING A UNIT ON:

_____ Number of days _____

Textbooks: (Title, Author, Chapter, or Pages)

_____
_____
_____

Bulletins: (Title, Source, Pages)

_____
_____

Film, Filmstrips, Slides: (Title & Source, Time & Cost)

_____
_____
_____

Charts, Flannel Boards, Tack Boards & Pictures:

_____
_____
_____

Tools & Equipment:

_____
_____
_____

Overhead Transparencies & Handout Materials:

_____
_____
_____

Real Materials & Specimens:

_____
_____

Field Trips: (Location & Contact Person)

_____
_____

Resource People: (Topic & Address & Phone number)

_____
_____

Suggestions For Next Year:

_____
_____
_____
_____

Figure 19.2   Realia Inventory Form

- Is the content up to date? . . . totally? . . . in part?
- Is the content logically sequenced?
- Is the material appropriate for the grade level of my students?
- Can each of my students handle the vocabulary used?
- Will this material motivate each of my students?
- Is this material geared to the abilities, needs, and interests of all my students? some of my students?
- Will this material fit into my time constraints?
- Do I have access to the equipment (hardware) necessary to use this material? Is it in good operating condition?
- Do I have the facilities necessary to use this material effectively?
- Do I have access to the funds necessary to purchase or rent this material?
- Is this material well produced technically? (Is it sound, clear, and audible? Is the print in the text easy to read?)
- Does the material have validity? (Does the author or producer indicate that it has been proven that it will do what it is intended to do?)

SUMMARY

The use of realia does make teaching more effective as well as more positive. They promote the application of basic principles of learning. Using realia helps to involve students in their own learnings. Likewise, the use of realia makes instruction more interesting and pleasant.

It takes time and effort to collect and prepare quality realia. Therefore, effective teachers develop a filing and storage system which facilitates the reuse of these realia readily and easily for future classes.

One caution—realia have not proven a "cure all" for teaching troubles, nor a "crutch" for poor teaching, nor a substitute for sound teaching plans or procedures. However, if properly planned for and correctly used, realia can make teaching more effective, more enjoyable, and more positive.

ENDNOTE

1. "Cone of Experience" from AUDIOVISUAL METHODS IN TEACHING. Third Edition by Edgar Dale, copyright © 1969 by The Dryden Press, reproduced by permission of the publisher.

CHAPTER 20

Concluding a Lesson

The O.P.E. Concept points out the fact that every lesson has a beginning and an ending. Up to this point, the "A" and the "B" of positive teaching has been discussed. The "A" stands for a stimulating introduction and the "B" for a clear presentation of new knowledges, skills, and/or attitudes. In order to present the A B C's of positive teaching, the final component must be discussed. The "C" is the Conclusion of a lesson. The Conclusion is also referred to as the "closure" of the lesson by some educators. A lesson summary is a part of the conclusion process.

What a teacher does at the end of a lesson is critical to "fix" and reinforce the day's learnings. There must be some definite concluding activity for every lesson. An effective conclusion performs many functions. It ties the lesson together by connecting all component parts of the teaching plan, it "rounds out" the educational experience, it makes learning more meaningful, and it emphasizes the major points of the lesson. Concluding activities, however, need to be varied.

WHY IS THE CONCLUSION OF THE LESSON IMPORTANT?

Students should leave every class period with something they did not have when they entered the classroom or laboratory (educational environment). If teachers would teach their students just one important, relevant, and useful concept or principle each and every time they met in the interaction process, in a school year students would learn a great deal. Following each learning experience, an effective conclusion of a lesson provides

1. a quick review of the key points stressed in the lesson

2. a basis for building the next day's lesson

3. a basis for determining whether the educational objectives were met

4. experience in thinking and decision making

5. a concise "package" of what students learned

6. a means to tie the lesson together

7. a means for reinforcing learnings

8. a basis for future use

9. a basis for objective evaluation of students' behavioral changes

The conclusion of the lesson may "stick" with the students longer than any other part of the lesson. It is important to remember that people tend to remember what was said last.

APPROVED PRACTICES
FOR CONCLUDING A LESSON

The following approved practices are presented to assist teachers in formulating conclusions for each lesson.

1. *Summarize in the light of educational objectives*
   Were the educational objectives achieved? Why? Why not?

2. *Draw conclusions (concepts or principles) from students through the use of oral questions*
   Ask, "What did you learn as a result of today's lesson? What conclusion could be drawn from the content presented? What concepts and/or principles were identified?"

3. *Identify and stress significant concepts—look at the "big picture"*
   Avoid trivial points; encourage students to identify relationships, form opinions, and/or make decisions.

4. *Make formulating a statement of the conclusion a group process*
   Do not accept the first thought presented. Secure some consensus of agreement from several students before accepting any statement as a conclusion of the lesson! Involve all or most of the students in the conclusion process; use oral questions to stimulate thinking.

5. *Once identified and agreed upon, write the conclusion(s) on the chalkboard or use the overhead projector.*
   Require students to record the conclusion(s) in their notes.

AN ILLUSTRATION
ON CONCLUDING A LESSON

To illustrate how conclusion(s) might be drawn, assume an economics teacher was teaching students the principle of fixed and variable costs.

Step 1.   The following study questions had been answered in class.

- What expenses are involved in operating a car?
- How can these expenses be grouped?
- What are the two types of expenses?
- Describe and give examples of the two major expense groups?
- Which group of expenses change as the car is driven more miles?

Step 2.   As a cumulating activity, the teacher projects the chart below.

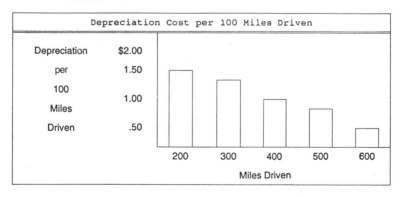

Figure 20.1   Depreciation Cost per 100 Miles Driven

Step 3.   The teacher then asks these questions to start the conclusion:

1. What was our objective for this lesson?
2. What was the "depreciation per 100 miles driven" if the car was driven 200 miles?
3. How much will be the "depreciation per 100 miles driven" if driven 600 miles?
4. Why the difference?
5. Would this be true on other types of vehicles?
6. Does the total annual depreciation change?
7. Why does the depreciation cost per 100 miles driven decrease as the car is driven more mileage?
8. What conclusion(s) can we draw from this example?

Step 4.   The teacher draws conclusion from students.

Conclusion:

The "depreciation cost per 100 miles driven" declines by spreading the annual depreciation costs over more miles driven.

To arrive at this conclusion, students had to think by forming definite relationships between each cost of depreciation for each 100 miles driven. This type of summary and conclusion activity promotes positive teaching.

The conclusion of a lesson should be completed in an exciting manner in a short period of time. It should stress the key points covered in the lesson and involve students in deriving the main concepts or principles evolving from the lesson. The conclusion should require and stimulate thinking on the part of the students. Moreover, it should be conducted in such a manner that the relevant points of the lesson will be retained by the students.

TECHNIQUES USEFUL
IN CONCLUDING A LESSON

One or more of the following techniques may serve to effectively culminate a lesson, a class period, or a unit of instruction [1].

1. Stress key points, information, or skills learned.

2. Review key points quickly.

3. Summarize in the light of the objectives by asking students if the objectives were achieved.

4. Summarize the major points.

5. Develop a list of approved practices or acceptable concepts discussed or studied in the lesson.

6. Have students point out key points or concepts learned.

7. Have students summarize the lesson orally.

8. Ask students what major points were learned as a result of the lesson.

9. Have student(s) review orally what was discussed.

10. Have student(s) review what was studied in lesson.

11. Stress the application of the information or skills learned.

12. Have students evaluate progress made towards achieving the desired goals (objectives).

13. Have student(s) tell how the new learning can be put to use.

14. Have the teacher tell students what will be covered in the next lesson. Introduce next day's lesson.

15. Formulate generalizations, concepts, and principles evolving from the lesson.

16. Have students write out a summary of the lesson.

17. Have teacher stress the relevance, value, and usefulness of the lesson for future use.

18. Have teacher stress the relationship(s) resulting from the lesson.

19. Have students leave class with at least one new fact, skill, or concept.

20. Use oral questions to draw conclusions from students.

21. Ask students the following questions.

What was the most important thing they learned today?

What were the stated objectives for this session? How well were they accomplished?

What have the students learned?

Was this a productive session? Why?

Did the students like the approach used today? Why?

What has the teacher been trying to accomplish today?

Has the lesson been building up to something during this class period? What?

Was what the students did today worthwhile?

CRITIQUING THE CONCLUSION

Learning how to present an effective conclusion can only be accomplished through actual experience and practice. This chapter has discussed how a lesson should be concluded. It is not possible to provide actual experience required to perfect a teacher's ability to effectively conclude a lesson by merely reading about it; however, Figure 20.2, a critique form with selected criteria, is presented to help assess how well a teacher can perform this important pedagogical task of concluding a lesson [2].

SUMMARY

There should be a conclusion to each lesson or class period, no exceptions. Students should be actively involved in the conclusion of a lesson. This part of a lesson is critical if students are to gain experience in analyzing, synthesizing, and evaluating subject matter.

The culminating activity(ies) should be conducted in a concise manner. There is no need to spend excess time, for example, on reanswering the questions for study. The intent of the conclusion of a lesson is to tie the lesson together, to provide a quick and concise review of key points covered, and to involve students in thinking by having them draw the main concept(s) taught in the lesson.

Did the Teacher in the Conclusion: How Well Accomplished?

1. Provide an opportunity for the students to
   explain in their own words the main points
   of the lesson?   _____

2. Review the objective at the beginning of the
   conclusion process?   _____

3. Give the students an opportunity to ask
   questions, make comments, or express ideas?   _____

4. Clarify the main points presented by making use
   of students' answers, comments, and/or ideas?   _____

5. Emphasize only the main ideas covered in the
   lesson presentation?   _____

6. Provide continuity between this lesson and
   future lessons or experiences?   _____

7. Allow students to draw concepts, generalizations
   or principles evolving from the lesson?   _____

8. Make the conclusion a group process?   _____

9. Record the conclusion(s) on the chalkboard?   _____

Figure 20.2   A Critique Form for Lesson Conclusion

The conclusion of a lesson, involving active student participation, can be one of the most effective teaching methods to provide students experience in reasoning, thinking, and decision making. A student should leave each class period with something new in the form of knowledges, skills and/or values, appreciations, or attitudes gained. The conclusion can serve as a positive learning experience not only for the students, but also for teachers by assisting them in determining what the students have learned, how well the students have learned, and what the students need to learn.

Finally the conclusion of the lesson will, in all probability, "stick" with the students longer than any other part of the lesson, if properly conducted.

ENDNOTES

1. Adapted from Andrews, D. W. and Juergenson, E. M. (1966). *Selected lessons for teaching agricultural science*. Interstate Printers and Publishers, Danville, Illinois, p. 10–11.
2. Cameron, Walter A. and Cotrell, Calvin J., *op. cit.*

INDEX